D0961387

RED ROULETTE

AN INSIDER'S STORY OF WEALTH, POWER, CORRUPTION, AND VENGEANCE IN TODAY'S CHINA

DESMOND SHUM

Scribner

New York London Toronto Sydney New Delhi

Scribner
An Imprint of Simon & Schuster, Inc.
1230 Avenue of the Americas
New York, NY 10020

First Scribner hardcover edition September 2021

SCRIBNER and design are registered trademarks of The Gale Group, Inc., used under license by Simon & Schuster, Inc., the publisher of this work.

For information about special discounts for bulk purchases, please contact Simon & Schuster Special Sales at 1-866-506-1949 or business@simonandschuster.com.

The Simon & Schuster Speakers Bureau can bring authors to your live event. For more information, or to book an event, contact the Simon & Schuster Speakers Bureau at 1-866-248-3049 or visit our website at www.simonspeakers.com.

Interior design by A. Kathryn Barrett

Manufactured in the United States of America

1 3 5 7 9 10 8 6 4 2

Library of Congress Cataloging-in-Publication Data has been applied for.

ISBN 978-1-9821-5615-2
ISBN 978-1-9821-5617-6 (ebook)

For Hong Kong and Whitney Duan.
I wish I had the right words; just know I care.

寧鳴而死, 不默而生

Better to speak out and die than keep silent and live.

—Fan Zhongyan (989–1052)

CONTENTS

INTRODUCTION

ON SEPTEMBER 5, 2017, WHITNEY DUAN, AGE FIFTY, disappeared from the streets of Beijing. She was last seen the day before in her sprawling office at Genesis Beijing, a development project she and I had built worth more than $2.5 billion. There, cocooned in a work space that visitors reached after running a gauntlet of security guards, meticulously landscaped gardens, and a dozen varieties of Italian marble, Whitney had masterminded real estate projects worth billions more. And now suddenly she was gone.

How had that happened? And who is Whitney Duan?

Whitney Duan was my wife and business partner for more than a decade. By that point, we were divorced, but for many years we'd been close collaborators and confidants and together had enjoyed the wildest of rides. We'd achieved our shared dream of doing great things in China for China. Coming from poverty, we'd been seized with a desire to make something of our lives. We were awed by our own success.

We'd built one of the biggest logistical hubs in the world at the Beijing Capital International Airport. We'd conceived and constructed the swankiest hotel and business center in China's capital—located on a choice swath of real estate near the city's bustling heart. We'd done stock deals that netted us hundreds of millions of dollars. We'd operated at the center of power in China, cultivating premiers, high-ranking members of the Chinese Communist Party, and their families. We'd counseled the up-and-coming officials who had all of China in their grasp. We'd pushed for social and political changes to make China a better place. By doing well, we believed we could do good. We'd done the math; our net wealth totaled in the billions.

But now she'd disappeared. From my home in England, I reached out to Whitney's housekeeper, who said that Whitney hadn't returned from work on that day in September 2017 and hadn't been seen since. It was as if she'd been vaporized.

I called people in the company we'd founded and learned that Whitney wasn't the only one to have vanished. Two senior executives in her firm—along with a junior assistant who doubled as a housekeeper—were also missing. None have been heard from since. I'd only just left Beijing in late July, having dropped off our son for a summer with his mother. I wondered: Might I have disappeared, too, if I'd stayed a few more weeks in China?

Unexplained disappearances occur regularly in China, where the Communist Party holds a monopoly on power. Despite legal protections enshrined in China's constitution, Party investigators flout those rules to seize anyone on the flimsiest of pretexts and hold them indefinitely. These days Chinese Communist operatives even perform snatch-and-grab operations overseas, targeting newspaper publishers, businessmen, booksellers, and dissidents. You've heard about America's extraordinary rendition of terrorist suspects. Well, this is China's version.

I called Whitney's parents, but they knew nothing. I asked friends, senior officials in the Communist Party hierarchy who owed their positions to her. None were willing to intercede on her behalf. People were so worried about being ensnared by Whitney's case and so afraid of the Party's Central Commission for Discipline Inspection, which I've concluded is the organization that is holding Whitney, that they were unwilling to lend a hand.

The more I asked around, the more I realized that every relationship formed among those who work within the Party system in China is saturated by calculations of benefit and loss. Whitney had been extraordinarily useful to her friends. She'd arranged for promotions for scores of people inside the Chinese Communist Party and the government. She'd managed their careers and spent countless hours strategizing with them about the next move. But now that she was in danger, they'd dropped her like a stone.

As I thought frantically about what to do, what clever approach would deliver back to my son the mother who'd gone missing and the ex-wife who'd had such a transformative effect on my life, I reflected on the years-long series of incredible events that had led to this.

When Whitney disappeared, her net worth vastly exceeded what either of us might have imagined back in the early days of our relationship. A woman of outsize talents in a patriarchal society, she'd played the roulette-like political environment of the New China with unparalleled skill, parlaying an alliance with the family of a political titan into almost unimaginable success. Until she didn't. She'd understood the real China, until she didn't. I was her business partner and husband. We scaled the heights together. This is my story, and hers.

CHAPTER ONE

FROM MY BACKGROUND, THERE WAS LITTLE REASON to believe that I'd find myself at the nexus of economic and political power in China at the turn of the twenty-first century. I wasn't born into the red aristocracy—the offspring of the leaders of the elite group of Communists who seized power in China in 1949. Far from it. My personality also didn't seem suited for the role.

I was born in Shanghai in November 1968 into a family split between those who'd been persecuted after China's Communists came to power and those who hadn't. According to Communist doctrine, my father's side belonged to one of the "five black categories": landlord, rich peasant, counterrevolutionary, bad element, and rightist. Before the Communist revolution of 1949, my ancestors were landlords. They were doubly damned if you factor in the additional charge of having relatives overseas. Anywhere else in the world these would be marks of distinction, but in China of the 1950s and 1960s, economic success and international connections meant you were, as the Communists said, "born rats." The family's lowly status prevented my dad from attending better schools and saddled him with a grudge against the world that he'd carry all his life.

My father's people were landowning gentry from Suzhou, a small city in the Yangtze River delta known as the Venice of China thanks to its luxurious gardens and picturesque canals. Family legend has it that as Communist forces advanced in 1949 in their civil war against the Nationalist Army of Chiang Kai-shek, the Shum clan dumped its valuables down a well on the family compound. That land was subsequently expropriated by the Communist government and today is the site of a state-owned hospital. At a reunion years ago, an elderly relative gave me a very specific location and tried to convince me to dig up the family treasure. Seeing as China's government considers everything under the earth to be state property, I demurred.

My grandfather on my father's side was a prominent lawyer in Shanghai before the revolution. As the Communists tightened their grip on the nation, he, like many of the well-off, had a chance to flee. But my grandfather balked at the prospect of becoming a lowly refugee. To him, Hong Kong, a favored destination for migrants from Shanghai, could never compare with his home city, then known as the Paris of the East. Buying into Communist propaganda that the Party would partner with members of the capitalist class to build the "New China," he decided to stay.

My father never forgave his dad for that fateful decision, holding that his naive belief in the Party cost my dad his youth. In 1952, Party authorities shut down my grandfather's law firm and drove the whole family, including my father's two brothers and a sister, out of its three-story row house in Shanghai, which Grandpa had purchased with gold bars before the revolution. My grandfather took everyone back to Suzhou. Everyone, that is, except my dad, who, at ten years old, was directed to stay in Shanghai to finish grade school.

The next few years were difficult. My father bounced between a series of relatives, scrounging meals and a place to sleep. He often went to bed hungry. One uncle was particularly kind to my dad, even though the revolution hadn't been kind to him. Before the Communist takeover he'd been a successful businessman. The Communists took over his company and assigned him a job as a rickshaw driver at one of the factories he'd owned. The Communists were masters at that kind of treatment, designed to destroy a man's most prized possessions—his dignity and self-respect.

As the scion of a capitalist lawyer's family in a Communist country, my father learned to keep his head down. Living on his own made him resilient and taught him to survive. Still, his troubles only strengthened his anger at his father for keeping the family in China.

Growing up hungry and alone in Shanghai instilled in my dad a fear of forming deep connections with those around him. He hated owing anyone anything and just wanted to rely on himself. That same outlook was instilled in me, and, even today, I'm still uncomfortable feeling indebted. Only later, after I met the woman who'd become my wife, would I learn how isolating this can be. In the ebb and flow of life, if you're never beholden to anyone, Whitney would say, no one will ever be beholden to you and you'll never build deeper relationships. Although I spent years fearing my father, I now see him as a lonely figure who battled the world alone.

My father's disapproved-of class background made it impossible for him to attend one of China's better colleges. Instead, he was assigned to a teachers' training school in Shanghai where he majored in Chinese. Tall for his generation, over six feet, my dad starred on the school's volleyball team. His dogged industriousness and his athleticism must have caught my mother's eye. The two met at the teachers' college in 1962. My mother was also attractive, tall for a Chinese woman—five-eight—and also an athlete; she ran track. Outfitted in drab Mao suits and captured without an iota of expression in the postage-stamp-size black-and-white snapshots of the day, they still made a handsome couple.

My mother's family had overseas connections, but she and her relatives in China dodged persecution. My maternal grandfather hailed from Guangdong Province near Hong Kong. Like many southern Chinese clans, his family had spread across the world. Seven brothers and sisters had immigrated to Indonesia, Hong Kong, and the United States. Before the Communist revolution of 1949, my mother's father had shuttled between Hong Kong and Shanghai, managing businesses in both cities. At one point in the late 1940s, he represented the ownership in negotiations with a workers' representative from the Shanghai Toothpaste Factory named Jiang Zemin. Jiang would ultimately rise to become the head of the Communist Party in 1989 and China's president in 1993. When the Communists took over Shanghai in 1949, my mother's family moved to Hong Kong, but after a falling-out with my grandfather, my grandmother returned to Shanghai with the three children, including my mom. The couple never divorced, however, and my grandfather supported my grandmother by wiring money back to China until the day he died.

My mother's family didn't suffer under Communist rule. After the 1949 revolution, the Chinese Communist Party used families like my mother's as a source for foreign currency and to break the Cold War trade embargo that the United States had slapped on China. The Party called these families "patriotic overseas Chinese," a signal to authorities inside China to go easy on those relatives who'd stayed behind. At one point, the Communists asked my grandfather to run the Hong Kong subsidiary of China's state-owned oil company, the China National Petroleum Corporation.

My grandmother on my mother's side was a character. A beauty in her youth, she came from a wealthy family from the coastal city of Tianjin, which before the Communist revolution had been the commercial and trading hub of northern China. Ensconced in a Shanghai row house, which that side of the family never lost, she rose each morning at 4:00 for calisthenics at a nearby park, bought a cup of soybean milk and a *youtiao*, a cruller-shaped piece of fried dough, for breakfast, and retired to her home to smoke—rare for a woman in those days—and play solitaire. Supported by my grandfather's remittances from Hong Kong, she never worked a day in her life and had servants even during the darkest days of the Cultural Revolution, when people who'd been educated in the West were murdered by the thousands for the crime of favoring Western ideas like science, democracy, and freedom. My grandmother escaped unscathed, shielded by the aura of her association with "patriotic overseas Chinese."

My grandmother remained outgoing and popular into old age. I loved going to her place on weekends. She'd grind her own sesame seeds into a tasty paste and serve up platters of steamed *baozi*, softball-size dumplings stuffed with meat and vegetables, a specialty of her hometown, Tianjin.

My mother had a far happier childhood than my father. Like my grandmother, my mother was a gregarious sort. She was popular among her schoolmates and possessed a sunny view on life. Her personality was almost the polar opposite of my dad's, especially when it came to risk. My mother embraced it; my dad shunned it. My mother later developed uncannily good investment instincts that allowed my parents to ride real estate booms in both Hong Kong and Shanghai.

In 1965, with the Party's permission, my parents married. Party authorities assigned them jobs as teachers at different secondary schools. That's what happened back then. The Party controlled everything. You couldn't pick your own job or your wedding day. At Xiangming Secondary School in Shanghai, my dad taught Chinese and English, which he'd learned by listening to lessons on the radio. He also coached the girls' volleyball team and they regularly contended for the Shanghai municipal championship. All those years of being careful paid off when the school's Party committee named my father a "model teacher."

My mother's school was an hour's bike ride from home. She taught math and was beloved by her students. One reason was her diligence; the other was that she was adept at looking at things from other people's point of view. My father was a my-way-or-the-highway type of guy. My mother was more flexible. This quality came in handy when teaching math, especially in Chinese secondary school, where the curriculum becomes demanding. Her ability to see problems from a student's perspective allowed her to better guide them to a solution. She also was a voice of moderation as political campaigns rolled through the school and students and teachers attacked one another for ideological transgressions.

During mass criticism sessions when a student was singled out, my mother would step in and end the confrontation before it got too violent. No other teacher at the school dared do that. But my mother's status as the daughter of a "patriotic overseas Chinese" gave her some cover to help. Her actions were like tossing a rope to a drowning person, a good deed her students never forgot. To this day, they still hold reunions.

My mother was the second of three children, wedged in between two boys. After my parents married, my uncles mocked my mom for choosing a man descended from one of the lowly "five black categories." They never let my dad forget that they were of an exalted status and had more money, courtesy of the monthly stipend from Grandpa in Hong Kong. One of my uncles bought the first motorcycle in his neighborhood with that cash and made sure my dad knew about it.

I was born in the middle of the Cultural Revolution. The Party sent my parents to the countryside to learn from China's peasants, a program thought up by Chairman Mao that destroyed the lives of millions of people and ended up driving China's economy into a ditch. My parents and I were lucky that we never lost our permits to live in Shanghai, unlike hundreds of thousands of Shanghai residents who were exiled to China's version of Siberia, never to return. My parents' schools allowed them to take turns living among China's peasants, so I was never alone.

I was born big and grew fast. I was worthy of my Chinese given name, Dong, which means "pillar." My size—I top out at six-five—and athleticism made me a natural leader among my peers. My parents also cultivated in me a love of reading. From my earliest days, I had the best collection of comics about Chinese mythical figures, the heroes of China's Communist revolution, and China's war against Japan. Raised on stories of Xiao Gazi, a kid who picked up a gun to kill Japanese invaders during World War II, I was naturally patriotic—and fond of storytelling. My gang of friends would crowd around to hear me recount those tales. I'd make others up as I went along. I still remember concocting a madcap adventure about a cave opening up to swallow the motorcade of a Chinese general.

Those comics, full of stories of people sacrificing themselves for the motherland and the Communist revolution, nurtured in me a deep love of China. They set the tone for my later life and fed a belief that I, too, should devote myself to building China. I was taught to see China as a great country, and to believe in its promise.

In Shanghai, we lived in the same house that Communist authorities had expropriated from my dad's father in 1952. It was an English-style row house on a lane off Huaihai Middle Road, a main boulevard in the old French Concession, a leafy district that before the revolution of 1949 had been administered by civil servants from Paris as part of France's imperial empire. The Communists often directed erstwhile property owners to live in a small corner of their old home, again a deliberate tactic to demonstrate the awesome power of the state.

We were allotted two rooms on the second floor. A doctor and his family occupied my grandfather's old living room on the first floor. The doctor had studied in England before the revolution and his flat overflowed with foreign medical journals. A family of distant relatives lived above us on the third floor. All ten people in the house shared a bathroom and a kitchen. One of Shanghai's premier bakeries was located around the corner and at all hours the tantalizing smell of baked bread wafted down our lane.

My parents slept on a double bed in one corner of our room. I had a single bed in another. A chest of drawers separated us. A small desk with our prized possession—a radio—was next to my bed. My father spent hours perched on a stool in front of it learning English. When my parents were downstairs cooking, I set aside my homework to tune into shows about Chinese heroes of the past, listening with equal intent to the narrator and for the footsteps of my parents ascending the stairs. They wanted me to buckle down on my studies. Like many Chinese children, I was a latchkey kid. I came home by myself at lunchtime and made myself lunch. At an early age, I threw together breakfast, too.

Angry with his lot and nursing his resentments, my father took his unhappiness out on me. He'd pull me into the middle of the room under a flimsy fluorescent light hanging by two wires from the ceiling to beat me mercilessly, with belts, or the back of his hand, or a rock-hard wooden ruler. Actually, I was a model child. I was one of the first in my class let into the Little Red Guard, a selective children's organization sanctioned by the Chinese Communist Party. I'd been appointed a class proctor and recognized as a natural leader. But my dad didn't care. He beat me anyway.

One day I forgot a homework assignment. Chinese teachers are very assiduous when it comes to informing parents of their children's miscues. That evening, my father thrashed me as if there were no tomorrow. The wife of the doctor downstairs heard my yelps, walked up the stairs, knocked on our door, and quietly asked my father to knock it off. He stopped. My parents respected that family, especially because the doctor had studied in the West.

His wife turned out to be my savior. Each time that my father lunged for me, I prayed that my screams would get her to climb the stairs.

My parents told me that I actually had it pretty good. Other parents punished their kids by making them kneel for hours on a ridged washboard, which split the skin on their knees. I'm not convinced. I still have nightmares about these beatings. I wake up in a cold sweat with my heart racing. My father and I have never had a reckoning about the past. He never gave a hint that, retrospectively, he was regretful about handling me so roughly.

While she protected her students at school, my mother never afforded me the same courtesy. Instead, she expressed her disapproval, not with beatings, but with words. Well into my thirties, she'd often remark that I was "dumber than a herd of livestock and denser than a bunch of vegetables."

"Stupid birds need to start flying early," she'd tell me, stressing that if I was going to make something of myself, I'd need to work a lot harder than other kids.

So, at home, I grew up in an environment of degradation and punishment. Compliments were as rare as eggs were at the time. My parents picked on me for my mistakes. "Don't get cocky," my mother said every time I tasted a little success. Eventually, most of my interactions with my parents became attempts to avoid criticism rather than win praise. It wasn't about embracing achievement. It was about escaping failure. I constantly worried that I wasn't good enough.

At that same time, from an early age I experienced this yawning gap between the world outside my home, where I was recognized as a leader, a raconteur, an athlete, even a nice person, and the world of our tiny flat, where my parents seemed thoroughly disappointed with me. Perhaps this is common among kids from China, where expectations are high and criticism constant, and where parents believe that children learn by failure, not through success. As I matured, the tension grew between these two worlds.

I'll always feel grateful to my parents, however, for helping me to read early and read a lot. Both knew exactly what kind of books would enthrall me. They started me with comic books. I soon graduated to *wuxia xiaoshuo*, the martial arts novels of the type that would inspire director Ang Lee's hit film *Crouching Tiger, Hidden Dragon*.

Growing up an only child in a society where at the time everyone had siblings, I spent a lot of time alone. So I read. The martial arts books, like the Harry Potter stories of today, pulled me into an imaginary universe filled with complicated relationships in the courts of kings, life-and-death struggles, love and hate, rivalry and revenge, plots and schemes. My favorite tales followed a similar trajectory. A child witnesses the murder of his parents. Misery follows as he begs for food and struggles to keep himself warm in the winter as he's chased by his assailant, who is intent on wiping the child's family from the face of the earth. Lost in the wilderness, he stumbles into a cave to find an itinerant monk who teaches him the secrets of wushu. After years of hardship, he returns home, exacts revenge, and unites the empire's martial artists to bring peace to all those under heaven. I saw myself in this story, battling and beating my own demons.

My elementary school was located near the Jinjiang Hotel, one of Shanghai's most famous pre-1949 landmarks and, at the time, one of only two hotels in the city that accommodated foreign travelers. Our proximity to the Jinjiang meant that the city's Propaganda Department often organized groups of foreigners to tour the school. The Chinese Communist Party divided the world into enemies and allies and, to win support internationally, aggressively cultivated "foreign friends" such as left-wing intellectuals, journalists, and politicians. Each time a group of "foreign friends" showed up at my school, the best math students would be trotted out to perform calculations on the blackboard and the best athletes would be summoned for a gym class—all part of a great Communist Chinese tradition of bamboozling incredulous fellow travelers into acknowledging the brilliance of Chinese Socialism.

One day a representative from China's vast Soviet-style sports bureaucracy came to our school. A group of the more athletic among us was told to strip to our undershorts. The bureaucrat studied my hands and feet and pronounced that I should be a swimmer. My father began taking me to a municipal pool near my primary school. He taught me to swim in typical Chinese fashion: he tossed me into the pool. I struggled to the surface and gulped down a lot of water. Within weeks, however, I was ready for a tryout with a local team. At the age of six, I won a spot.

Swimming practice was held seven days a week at a pool forty minutes' walking distance from my house. Each morning I got up at 5:30, made myself breakfast, and headed out through Shanghai's serpentine alleys to the pool. I used to challenge myself to find shortcuts. Entering a new alley, I'd never know where I was going to come out. I learned fast that there were many routes to get to the same place. We swam from 7:00 to 8:00, after which I walked to school. We often had a second workout in the afternoon. Meets were held on weekends. I soon became number one at the backstroke and number two at the crawl in my age group. A neighbor's kid was my chief competition; he ultimately made China's national team. We used to walk to the pool together. In the changing room, on the mornings after my dad had whipped me, I tried to hide the welts on my arms, back, and legs. But he noticed them. I told him he was lucky that his father didn't beat him. He gave me a sad smile.

Our trainer, Coach Shi, was a typical Chinese coach: short, squat, with a bad temper. Shanghai's winters were cold, but because the city is situated south of the Yangtze River, under rules set by the central government none of the buildings were heated. Coach Shi would kick off workouts on winter mornings by having us do the butterfly to break up a thin layer of ice that had hardened overnight on the pool's surface. Coaches would sometimes pour hot water from big thermoses into the pool just to watch us, like fish wriggling after food, thrash around in the warm spots in a vain attempt to avoid the chill. They thought this was hilarious.

There were benefits to being on the team. Following afternoon workouts, we got a decent meal. Rice and meat were still rationed in China, but in the team's canteen we were treated to lean meat, not just fat, good-quality vegetables, and, something we all treasured: the occasional egg. Once a year we were given a chicken to take home. I became adept at pocketing extra food, which I'd dole out to my fellow team members in exchange for their loyalty. Food was precious in those days; it was one way to become leader of the pack.

Swimming contributed enormously to who I am today. It taught me self-confidence, perseverance, and the joy of a purposeful endeavor. Through swimming, I met people far outside my normal social circle. I still feel its imprint.

I had only the haziest sense of politics as a boy. I remember walking past political posters calling for class enemies to be mercilessly punished as the Cultural Revolution sowed countrywide chaos. I heard soldiers in an army barracks near my school chanting slogans against ideological deviation and in praise of Communist China's founder, Chairman Mao Zedong. I saw political prisoners wearing dunce caps being driven through the streets in open trucks, heading toward execution.

Then on September 9, 1976, Mao died. My eight-year-old classmates and I had little understanding of what it meant. When the school announced it, our teachers began crying, so we started crying, too. The rule came down that we weren't allowed to play or smile. Several of us were reprimanded for making too much noise.

About a year later, a senior Chinese leader named Deng Xiaoping returned to power after years in internal exile. Deng masterminded the arrest of the Gang of Four, a group of ultra-leftists who'd gathered around Mao. And in 1979 he launched historic reforms that would transform China into the economic power it is today. But my family wasn't going to live through those epochal changes. My parents had other plans.

CHAPTER TWO

IN THE SUMMER OF 1978, WHEN SCHOOL WAS OUT, MY mother and I went to Hong Kong. She told me that we'd be going on a short trip, so I didn't say goodbye to any friends. On that journey, there were plenty of firsts, among them my first plane ride and my first Coke. Neither was very impressive.

We waited to enter Hong Kong at a sleepy border post called Shenzhen, a township of thirty-six thousand people. (Today its population is almost 13 million and it's home to the technology giants Tencent and Huawei.) We needed permission to leave China. Each day my mother pleaded our case to grim-faced Chinese border guards who were in charge of managing the flow of people out of China. After two weeks, they finally let us go. Only later did I realize that my family wasn't planning on just visiting relatives. We were waiting for permission for a "short-term" exit visa that really meant long-term emigration.

The plan to leave Shanghai began by accident. Following the end of the Cultural Revolution in 1976, China again looked to overseas Chinese for the capital needed to save its economy. Officials from the Shanghai bureau for Overseas Chinese Affairs asked my mother to persuade her father to get some of our wealthier relatives in Indonesia and elsewhere to invest in Shanghai. That started a discussion with the authorities in Shanghai about getting an exit visa to leave China to visit Grandpa in Hong Kong. At home, my parents looked at this not as a way to get investment into Shanghai but as a chance to get out of China. My father had spent his whole life nursing that grudge against his dad for failing to leave China when he had the chance in 1949. He wasn't about to make the same mistake now that the opportunity had come around again.

We entered Hong Kong with ten Hong Kong dollars, or a tad more than two US dollars, in my mom's pocket. We landed in a 750-square-foot two-bedroom apartment owned by my mother's father. Grandpa slept in one bedroom. My mother's elder brother, who'd immigrated seven years earlier, occupied the second bedroom with his family of four. Mom and I squeezed into the tiny living room. I slept on a rollout couch. I missed our two-room place in Shanghai. Cramped as it was, at least it was home. In Hong Kong, all I had was a place to sleep.

My mother dove into life in Hong Kong. Her father had spoken Cantonese to her when she was young, so she passed as a local. She parlayed her math major into a job as an accountant at a textile plant and boosted her skills with bookkeeping classes at night.

My mother returned to Shanghai several times to plead with the authorities to let my dad join us. The cost of those trips all but bankrupted her. Thanks to Deng Xiaoping, the authorities in Shanghai were done prosecuting people for having relatives or living overseas. Still, the Chinese government was loath to allow families to leave together, wanting to maintain leverage over people abroad by making family reunification hard. Finally, after two years, my mom succeeded in nagging so tenaciously that the authorities relented. To this day, she remembers the name of the official who let my dad go.

I was nervous, knowing that my father was coming to Hong Kong. But the beatings stopped. All of my relatives crammed into my grandfather's apartment gave me a measure of protection. Besides, my parents were so busy making ends meet that, like ships passing in the night, we didn't see each other much. However, our relationship didn't really improve. My dad was always a stern presence in my life; he was never tender. After my father moved to Hong Kong, I stayed on the rollout couch and my parents moved to a tiny bed behind a makeshift curtain.

For my dad, the transition proved tougher than it had been for my mom. He was thirty-seven and didn't speak the local dialect. In Shanghai, he'd been an award-winning high school teacher, but Hong Kong didn't recognize mainland China's teaching credentials. While my grandfather was kind to my father, my uncle and his wife looked down on him and constantly called attention to his being unable to find any job besides pushing around frozen meat in Hong Kong's biggest cold-storage warehouse.

Still, if nothing else, my father's pigheaded perseverance gave him the strength to succeed. After work, he, too, attended night school, eventually earning an MBA. He worked weekends, when he was sick, and often didn't punch out until late at night. In a business where stuff routinely falls off the truck, my dad earned a reputation for honesty. He moved up the ranks and after seven years became the firm's general manager. I still remember the night his boss invited us to celebrate my father's promotion. I got my first ride in a Rolls-Royce. I was mesmerized by its translucent walnut interior.

It took me years to acknowledge it, but witnessing my parents' labor in Hong Kong to get us back up the ladder affected me profoundly. We were in desperate straits. For three years, we squatted in someone else's living room. We had no bathroom of our own. We were barely making ends meet. But my parents both knew what life felt like at the other end of the tunnel. They understood what they had to do to make it through. So they went for it. I learned this lesson at their feet.

My grandfather's apartment was located in Mei Foo Sun Chuen, a solidly middle-class real estate development of ninety-nine towers on the Kowloon side of Hong Kong. Eventually, my father could no longer stomach living with the in-laws, so we moved into our own place in a run-down neighborhood called Yau Mai Tei, a haunt for gangsters, drug dealers, and prostitutes, also on the Kowloon side. My father's boss offered my dad the place rent-free. We lived on the second floor of a dingy low-rise building in a bare one-room studio partitioned by plywood boards. A shower and a leaky toilet occupied one corner. At least we didn't have to share them with two other families.

At night, rats had the run of the place, scampering over me and my parents as we slept. After school, I'd inch up the dark stairwell and down the gloomy corridor never knowing who or what was around the corner. Once inside the apartment, I often double-locked the bolt. There were times when I fell asleep and my parents had to pound on the door to wake me up to get in.

Moving to Hong Kong was a shock. Part of it had to do with

the way my parents handled it. They never told me they intended to immigrate. I thought I was just on an extended vacation with some school thrown in. Only after I finished my first semester at elementary school did my mother tell me we were staying.

Hong Kong's culture differed significantly from that of China. In Shanghai, my buddies and I always had our arms over one another's shoulders and we were always into each other's business. The whole concept of privacy didn't really exist on the mainland. In the 1970s and 1980s, boys, even men, thought nothing of walking down the street holding hands.

Hong Kong was another world. I remember the first time I tried to put my arm around a Hong Kong kid my age. He was a schoolmate who lived in the same housing development. I thought since we were buddies, it would be only natural for me to drape my arm across his back. He jumped like he'd been electrocuted. "What are you doing?" he screeched. I was really surprised. That was the first time it dawned on me that people associated with one another differently in Hong Kong. They had a more expansive sense of personal space and a less intrusive interpretation of friendship. Friendships on the mainland were, for lack of a better word, sticky. People barged into your life. If you looked fat, they'd announce it. If you were having financial troubles, they'd demand details. If you wanted a partner in crime, they'd volunteer. Hong Kong's relationships weren't as meddlesome. People gave one another room.

In addition to having to figure out a new way of connecting socially, I had to relearn how to talk. When I first went to school in Hong Kong, I couldn't understand either of the two languages of instruction. Elementary school was taught in Cantonese.

Although technically a Chinese dialect, Cantonese was almost totally unintelligible to someone like me, who'd grown up speaking Shanghainese and Mandarin. And then there was English. I had a hard time even mastering the alphabet. My parents asked a cousin of mine to tutor me in English. She came to our apartment and helped me with spelling. "Apple" . . . "bee" . . . "orange." I couldn't seem to remember anything. I spent a long time with her fighting to get the basics down. I was basically mute.

I bounced around in primary school. The year after Mao died in China, all elementary students in Shanghai were made to repeat a grade because schools spent so much time commemorating his life that all of us fell behind. So in Hong Kong, I spent the first semester in third grade at St. Clement's Elementary School, an Episcopal school. But the next semester my parents switched me into a school for the families of police officers because the school had lower standards that allowed me to skip a grade. My parents also thought I'd be better disciplined at a school for police families. The opposite was true. That school was rough. Boys fought boys; I'd seen that before. But girls fought boys, too. I remember one boy taking a swing at a girl. She dodged his fist and then counterpunched him—bang!—in the face. *What a shot*, I thought. Kids from my class would disappear into juvenile detention for carjacking. This was just a few years after Hong Kong had established the Independent Commission Against Corruption to deal with endemic malfeasance in law enforcement. Cops and crooks, in Hong Kong at least, were cut from the same cloth.

I got picked on because I was a big target and I didn't fit in. Older kids were particularly aggressive, and I spent break times between classes in hiding. I wasn't a tough kid and I didn't know how to fight. Despite looming over the bullies, I ran from them. Being from mainland China didn't help. Soon after my family moved to Hong Kong, a local TV station began airing a comedy that featured an immigrant fresh from China named Ah Chan, a rough-edged hick, too dumb and too lazy to adapt to the territory's fast pace. At school, I became "Ah Chan." At home, my cousins laughed at me for not being quick enough to match Hong Kong's tempo. Over time, I sped up, letting myself be molded by others. This would happen again and again. Something about me prompted in others a desire to change me. I was often a willing accomplice, to a point.

In Hong Kong, I also confronted the reality of being poor. In Shanghai, we lived like everybody else. But in Hong Kong, my parents scraped together money to make ends meet while at school my classmates always had spare change. So instead of taking the bus to school, I walked two miles each day so I could pocket the bus fare and afford a snack. At an early age, modeling myself subconsciously on my parents, I learned what had to be done to get by. I promised myself that when I grew up no one would look down on me.

The switch to Hong Kong was the first of many for me and, like swimming, moving became a constant in my life. Over the decades I'd move from Asia to America, back to Asia, and to Europe. This constant motion taught me to adapt, even to dramatic changes, and made me comfortable with people from all over the world. Losing my home at an early age taught me to find a piece of it wherever I'd be. I learned to roll with the tide and adapt to different cultures. I became a chameleon, adept at changing skins to match the place. If nothing else, my constant wandering gave me the assurance that new things wouldn't kill me and that, no matter what, I was going to survive.

With some determination, I got a handle on Cantonese and English. I transferred back to St. Clement's. And I kept reading throughout. St. Clement's ran two shifts of students and my classes started at 12:30 and went to 6:00. I'd spend the mornings in a library near my house, inhaling novels and nonfiction.

When I was twelve, I tested into Queen's College, the territory's oldest and most prestigious all-boys public secondary school, with illustrious alumni such as Sun Yat-sen, the father of modern China. At five-eight entering first form, the Hong Kong equivalent of seventh grade, I was the tallest in my class.

Soon after school began, a phys-ed teacher asked who among us could swim. A few of us raised our hands. I hadn't swum since we'd moved to Hong Kong. He took us to a public pool in Victoria Park across from the school. "Show me what you can do," he said. I jumped in and did laps. Like that, I made the team.

I won meets and broke school records in the fifty- and one-hundred-meter sprint. By fifteen, I'd joined a competitive swimming club. One day, I was training at a public pool and a coach on the Hong Kong national team happened by. "You look good," he said, and invited me to try out. I won a spot on the city's youth squad.

As it had in China, swimming taught me resolve and persistence. We didn't have really cold winters in Hong Kong, so I never had to break any ice. But rain or shine, cold or hot, we always swam, and the pools were always outdoors. There were days when I felt good and days when I didn't. And on the days when I didn't, when the guy behind me touched my feet with his fingers,

I'd push myself to make sure I wasn't the one blocking the lane. And at the end of practice, I'd climb out of the pool with a sense of accomplishment. As it had with my father, doggedness became one of my greatest strengths. *Things may seem insurmountable,* I told myself, *but you'll always get out of the pool.*

Being a member of the team expanded my social circle. We practiced and competed all over the territory. The rich kids on the team came to practice in chauffeured BMWs; the poorest grew up in public housing. I swam in youth team competitions in Japan and up the Pearl River in Guangzhou. The trip to Japan marked the first time I'd left Greater China.

My grades during my first year at Queen's College were horrible; I ranked thirty-third out of forty kids in my class. I'd studied hard to get accepted, but once in I stopped pushing and had fun. Instead of doing homework, I spent hours playing soccer and basketball in nearby Victoria Park. Too busy working, my parents yelled at me about my lousy marks but otherwise didn't have time to spare. I began to improve a bit, however, and at the end of my third year I was in the middle of the pack.

By the time I got into Queen's College, I'd morphed from a Shanghai native to Hong Kong local. I was spending a lot more time with my peers than with my parents. Outside our family's tiny apartment, my self-doubt disappeared and I brimmed with self-confidence. I was a good swimmer; I was tall and well liked. I spoke Cantonese like a native and I was at home at my new school.

My view of myself has always been colored by a certain type of vanity. From an early age, people stared at me. That's natural in China and Hong Kong, where the average height for men is five-seven and I was always head and shoulders taller than both my peers *and* most adults. People forever commented on my looks in that very blunt, very Chinese kind of way. If you've got lots of acne, they'd say, "Wow, so many pimples." In my case, it was: "Wow, so tall and handsome." It made me extremely self-conscious. It also saddled me with a powerful desire not only to live up to their image of me as "so tall and handsome" but also to ensure that they didn't look down on me.

Most days, I went home from Queen's College with a bunch of classmates who like me lived on the Kowloon side. We took a bus from school to Hong Kong's high-end Central District and then got on a ferry to cross to Kowloon. We usually goofed around on the trip, but one day something caught my eye. I saw a Westerner working on a Chinese construction crew. He stuck out like a sore thumb, with his pale face and his hard hat surrounded by Chinese coworkers, their skin darkened by Hong Kong's subtropical sun. *Wow,* I thought, *that could be me in ten years, everybody passing me by, looking at me strangely.* I promised myself that I never wanted to be someone like that, sticking out like an oddity. Until my mid-forties, I was driven by the fear of looking bad. That's what Chinese mean when they use the term "to save face." I was consumed by a desire to avoid disappointing people and to fit in. Still, I always felt people's eyes trained on me.

Making huge sums of money wasn't really the goal here. My mother always said money wasn't a cure-all and I believed her. But to me, saving face was. I was wired at all costs to avoid embarrassing myself and, by extension, my family.

Even though I was a middling student, I believed I was middling by choice rather than lack of ability. We had a school debate team. Because my grades were so-so, I was never asked to participate. But I attended the debates and would counter the arguments of each side in my head. Naturally, I thought my points were better than those of the speakers at the front of the room.

During my fourth year at Queen's College, when I was sixteen, I realized that unless I did well on the Hong Kong Certificate of Education exam scheduled for the end of my fifth year, I'd be forced to attend a far less prestigious school. I knew my parents didn't have the means to save me, so I decided to apply myself to my studies and try to get good grades.

It took my teachers a while to get used to the new me. I'd gained a reputation as a class clown, chitchatting non-stop. In music class, I refused to learn how to read notes. But I was always a strong reader. In Chinese-language class in the fourth form, I wrote an essay about the Chinese poet Xu Zhimo. Xu was a dashingly handsome writer, famous for his romantic liaisons as much as his lyrical poetry. Xu wrote in the 1920s, when warlords had carved China into fiefdoms and Japan threatened to invade. Xu contended that art didn't need to serve society or the greater good; it was enough to appreciate beauty. I took issue with Xu's view of art for art's sake. How could he wax poetic about beauty when China was collapsing in chaos? I asked.

At the end of one class, my Chinese teacher told me to stay behind. "Did you really write this essay yourself?" she asked. "Did you come to these conclusions on your own?" She thought I'd plagiarized it. But it was my own work.

By that year's end, I was in the top ten in my class. At the end of my fifth year, I was in the top five and I passed the exam, which allowed me to stay at Queen's College and move into the sixth form—Hong Kong's equivalent of senior year in high school.

Crawling up the class rankings at Queen's College taught me a lot about my capabilities. I'm not lazy per se, but I do have a tendency to slack off. Once accepted at Queen's College, I took it easy. I only did what was necessary. But that's because somewhere inside me, I had this innate belief that when I needed to I could step on the accelerator and get the job done. These traits stayed with me throughout my professional life.

After I completed the sixth form, my swim coach told me that if I practiced more, I might be able to make the qualifying time to join the Hong Kong team for the fifty-meter freestyle in the upcoming 1988 Seoul Olympics. Queen's College's principal met with my dad and everyone agreed that I'd be given time to train. I was surprised that my father consented, but he'd always been impressed by authority. Whatever the principal suggested was fine with him.

I took full advantage of this extended vacation. While my classmates gazed jealously from the school's windows, I practiced my jump shot in the school's playground below. The teachers didn't like it, but I'd been given a license to play—from the principal, no less. In the end, I failed to make the cut, missing by less than a second—a flash in real life but an eternity in sport. I never recouped those years of lost training when we first moved to Hong Kong. Still, I wasn't particularly crushed by not making the team. I enjoyed the process. *No matter how bad things become,* I'd tell myself, *you'll always get out of the pool.*

During the summer as a seventeen-year-old, I earned money for the first time, teaching swimming to kids at Hong Kong's South China Athletic Club. I taught from 7:00 in the morning to 7:00 at night. My students peed in the pool with such impunity that I contracted a nasty rash. Still, with the equivalent of one thousand US dollars in my pocket, I began indulging a newfound taste for fashion. This was a huge change for me. Ever since we'd moved to Hong Kong and my mother had worked as an accountant at a textile mill, she'd clothed me in knock-offs and rejects. Now, with the guidance of a friend from the Queen's College swimming team named Steven, I discovered the world of style.

Steven came from a well-off family and always had money to burn. He took me to buy my first branded piece of clothing—an orange polo shirt from Ralph Lauren. I moved up quickly to Yohji Yamamoto and Issey Miyake. Steven taught me to shop, and I soon picked up the subtle art of nonchalantly peeking at the price. My mother always said money isn't everything, but you can't do without it. Now that I finally had some in my wallet, I noticed the freedom it afforded—to satisfy my wants, to explore the world, to indulge my curiosity.

Other developments underscored the value of having resources. My parents had bought a new apartment. Although it was only 540 square feet, for the first time in my life I had my own room. It became my sanctuary.

My parents were—and remain—incredibly frugal and I took after them in that respect. When I cook today, I cut vegetables and meat with the goal of not wasting even a teaspoon's worth. I still clean my plate at every meal. "Each grain of rice is hard won," goes a line from a Chinese poem that we memorized at school.

We'd lived in that ratty apartment that belonged to my father's boss for two years. One day, my dad and his boss had a falling-out. My father's overdeveloped sense of personal honor was susceptible to any slight—a sensitivity that was amplified by the fact that we were living rent-free. When my father and his boss bickered, we moved out, bought the new apartment with a big chunk of my parents' savings, and my dad quit.

My dad didn't have a new job lined up and it took him a year to find steady work. He joined a trading company, but that didn't pan out. He dabbled in other ventures, but they went belly up. Finally, after a year, Tyson Foods, the American chicken giant, impressed by his background in cold storage, hired him as its first employee in Greater China. Tyson wanted to sell into China and my dad recognized that there was gold in all the parts that Americans didn't eat. Chicken feet, chicken ass, chicken innards, chicken gizzards, chicken neck, chicken heart—the Chinese coveted them all. Tyson flew him back to the United States, where he suggested production line changes to salvage these nuggets. My dad's friends and colleagues laughed at his new line of work. In Chinese, *mai ji*, or selling chickens, is slang for pimping prostitutes. But the joke was on them. Within a few years, Tyson was selling 100 million dollars' worth of junk chicken in Asia, filling the bellies of Chinese consumers with Yankee-grown "phoenix claws," the Chinese term for chicken feet.

From my father's experience at Tyson, I first learned about the vagaries of US-China relations. The Arkansas chicken pipeline into China was hostage to politics. Anytime you had tension with the United States, the Chinese government would suddenly up the required quarantine period for chicken feet from two days to two weeks. Faced with losing tons of product to spoilage, my dad had to conjure ways to get around the regulations and get the stuff into China. He was such a magician that Tyson named my father "salesman of the century."

Tyson also provided my dad further proof that life wasn't fair, especially to him. When he retired in 2003, Tyson didn't offer him a pension. He was an international hire, the corporation said, so he wasn't eligible for benefits. My mother pushed him to demand better treatment, but he never did. He's just not that kind of guy.

At the end of the sixth form, Steven, my swim teammate turned fashion adviser, went to the University of Southern California. As I trained for the Olympics, I felt abandoned. Instead of writing letters, we exchanged tapes. I'd close the door to my room and pour my heart into my recorder. Steven gave me a detailed rundown on the process of buying a car in the United States; his mother had given him a choice between a Volvo, a BMW, or a Mercedes, and he was having trouble deciding. Why, my parents asked, are you talking to a machine and not to us?

Life in Hong Kong reinforced the independent streak I'd already developed in Shanghai. My parents were so challenged adapting to their new lives that they had neither the time nor energy to inject themselves into my world. Our social circles gradually grew far apart. I befriended local kids, while my parents' friends were all recent immigrants from mainland China, like them. My parents criticized me for being different. "You're not like either of us," my mother complained. But in a way she was wrong. My father had been forced to become independent, too, in Shanghai in the 1950s. And, like my dad, I, too, knew that, when called upon, I was capable of hard work.

Family life with Mom and Dad settled into a cold war. I didn't enjoy being around them and I suspect they felt the same about me. On Saturdays, as was the Hong Kong habit at the time, they both worked a half day. To avoid them, I'd pretend to sleep in. Afterward, I'd go to swimming practice and spend the rest of the day away from home.

Although the beatings had stopped, my father continued to yell at me. He'd burst into my room in a frenzy and start screaming. If I was late getting up for school in the morning, he'd bang on the door. On Sunday morning, I'd listen to *American Top 40* on the radio and he'd bang again and command me to turn it down. "Why do you have to listen to that junk all the time?" he'd ask.

I began clubbing and drinking beer. When I started to drink, two things surprised me. One was my tolerance for alcohol. After one bottle, my friends were already getting tipsy, but I felt nothing. Back then, this was both upsetting and expensive; later, in my business life, my ability to hold my liquor would serve me well.

The other surprising aspect related to my self-consciousness, or lack thereof. When I drank, I became less self-conscious, more approachable, and more outgoing. Because of my size, I was pretty imposing, even as a teenager. People felt intimidated around me. Add to that the fact that I wasn't naturally gregarious. But when I drank, I relaxed. People noticed that I became a different person, more accessible and warmer. I opened up. Ever curious, I was interested in the ways that alcohol changed me and my relations with the outside world. Inside, I yearned to be more social. Alcohol allowed things to happen.

I also began to try to date but had no idea what to do. Once a girl from a sister school cold-called me and asked me out. I was so nervous that I got a worldly friend from a police officer's family to accompany me. We all met at a McDonald's. I couldn't think of anything to say. Single-sex education might have its good points, but it made me uncomfortable around girls.

Despite constant tension with my folks, we maintained one Hong Kong tradition. Almost every Sunday, we went out for dim sum brunch. We'd go with a big group and the adults would talk business. They were all old school chums of my parents from Shanghai who'd also immigrated to Hong Kong. China was opening up to foreign investment and my parents' friends ran trading companies involved in cross-border deals. My father's friends noticed that I liked listening in. Business in China interested me. I'd started reading the *Wall Street Journal*'s Asian edition. I'd read Lee Iacocca's autobiography and, also, Donald Trump's *The Art of the Deal*. I liked the idea of doing business, of building something that hadn't existed before, of leaving a mark.

In Hong Kong, business was pretty much the only career path. We didn't have politicians and the civil service didn't interest me. You couldn't afford to become an artist; the colony was a cultural desert anyway. In Hong Kong's hypercompetitive environment where people were primed to get ahead, business was the main avenue to prove oneself.

Steven's departure to the United States reinforced my desire to get out of Hong Kong. But when the cousin who'd taught me English offered to host me in Australia, where she'd gone to study, I refused. In my view, Australia was an oversize rock. I was bent on following Steven to "the land of the free," preferably to the golden coast of California. I'd been raised on American movies and music. My first cassette tape was from the band Bananarama; the trio might have been British, but to me their New Wave sound was pure Americana. It never occurred to me to go anyplace else other than the United States.

At the end of seventh form, I applied to the University of California, Berkeley (Cal Berkeley) and UCLA, along with Washington University in St. Louis and the University of Wisconsin. Cal and UCLA rejected me, but I was accepted by the other two. At the time, Washington University cost $10,000 a year while Wisconsin's tuition was half that. *U.S. News & World Report* ranked the pair seventeenth and eighteenth respectively. My father announced that I'd be attending number eighteen Wisconsin. My parents were doing better financially; nonetheless, an extra $5,000 a year meant a lot in those days.

In the late spring of 1989, as I waited to head to the United States, I returned to Shanghai to visit relatives. In cities across mainland China, demonstrations had erupted following the death of the ex–Communist Party General Secretary Hu Yaobang in April. He'd been removed from his post in 1987 because he'd refused to crack down on student protests. Millions of people flocked to these new demonstrations, using Hu's death as an excuse to demand more freedom and government action to stem widespread corruption that had allowed families of high-ranking Communist Party leaders to enrich themselves. In Shanghai, hundreds of thousands of people marched for change. I did, too, somewhat by accident. One day in late May 1989, I was on Nanjing Road, Shanghai's main shopping thoroughfare. The street was packed with demonstrators, blowing whistles, chanting for freedom, and carrying placards calling for a more open China. No cars could pass, and the sidewalk was chockablock with spectators. The only way to move was to join the march. I slipped into the flow. People stared at me like I didn't belong. It must have been my clothes; Hong Kong people dressed differently than mainlanders in those days, especially this gangly teenager with an interest in style.

In Shanghai, I stayed with an uncle who'd suffered during the Cultural Revolution. One evening as he and I watched the TV news, tears came to his eyes. "It's not going to end well for these youngsters," he predicted. "They don't understand," he said. "The Communist Party rose to power by manipulating protests, ginning up mass movements, and then suppressing them ferociously once they'd served their purposes.

"A newborn calf doesn't fear a tiger," he said. "You cannot beat the Communists this way."

I left Shanghai for Hong Kong on June 2, 1989. On the night of June 3, the Communist Party declared war on China's people across the country. In Beijing, army troops massacred hundreds of students and other demonstrators as they expelled the protesters from Tiananmen Square. Demonstrations in Shanghai were suppressed peacefully, earning Jiang Zemin, Shanghai's Communist Party boss, a promotion to the Party's top position nationwide after the Tiananmen Square massacre.

In Hong Kong, my father and I watched the crackdown in Beijing live on television. Both of us broke into tears. For us, it was one of those 9/11-type moments. We remember vividly where we were. Given my dad's early experience with the Communists, he always believed that the Party was evil to its core. He'd seen it turn on a dime against its own people. He'd expected the worst.

As the events in China unfolded and the Chinese government issued a most-wanted list of student leaders who were just a few years older than me, my parents emphasized that they'd started their lives anew in Hong Kong so I could have a better future. All of their sacrifices, they said, were made so that I might avoid the fate of people on the Chinese mainland.

I was too young and too sheltered to understand what the chaos was all about. The whole affair made me want to leave Hong Kong all the more, to get out from under my parents, to find freedom and adventure, anywhere, even in Wisconsin, USA.

CHAPTER THREE

IN LATE AUGUST 1989, I FLEW TO LOS ANGELES International Airport on my way to Madison. Steven picked me up in his new light blue BMW 3 Series. We visited UCLA and USC, saw the sights in Los Angeles, and, after a couple of days, he accompanied me to Milwaukee, where he had relatives.

His relatives took us out to a Japanese restaurant. I'd been to Japan with the Hong Kong swim team, but it was in the midwestern heartland where I first tasted sushi. I capped off the delicious meal by popping a massive blob of wasabi, fiery Japanese horseradish, into my mouth. I don't know what made me more distressed, the embarrassment or my exploding sinuses.

From Milwaukee, we took a puddle jumper to Madison. Out the window, all I saw was green. I'd lived my entire life in concrete jungles in Shanghai and in Hong Kong. Here I was, wondering if I'd be attending college in a forest. Steven helped me settle into my dorm room. We met my roommate, a barely communicative wrestler from Minneapolis. After a day, Steven went back to USC.

At Wisconsin, my schedule that first semester afforded me a lot of free time. With no friends in the beginning, I spent the afternoons lifting weights in a gym across from my dorm. The university's swim team worked out in a pool next to the gym. One day, I checked out the practice and approached the coach. I had no idea how competitive Big Ten swimming was. I asked him if I could join the team. He told me to come back the next day for a tryout. The next afternoon, I returned, dove in, and started doing the crawl. After a few laps, he barked, "You're in." I guess those winter mornings breaking ice in the Shanghai pool had served a purpose.

The swim team kept me emotionally grounded my first year. I was the only Asian among a group of white swimmers, but I felt accepted as part of their group. We threw parties and drank plentifully. The coach, a barrel-chested midwesterner in his early fifties named Jack Pettinger, looked out for me, inviting me over for Thanksgiving when most of the international students were left to fend for themselves. Coach Pettinger came to my dorm to pick me up. I had no concept of automobile etiquette in America. In Hong Kong, my parents never had a car. So when he drove up, I got into the backseat. "Heh, do you think I'm your chauffeur?" he barked. "Get in here with me." In China, you don't sit next to the senior guy, so I thought in America you did the same. I was trying to be respectful. Turns out, I had a lot to learn.

Because I'd completed the seventh form in Hong Kong, I entered Wisconsin as a sophomore. At USC, Steven was on the dean's list, so I aimed for that at Wisconsin. My first year I barely missed it, but I never got close again. I was invited to a few frat parties, but each time I went I stuck out like a sore thumb—or, at least, I felt that way. Chinese kids would only begin coming to Wisconsin in big numbers after 2000. And this was 1989.

New to America, I was pretty clueless when it came to the latest TV shows that always seemed to be the center of conversation. I had trouble getting—much less cracking—any jokes. I noticed that many Americans seemed to have a different view of friendship than people did in Asia. There was a fluffiness to American relations. Acquaintances at Wisconsin would greet me enthusiastically and act like we were best buddies. But if I was looking for someone to be more substantially involved in my life, I had a nagging sense that they wouldn't be there.

Still, throughout my first semester I avoided people from Hong Kong. Living in the dormitory and working out with the team, I didn't come into contact with many. When I did, I tended not to make friends. Once I went to a dance party organized by students from Hong Kong. I started speaking English with everyone, not our native Cantonese. People thought that I was showing off and I didn't get invited back. In reality, I was just trying to fit in as I shuttled between the dorm, the classroom, the cafeteria, and the pool.

My second year, I moved off campus and quit the swim team. The coach wanted me to keep at it because my presence upped the team's cumulative GPA, but I needed to study. I'd chosen to double major in finance and accounting, which added a year and increased my workload. I befriended classmates from Asia. My roommate was from Indonesia and through him I met a large circle of Japanese, Taiwanese, and Korean students. I dated both American and Asian women. And I discovered on trips to Chicago some of the big-city feel that I'd been missing. Even on my limited budget, I developed a taste for fine food and wine. One day during my senior year, I spotted a review of a Chicago restaurant called Everest, which touted a seventeen-course tasting menu. My curiosity was piqued, and I immediately booked a table with a girlfriend. On the day of our meal, we fasted and showed up famished. The sommelier patiently walked us through the wine-pairing list. Near the end of the meal, I asked our waiter when the main course was coming. All of the portions had been tiny servings on enormous plates. So went my introduction to nouvelle cuisine.

Having arrived in the United States immediately after the June 4 crackdown in China, as a student from Greater China I was eligible, thanks to an Executive Order signed by President George H. W. Bush, for a green card. I passed on the chance. I felt too different in America and suspected I'd hit a glass ceiling if I remained. Frat culture permeated the business world, and from those parties I'd attended I sensed that I'd have little traction with my American bosses and peers. After four years at Wisconsin, I graduated in May of 1993 and flew home.

My experience in the United States changed me profoundly. In Hong Kong and China, I already stood out because of my height and the way I dressed. But time in America made me even more individualistic and more comfortable being me. My parents didn't like that. They regretted that I hadn't stayed in Hong Kong. "You would've turned out better," my mother announced after I returned. "You wouldn't have gotten so opinionated. You would've fought with us less." They both told me that sending me to America was the worst decision they'd ever made.

But for me, living in Wisconsin was liberating. It set me on the path to becoming a global citizen. I made friends with people from all over the country and all over the world, people of different colors, religions, and beliefs. Without that first journey to the States, I wouldn't have succeeded like I have. Even my English was transformed. Seasoned by midwesterners and foreigners alike, my accent ended up more like Arnold Schwarzenegger's than a Hong Kong Chinese.

Back home, I hustled to get a job, sending out twenty applications to investment banks. Within days I had interviews with Morgan Stanley and Goldman Sachs, but I botched both. When the Morgan Stanley interviewer told me to return home and wait for his call, I ignorantly suggested that he just leave a message on my answering machine and announced that anyway I was planning on a vacation before I started work. At the Goldman interview, I got into an argument about racism and raised my voice. Neither called me back.

I settled on a position as a stockbroker with the brokerage firm Citibank Vickers. I thought the job would be the most exciting in the world. All of us in that generation had watched Michael Douglas as Gordon Gekko in the blockbuster *Wall Street* memorably declare, "Greed is good." But I soon discovered that being a broker wasn't all that it was cracked up to be. In Hong Kong, at least, it was about who, not what, you knew. If you had well-heeled contacts, you could make it. But as a junior broker with a limited social circle, I was always waiting for my boss to toss me trades that were too small or too tedious for him to execute. Clients called me to gossip, not to buy or sell. I soon realized that it didn't matter whether I or the guy next to me sold a share of Hongkong and

Shanghai Banking Corporation or any other stock. *What is the difference,* I asked myself, *between this and selling shoes?*

Still, my colleagues and I mimicked the over-the-top, partying culture that we'd seen in the movie. The Hong Kong Stock Exchange closed every day at 4:00, and after the gym we'd head out to Lan Kwai Fong, a curved street featuring a string of bars near Hong Kong's Central District. That was the culture. As a newly minted broker, I told myself that partying served a professional purpose. A good contact list was a key to success. I buzzed around, as the Chinese said, like a headless fly, hitting the bars and looking for business connections. I didn't actually end up making many.

I ran into credit card problems and had to ask my parents to bail me out. Sometimes I didn't get home until after dawn. I'd moved back in with my folks, who, riding Hong Kong's real estate market, had upgraded again to another apartment in a better neighborhood. After multiple late-night episodes, my parents threw me out. I moved into a five-hundred-square-foot rental in the Tianhou neighborhood two blocks from Queen's College. I knew the area and it felt like home.

After nine months as a stockbroker, I started looking for another job. I wanted something where I could apply my education—a position that offered a career path. In June 1994, I interviewed at a private equity firm called ChinaVest. The firm took up the entire penthouse of an office building in Central. Very exclusive, I thought. They asked me my understanding of private equity. I'd looked up the term the previous day and my college finance textbook only had three lines on it. Private equity was a new concept. I regurgitated what I'd memorized and got the job.

ChinaVest had been founded in 1981 by Bob Theleen, a smooth-talking former CIA officer; his wife, Jenny, who was raised in Singapore and educated in France; and two other Americans. My hiring was directly connected to changes unfolding inside China. The years between 1989 and 1992 had been bad ones for China. Following the Tiananmen Square crackdown in 1989, a reactionary wing of the Chinese Communist Party, led by Premier Li Peng, had rolled back market-oriented reforms, cracked down on private businesses, and poured money into the inefficient state-owned sector. China's economy slowed dramatically. But in 1992, China's paramount leader, Deng Xiaoping, impatient with the conservatives, left Beijing and traveled to the southern city of Shenzhen on Hong Kong's border to urge a resumption of market-oriented changes. Deng's "southern journey" unleashed a new round of capitalist zeal. Hong Kong was the prime beneficiary. In 1993, Wall Street visionary Barton Biggs came to the territory after six days in China and pronounced himself, "tuned in, overfed, and maximum bullish" on China. After Biggs's declaration, more than $2 billion roared into stocks on the Hong Kong Stock Exchange, chasing companies with business in China.

Theleen and his team capitalized on this boom, bartering their expertise on the Chinese way of doing business for equity stakes in firms seeking to establish a presence on the mainland. They invested in food chains TGI Fridays and Domino's, along with electronics companies from Taiwan. They took a controlling stake in Tait Asia, a subsidiary of the oldest trading company in the region and a specialist in fast-moving consumer goods, including beer and cigarettes.

I worked for my first boss, Alex Ngan, at ChinaVest for a few years, creating spreadsheets, taking notes in meetings, and writing investment memos. He was a taskmaster, but the work was fascinating. Senior executives from a wide array of industries would come to our office and pitch their ideas. It was an education, a deeper version of the conversations I'd overheard as a youth with my parents over dim sum. Even better, I was getting paid to eavesdrop and I was the youngest person in the room.

I became the firm's representative to Tait Asia, which held the accounts for Heineken beer and Marlboro cigarettes. The appetite for these goods in China was extraordinary. In the space of a few years, Heineken's sales in China went from zero to $40 million, and Tait Asia had the distribution rights.

China had enacted heavy duties on imported beer—upward of 40 percent—to protect Chinese breweries. Tait Asia brought beer into Hong Kong and resold it to companies that figured out a way to move it into China duty-free. We didn't want to know how that happened as long as sales and profits increased. It wasn't just ChinaVest, of course. Anyone doing business in China did it this way, circumventing the rules in search of profit. I quickly learned that in China all rules were bendable as long as you had what we Chinese called *guanxi*, or a connection into the system. And given that the state changed the rules all the time, no one gave the rules much weight.

At one point, a Chinese naval officer offered Tait Asia a Chinese warship to smuggle the beer. I was floored. I'd grown up in China with a glorified image of the People's Liberation Army and had been taught that the army had battled Japan during World War II, freed China from the corrupt regime of Chiang Kai-shek, and fought US forces to a standstill in Korea. And now the Chinese navy was trafficking in beer?

I was very junior at the firm and new to everything. But I found it perplexing to see ChinaVest so thoroughly unconcerned by how Tait Asia, which it had invested in, was getting beer into China. We'd intentionally created a black box inside of which a lot of money was changing hands. Because of US regulations, ChinaVest's leadership needed to pretend not to know. A lot of Western businesses in China adopted a similar, don't-ask-don't-tell business model. Abysmal working conditions in factories making high-end sneakers? "Who knew?" Prison labor making blue jeans? "There must be a mistake." In business with the army or the police? "We weren't aware."

I was just starting out in business and learning the ropes. I wasn't really in a position to make judgments. If my bosses thought it was okay, I thought it was okay. And the more I got into the China business, the more I saw everyone, American businesses, Hong Kong businesses, European businesses, and, of course, Chinese businesses, bending and curving around the rules. I was at the start of my career and this was my earliest lesson in the China trade. It set the tone for my future work and showed me the path forward in China.

Theleen was a master at wowing Westerners with his knowledge of Asia. In the fall of 1994, ChinaVest held a meeting with its key investors in Beijing, including representatives from family offices from the Midwest and large investors such as the Ford Foundation and the California Public Employees' Retirement System. Bob wanted to put on a show and sent me to China to help organize the affair. At the airport, I greeted the guests in three

Red Flag limos, China's clunky version of the Lincoln Continental. We put our visitors up in the Diaoyutai State Guesthouse where Richard Nixon and Henry Kissinger had stayed during Nixon's famous first trip to China in 1972. Each time we hit the road, our drivers would switch on their sirens to clear the route. Our guests were floored by the experience. Many were on their first trip to China and weren't accustomed to this type of treatment, where the intent was to dazzle with flattery. One, the scion of a wealthy family from Ohio, turned to me and declared, "This is another world." Theleen had learned this trick from the Chinese, who are masters at shock-and-awe hospitality. In so doing, Bob achieved his goal of making China seem like a riddle that only ChinaVest could solve.

When the group checked out, the guesthouse presented me with a big bill. Some of our investors had availed themselves of the retro 1970s-era Chinese pens, writing pads, glassware, and ashtrays decorating their rooms. It was a small price to pay for these firms' continuing business.

I began returning to China looking for investment opportunities for the firm. I went to Luoyang in Henan Province, famed for peonies and the Longmen Buddhist grottoes, but by the time I arrived in the summer of 1995 it was a grimy post-Communist dump. There I visited a motorcycle factory; the industry was just beginning to take off as Chinese swapped pedal bikes for scooters. In coastal Fujian Province, I dropped by a TV monitor factory that would grow into the biggest manufacturer of computer screens in the world. In the boondocks of central Anhui Province, long known as one of China's poorest, the only decent place I could find to sleep was a police dormitory. Arriving back in the provincial capital of Hefei, by no means a garden spot, I celebrated my return to civilization in a shabby four-star hotel.

China was so poor that none of its nascent private businesses had high-enough revenue to be investment targets. Still, I could feel the energy, suppressed for decades by Communism, waiting to be unleashed. All that aspiring entrepreneurs needed was for the government to give them a chance.

I also felt that I was finally participating in something bigger than myself. I'd come to a love of China early. So, naturally, I wanted to be a part of this new China story. No one knew how it was going to turn out and, in returning to my homeland, I certainly didn't know whether I was going to accomplish my goal of making something of myself. But it felt like the right thing to do.

The first private mainland Chinese technology company ChinaVest took a stake in was AsiaInfo, a firm that was building the backbone of China's Internet. Two Chinese students, Edward Tian, who had a PhD in natural resource management from Texas Tech, and Ding Jian, who had a master's degree in information sciences from UCLA and an MBA from Cal Berkeley, founded the firm in Texas in 1993. AsiaInfo's selling point was its ability to marry software and equipment from Dell, Cisco, and other firms to build a system that would connect Chinese to one another and China to the rest of the world. The Internet came to China in 1994. By the end of that year, thirty thousand people were online. Today almost 1 billion people have access to an Internet connection there, accounting for 20 percent of the world's users.

Tian wasn't a tech guy, but he was a gifted salesman. As I listened to his pitch, I was moved by his passion to help China embrace the telecommunications revolution that was sweeping the globe. Tian framed his return to China as part of the century-old flow of patriotic Chinese journeying home to build the motherland after their education overseas.

Tian said he'd been inspired to found AsiaInfo after he saw a speech by senator (and future vice president) Al Gore in 1991 during which Gore described the Internet as an "information superhighway." Just two years earlier, Tian had watched from the United States as student protesters had massed in cities across China in 1989 and, like me, had wept as the People's Liberation Army had killed hundreds in Beijing. Tian's response, like that of many Chinese, was to embrace capitalism, the free flow of information, and entrepreneurship to build China. Tian combined the promise of new technology with the promise of a freer China. "With our technology," Tian vowed, "enlightenment can flow through the taps like water." When he spoke about patriotic Chinese students returning home to modernize the motherland, I saw myself as part of a bigger story. In retrospect, I now realize that this was a calculated spiel, designed to impress Western investors and charm Chinese officials. Tian knew how to craft a story that could appeal to both audiences. Still, his success in China would become a beacon to tens of thousands of returnees like him, and me.

I was the analyst on the deal. Tian demanded what my bosses at ChinaVest thought of as an unreasonable amount of money. He claimed that AsiaInfo had a valuation of $100 million even though its revenues barely touched $15 million. The company was growing fast, but it was managed by a bunch of techies with no experience drawing up a spreadsheet. In three years, Tian predicted, AsiaInfo would grow its revenues by 600 percent.

Other firms were interested besides ChinaVest. In the end, the investment firm Warburg Pincus invested $12 million, we put in $7 million, and Fidelity Ventures about $1 million, breaking the record for the biggest private equity investment in China at the time. When AsiaInfo listed its shares on NASDAQ on March 3, 2000, they rocketed from $24 to more than $110 before settling at $75, a gain of 314 percent. Each of ChinaVest's partners on paper was richer by $8 million. And China's wild ride had only just begun.

Getting to know some of the participants in the AsiaInfo deal gave me a taste of the recipe China would follow as it powered its way into the future—one centered on marrying entrepreneurial talent with political connections. Edward Tian was a key ingredient. Even before AsiaInfo listed in New York, a Chinese state-owned company founded by Jiang Mianheng, the son of China's Communist Party boss, Jiang Zemin, had lured him away to join a firm called Netcom that had been given the mission of leapfrogging China into the forefront of information technology by laying fiber-optic cable throughout the country. Some of the cities Netcom wired with broadband had never had phone service before. Over a ten-month period in the early 2000s, Netcom workers laid six thousand miles of fiber-optic cable and connected China's seventeen largest cities to the World Wide Web.

Tian's ability to manage a telecommunications firm and articulate a vision was essential to the success of this staggering task. But Tian's efforts with Netcom wouldn't have succeeded without Jiang Mianheng. It was this combination of Tian's can-do spirit and Jiang's political pedigree that would drive China's rise. The marriage of know-how with political backing became a template for China's march into the future and a way for ambitious men and women like me to make something of our lives.

The AsiaInfo deal also showed that foreign firms could play this game as well. They were just as interested in using the sons and daughters of high-ranking Chinese officials to curry favor inside the system.

One of the bankers brought in by AsiaInfo to work on the transaction was a young man named Feng Bo. Feng's father was a writer and editor named Feng Zhijun, who'd been labeled a "rightist" in a political campaign in the 1950s and sent to a labor camp. In 1976 with the arrest of the Gang of Four, the ultra-leftists who'd gathered around Mao, Feng Zhijun was freed and became a leading member of the China Democratic League, one of the eight political parties that the Chinese Communist Party had maintained after the 1949 revolution as the window dressing of a pluralistic system. Feng Zhijun served on the Standing Committee of the National People's Congress, China's rubber-stamp legislature, for ten years and had access to inside information about policy changes that impacted foreign firms.

Feng's son, Feng Bo, had been a so-so student. In 1987, after Feng Bo performed poorly on the college entrance examination in China, his father sent the eighteen-year-old to the United States to stay with an American friend, hoping he'd gain some direction. Feng Bo landed in Marin County, California, took remedial English classes at the College of Marin, and learned to surf at Stinson Beach. To make ends meet, he worked as a busboy, waiter, sushi chef, and Chinese cook. He dabbled in avant-garde photography and dreamed of directing art house films.

In Northern California, Feng Bo met Sandy Robertson, the head of Robertson Stephens, a boutique San Francisco investment bank that rode—and eventually crashed in—the dot-com bubble.

Robertson learned of Feng Bo's political pedigree, trained him, made him an executive vice-president in his firm, and encouraged him to use his family connections to find Internet-related investments in China. In an April 1994 letter to Ron Brown, who was then serving as the secretary of commerce for the Clinton administration, Robertson reportedly boasted about Feng Bo's family ties. Along the way, Feng Bo married an American woman and they had two children.

For me, Robertson's cultivation of Feng Bo peeled back the curtain on the inner workings of a political system that mouthed Communist slogans while the families of senior officials gorged themselves at the trough of economic reforms. These sons and daughters functioned like an aristocracy; they intermarried, lived lives disconnected from those of average Chinese, and made fortunes selling access to their parents, inside information, and regulatory approvals that were keys to wealth.

Following the AsiaInfo deal, ChinaVest hired Feng Bo as our first Beijing-based rep. In the fall of 1997, after only a year at ChinaVest, Feng Bo left to pursue his own investments. Feng Bo ultimately divorced his American wife and married Zhuo Yue, a granddaughter of Deng Xiaoping. It seemed to me that Feng Bo leveraged his connections to the Deng family into substantial wealth. He also became a show-off, exchanging his dream of avant-garde filmmaking for the trappings of immense wealth. For a time, he cruised Beijing in a red Rolls-Royce convertible with military plates. Even people in his circle thought that was a bit much. China's red aristocracy was generally more subdued.

Soon after Feng Bo left ChinaVest, the firm held a management gathering. Right before the meeting, founder Bob Theleen's wife, Jenny, pulled me aside. "Hey, Desmond, how about moving to Beijing?" she asked casually. "You could be our new China rep." I thought she was joking, but the look on her face was serious. I jumped on it. At twenty-nine my life—born in China, educated in Hong Kong and the United States, and now heading back to the mainland—had come full circle. A few minutes later, Bob announced my promotion to the group.

CHAPTER FOUR

TRANSFERRED TO BEIJING IN LATE 1997, I DISCOVered a new China. Since Deng Xiaoping had resumed reforms in 1992, the economy had doubled, and it would double again by 2004. The country burst with rags-to-riches tales—stories of instant millionaires and financial sensations. The go-go energy of the place was infectious. Private business ownership boomed; it seemed as if everyone wanted to be his or her own boss. Mainland Chinese had spent decades living under the enforced poverty of Communism. Then in the 1990s, people rediscovered money, property, cars, and luxury goods and didn't look back.

The Party encouraged consumption and, in effect, offered the people an unwritten social contract encapsulated in Deng's formulation: "To get rich is glorious." Basically, the Party said, give us your freedom and we'll let you make money. That was the trade.

Still, most businesses remained small. A private firm with $2 million in revenue was considered substantial, except in the South, where manufacturers were building export giants selling sneakers, Christmas lights, toys, and microwaves to American consumers. Wanxiang, which would grow into one of the biggest auto parts makers in the world, was just getting started, and Jack Ma, a former English teacher who would found Internet sensation Alibaba, was on the hunt for angel investors. Jack and I met at the Ritz-Carlton's coffee shop in Hong Kong and he laughed at my request for a business plan. "Goldman Sachs is offering me five million dollars on the basis of an idea," he declared. "Why do I need to give you a business plan when we're just talking three million dollars."

The Communist system of central control and economic planning struggled to adapt to the changing China. Old laws no longer had relevance. But when the Party wrote the new laws, the ministries intentionally included vast gray areas so that if the authorities wanted to target anyone for prosecution, they always could.

The dismantling of the state-run work unit system in the cities where people had lived in apartments provided by the factory, sent their kids to the factory school, and worked together on the assembly line opened up a vast sector for new investment and new wealth: real estate development.

Corruption flowed through the system as Chinese Communist Party officials and their families made ample use of their connections to assign lucrative plots to friendly real estate developers. Party leaders used corruption investigations to purge their political foes. I arrived in Beijing as a case against the capital's mayor was wending its way through the courts. Mayor Chen Xitong had been accused of embezzling millions of dollars in a scheme to build vacation homes for the Party elite. His real "crime" was that he led the "Beijing clique," a Party faction that opposed the "Shanghai clique," overseen by Party chieftain Jiang

Zemin. In 1998, Chen was sentenced to sixteen years in prison. Chen's downfall was memorialized in the lightly fictionalized potboiler *The Wrath of Heaven*, which reflected the ever-widening gap between the official version of an honorable Party leadership and the street-level view of that leadership as a self-selected cabal of money-grubbing apparatchiks whose lives were far removed from those of ordinary folk.

As ChinaVest's representative in Beijing, I could feel the roar of China's engine stoked by decades of material scarcity. China's Communist system had failed to satisfy the material demands of China's people. But that was changing, and fast. Televisions, refrigerators, fans, microwaves, and washing machines were flying off the shelves. Still, I had trouble getting anyone to lift the hood for me so that I could become expert in how China really worked. Our investments were limited mostly to foreign-funded enterprises, which were building factories, cobbling together distribution chains, and transferring technological know-how as they turned China into a manufacturing powerhouse. This activity would only intensify as China negotiated the terms of its accession to the World Trade Organization in 2001.

I was unprepared for the job. I knew no one in business or in the Party. I was barely thirty years old. I couldn't even drink Moutai, a highly potent liquor that was brewed from sorghum, tasted like jet fuel, and was baked into China's national myth as the drink of Communist Party luminaries. I had to admit that I had no idea how to interact with adult mainland Chinese. They were another breed. I felt like an alien landing on another planet.

For one, I couldn't make small talk about politics, a necessary skill in the China business. I came from a very different socioeconomic situation. I had a career path, while the focus of my Chinese interlocutors was on making extra cash. My horizon was limitless. I could travel to Hong Kong at any time when for them a foreign trip was the highlight of the year. I could shop wherever I wanted. I knew brands that they'd never heard of. But I couldn't smoothly pass "red envelopes" stuffed with cash. All of those things added up. I was a foreigner in my homeland. I'd forgotten that singular stickiness of Chinese human relations that I'd known during my Shanghai youth.

Returning to Shanghai, I met a senior manager at the Fuxing Group, an up-and-coming conglomerate. We had a pleasant chat over tea about their businesses, but it was clear he wasn't interested in ChinaVest's money. Fuxing was already rumored to be in bed with the family of President Jiang Zemin. They had no reason to let a foreign firm peer behind the curtain to see how they operated. Within five minutes of meeting me, that guy probably concluded: *This idiot doesn't know anything about China*. He was right.

In Beijing, I lived in the bubble of a Western expat. I had a well-appointed apartment across the street from the Ministry of Foreign Affairs. A driver squired me around in a black Red Flag limo. A friend joked that I was so well looked after that I had a nanny secretary managing my office, a nanny cook managing my kitchen, and a nanny girlfriend—a Shanghainese model—managing my bedroom.

My social interactions were mostly confined to Westerners, English-speaking Asian expats, and those Chinese who wanted to mix with expats. ChinaVest's office was in the Swissôtel, which housed other Western firms. I worked out at the hotel's gym, surrounded by expats, and partied at the Hard Rock Cafe, which had opened a Beijing branch in 1994, again with expats.

I patronized a bar called the Half Moon Café in a back alley near a run-down diner that served Sichuan hot pot. Frequented by Westerners and the raggedy denizens of Beijing's demimonde, Half Moon Café featured live jazz performed by Chinese musicians who were rediscovering an art form that had been popular before the Communists banned it as "bourgeois" after the revolution in 1949. The bar was owned by Jin Xing, a Chinese dancer and choreographer who'd studied in New York in the 1980s with modern dance legends Martha Graham and Merce Cunningham. In 1995, Jin Xing had undergone the first public sex change operation in Chinese history to become a woman.

Whenever I'd arrive at the bar, the bartender would notify Jin and she'd sidle over. Unfortunately, she always seemed a little too pleased to see me, so I cut back my forays to the Half Moon. But that was Beijing. Everyone was on the make, yearning for something new, often money, but also personal freedom, and what Chinese imagined to be a Western lifestyle.

Banned for years from leaving China, Chinese began to emigrate in large numbers. Young, attractive Chinese women weren't immune to the desire to get out. At a foreigners' party, I met one and, searching for a common interest, we landed on swimming and agreed on a dip at the Olympic-size pool in the China-Japan Friendship Center on the east side of town.

My date emerged from the changing room in one of the skimpiest bikinis I'd ever seen. Suffice it to say, in a public pool in 1990s China the masses, unaccustomed to such bold exhibitionism, were agape. As her escort, I was both mesmerized and mortified. Soon thereafter, she married a German businessman and decamped to Düsseldorf. Experiences like these gave me a flavor of what was happening offstage but also combined to make me feel even more out of touch. Although I'd been born in the country and spoke three dialects like a local, I felt I was on the outside looking in.

In late 1999, I met an entrepreneur and son of a general in the People's Liberation Army named Lan Hai. Lan was a visionary in the telecommunications industry and had been a major software provider when paging was all the rage.

In the mid-1990s, pagers were a status symbol in a changing China, like they'd once been in the West. While it took months—and often a bribe—to get a landline telephone from a lumbering state-owned phone company, paging technology, sold by private firms, allowed people to leapfrog ahead. Scores of paging firms opened up vast call centers, firing messages nationwide. By the late 1990s, close to 100 million Chinese had pagers. Then another disruptive technology—mobile telephones—arrived with messaging capabilities built in, and paging began to lose out. Lan's firm, PalmInfo, attempted to give these call centers a new lease on life, offering secretarial and banking services. ChinaVest was interested in PalmInfo and we ultimately helped Lan raise $4 million. In late 1999, Lan offered me a job, spurring another big change in my life.

Lan's offer came when I'd already begun having doubts about a career in private equity. I felt as if I were standing on a riverbank watching the flow of a modernizing country rush by. Having become an associate at ChinaVest and then its chief rep in Beijing, I saw how my life would unfold. I figured I'd be promoted to partner by forty and a few years later I'd be renting a mansion in Hong Kong like my bosses were. Such a scenario left little room for imagination. In the private equity industry, we always said we were thirty thousand feet from the trenches. But I itched to be down there fighting, not just as an investor but as the builder of a business. I wanted to be part of the China story, not simply someone seeking to profit from it. What's more, I'd always enjoyed exploring the unknowns—from the alleyways of Shanghai to the American heartland. I wanted a new challenge. I wanted to do something tremendous. And I was living through a period of time in China when the tremendous was possible. I also felt that to be a good investor, I needed experience as an entrepreneur. In the venture capital industry at that time, everyone could run the numbers, but only a few could run a business. I wanted to be that guy.

I joined PalmInfo as its CEO in the beginning of 2000 and Lan moved over to become our chairman. Flush with money from ChinaVest, we took over a whole floor in a glitzy office building next to the Kempinski Hotel on Beijing's upscale east side. We poached senior staff from Motorola's operation in China and made one hundred additional hires. We even opened a satellite office in Irvine, California. We wanted to show that we were a high-flying concern. Our business cards listed a dozen subsidiaries. "Hmm," sniffed a senior executive at a state-owned telecom company as she fingered my business card, "so now you're an international conglomerate."

At PalmInfo, our results left something to be desired. Our burn rate was extraordinary and our revenues were feeble. We couldn't convince Chinese banks to buy our service. And even when companies were interested in the technology, we had competition. We were using proprietary software, but after one of our employees quit, a new company opened up selling the same service at a lower price. Who could we rely on to protect us? Nobody. China was the intellectual property rip-off capital of the world, churning out pirated software and DVDs with abandon; no Chinese law enforcement agency in the year 2000 was interested in taking our case.

In the late spring of 2001, eighteen months into the venture, it was obvious we needed a change. We downscaled to a smaller office. We fired our new hires. It was obvious that I, too, was redundant. So I quit. With nothing holding me in Beijing, I headed to Shanghai, where my parents had moved from Hong Kong.

My father's career was going in the opposite direction of mine. He'd grown Tyson's business in China from nothing to more than $100 million a year. He was so successful that Tyson decided to open an office on the mainland and send my dad back to Shanghai as its chief representative. My father saw his return home as a triumph. He'd left China as a schoolteacher under the cloud of a bad class background. He'd worked his way up from a laborer in a warehouse to the representative of a multibillion-dollar business. He was returning to China as what his friends called a *meiguo maiban,* an American comprador, the pre–Communist era term for the Chinese rep of a US firm. It was a double-edged appellation because it, jokingly, implied that my dad was a running dog of Yankee imperialism while it also acknowledged his success. My dad took the sobriquet as recognition that he'd made it. A corner office in a glass skyscraper and a swank apartment in the city center further boosted his ego.

Shanghai's boom extended far beyond the sale of chicken parts. The Xiangming Secondary School where my father had taught had been demolished to make way for a high-end karaoke bar. I moved into a second apartment that my parents had purchased as a weekend getaway in a suburb of Sheshan. There, developers were building Shanghai's finest private golf club.

Everything was going up except me. I'd grown accustomed to progress, but I had to admit defeat. For the first time in my life, I read self-help books, consuming everything from Dale Carnegie's *How to Win Friends and Influence People* to the Chinese philosophers Confucius and Mencius to the Buddhist spiritual teacher Nan Huai-Chin. I undertook a journey of self-criticism and self-discovery. It was then that I finally grasped the meaning of the Chinese proverb "if you want to jump, you must first learn to bow."

Nan Huai-Chin was a former kung fu champion who left a promising military career in the middle of World War II to enter a Buddhist monastery. In 1949, Nan fled the Communist revolution to Taiwan, where he became one of the most popular writers on religion and Chinese philosophy in the Chinese language. I realized that I'd been so busy aiming at the next target in my life that I'd never stopped to reflect. Reading Nan, I became far more interested in why I'd failed than in why PalmInfo had failed. What was it that I lacked?

I concluded that I'd been moving too fast, gliding through things without focus. Details had bored me, but the more I studied the more I understood that details mattered. The PalmInfo imbroglio had left me with a bad case of insomnia. I began to meditate, and I learned how to cleanse my mind so I could sleep. I worked on moderating my breath, a skill that would serve me well as life became more harried. Nan's exhortation to look beyond oneself set the foundation for my later interest in charitable organizations. I shed the outward trappings of my expat life in Beijing. I broke up with my girlfriend. Meanwhile, my parents lent me money to make ends meet.

In Shanghai, I still worked occasionally for PalmInfo. We'd been discussing a merger with another company named Great Ocean that had been selling hardware to the telecom industry. Our software complemented their products and we shared many of the same clients. Great Ocean wanted to take on new investors because it was perennially short of cash. State-owned telecom clients were always slow to pay up after they bought Great Ocean's hardware. On a trip to Beijing in the winter of 2001, we visited Great Ocean's offices in the Oriental Plaza next door to the iconic Beijing Hotel. There I met someone who was introduced to me as Duan Zong, or "The Lady Chairman Whitney Duan."

I'd been running around China for almost six years, but I'd never encountered such an independent-minded female entrepreneur. I first saw Duan Zong around a conference table with a dozen people in the room. She sat at one end and I at the other. She talked fast and brooked no dissent. It was impossible to get a word in edgewise. China is a very patriarchal society, so it was striking to see a powerful woman dominate the room. In addition, in my experience, Chinese heavyweights, especially women, were understated. I'd never seen somebody in a business milieu as full frontal as The Lady Chairman Whitney Duan.

As we saw each other more to discuss the merger, Whitney began passing casual judgments on the way I held myself in the blunt manner of many Chinese who, if you've gained a few pounds, will not think twice about declaring that you've become fat. "Your feet are higher than the table," she observed one day as I sat with my legs crossed, one foot bobbing in midair. In China, she declared, when you meet with officials you're not supposed to be so informal, so Westernized. "Be like a kid in a classroom," she instructed me. "Perch yourself on the edge of your seat." And don't speak until spoken to.

I'd never met anyone who tossed out observations and instructions with such self-confidence. Clothed in a Chanel suit with an Hermès bag, she conveyed an image of affluence and success. Searching for a new path and racked with self-doubt, I found purpose in Whitney's rules. I wanted to be like her.

At five-seven, Whitney was tall for a Chinese woman. She had a sweet voice and during her college days she'd been the lead singer in the school's choir. We started going to karaoke parlors with our colleagues, and when she snagged the mic everyone's jaw dropped listening to her croon.

I wouldn't really describe her as a beauty. She clearly had been gorgeous in her youth. By the time we met she was in her mid-thirties and had put on a few pounds. Still, she was a force of nature. Her eyes sparkled with insight and energy. Compared to my past girlfriends, intellectually and spiritually, Whitney was on a completely different plane. She'd read the books I was reading. She had a philosophical understanding of how China worked and could explain to me why people in China reacted differently than people outside its borders. She built a bridge that reconnected me to my beloved homeland. Given that this was a transformative period of my life, I was wide open to her charms.

Whitney gave the impression of having gained access to the engine of China's growth. For me, she was the first one who lifted the hood. She knew the officials whom I'd only read about in newspapers. She knew others whom I'd never heard of. This was a new world. I wanted to learn and Whitney seemed eager to be my guide.

I began visiting Beijing again. The more I saw of Whitney, the more I was impressed. She could reel off complete paragraphs from the works of Chinese philosophers, Confucius and Mencius, and the French enlightenment thinker Montesquieu. She signed me up to help her company raise money. I began advising her on financial matters.

We dated and did fun things like hiking and catching a movie. But what set our relationship apart were our discussions. Aligning our goals constituted her idea of romance. I'd never experienced this approach to a relationship, nor had I ever encountered anyone who was so certain that her way was the right way. Early in 2002, we met at the marble-encased coffee shop of Beijing's Grand Hyatt and talked for three hours. Whitney grilled me on my approach to marriage. She steered me, in a way no one else had in the past, to look clinically at my personal life. I'd never been much of a ladies' man, but I was more Western in my outlook toward relationships. If things happened, go with the flow. As Hollywood romances say, follow your heart. Whitney had no truck with that approach. "You," she announced, "need a better approach." She and I actually did a SWOT analysis, a checklist used to assess a business. Separately, we broke down the Strengths, Weaknesses, Opportunities, and Threats to our emotional ties. Then we compared notes.

Whitney's argument appealed to my analytical side. She

seemed to have a magic formula for success, which was especially intriguing because my formula had clearly lost its mojo. Whitney's view of passion, love, and sex was that we could grow into them, but it wouldn't be the glue that would bind us. What would cement the relationship would be its underlying logic—did our personalities match; did we share values, desire the same ends, and agree on the means? If so, everything else would follow. Early on, we both agreed on the ends. We wanted to leave something behind, to make a mark on China and the world. This had been my goal for years and Whitney shared it. As to the means, Whitney exuded confidence that she'd found the ticket to success. I put myself in her hands.

Ours was more a connection of the spirit and the brain than the heart. It felt like an arranged marriage, the difference being that we, not a matchmaker, were doing the arranging. The logic was persuasive. We complemented each other. I could read a spreadsheet and move easily in Western circles. Whitney had access to a hidden China. She made me realize how little I knew of that world even though I was a native and had done business in Beijing for years. She was my entrée into another dimension, one that was completely unfamiliar to me. I was entranced, wowed, literally swept off my feet.

Looking for the next step in my life, I followed Whitney's formula for success. Like I had with my cousins in Hong Kong, I allowed her to mold me. I became her project, Eliza Doolittle to her Henry Higgins. To appear more mature, I tossed out my contact lenses and opted for glasses. My casual look gave way to suits. She told me I needed heft, so I tried my best to conform to the Chinese aphorism "an old head on young shoulders."

One day we were riding together in a car and I was looking out the window as I did sometimes, with my mind blank.

"What are you thinking?" she asked.

"Nothing," I replied.

She sat up, turned to me, and declared, "That's not right. Your mind should always be working."

She was constantly planning the next step, whom to call, what to say, how to operate. She wasn't one move ahead; she was ten. I embraced that way of thinking, too. After a while, it became second nature. Such an approach to life did have a downside, though. In the early days, we thoroughly enjoyed each other's company. But the more we focused on the future, the more our minds lost the capacity to be in the now. We paid less attention to us, and more on the outside world.

Whitney gave me a crash course in China's political system. In the West, political parties only wielded power when they won elections and took control of the government. In China, the Chinese Communist Party had no competition. The Party secretary in a county, city, or province outranked the county chief, mayor, or provincial governor. Even China's military, the People's Liberation Army, was legally not the army of the Chinese state. It was the Party's army.

I did my best to broaden Whitney's horizons as well. I educated her about wine and Western food. I took her to the gym and used my years of training to help her shed a few pounds. We worked out together in the Grand Hyatt's health club and swam in its swimming pool, outfitted like a tropical rain forest with palm trees and shimmering lights. But Whitney dreaded our workouts. After a few months, she gave up.

We shared our spiritual sides, too. Whitney was a devoted Christian and found comfort in her religion. For a long time, she tried to convert me. She brought me to church and had me read the Bible, telling me it would strengthen our relationship. I also read the Koran and the holy texts of the Baha'i faith. I searched for a spiritual path, but, in the end, her Christianity found little traction in my soul.

Under Whitney's guidance, I shelved my desire for fiery passion and embraced her argument that intimacy would deepen over time, partially because I was spellbound by the glorious life to which a partnership with her might lead. Of course, we had our tender moments. In a society that still frowned on overt expressions of affection between men and women, we often held hands. In her private moments, Whitney had a girly, easygoing side that I found endearing. Throughout our relationship, she called me by my English name, Desmond. I called her Xiao Duan, or Little Duan. Within a year of meeting, we'd moved in together.

Looking back, a few things explained Whitney's pragmatism about love and her desire to be involved with me. For one, in China she was no longer a young woman. When we met, she told me she was thirty-four, about a month younger than me. She was late to the marriage market in a society where women on average marry at twenty-five. What's more, she traveled in circles where single women were prey.

Men in power constantly chased women. Unmarried women in China with a little money were all assumed to be sleeping around. Whitney had already turned down one marriage proposal from a high-ranking member of the Chinese Communist

Party who was twenty years her senior. If she stayed single, there'd be more. Being attached to someone was a shield. But even after we started going out, the advances didn't stop. Communist China had spent decades repressing the desires—material and sexual—of its people. Now they were erupting at the same time. "Even the air in Beijing contains hormones" went an expression at the time.

That I was tall with a not unpleasing appearance probably factored into Whitney's decision to be with me. My Western education and background in finance brought advantages, too. My status as an insider outsider—Chinese but Western educated—was valuable. But the most important thing to Whitney was trust. Whitney didn't just need a business partner; she required someone she could rely on completely. She was about to start a high-stakes chess match at the apex of power in China. It was a life-and-death game and she needed to have 110 percent faith in whoever she partnered with. That's why a normal business partnership wouldn't have sufficed. She needed complete commitment to her cause.

CHAPTER FIVE

WHITNEY SEEMED AT HOME IN THE CAPITAL, BUT I soon discovered that she'd only recently arrived in Beijing. She was born in Shandong Province, a coastal region known for its tough soldiers and as the birthplace of the philosopher Confucius. Her mother was a homemaker who'd fallen in with a Chinese offshoot of evangelical Christianity that favored speaking in tongues. Evangelical Christianity had found fertile soil in China's countryside for generations. China's bloodiest peasant rebellion was led in the 1850s by a Christian convert who hallucinated that he was the younger brother of Jesus Christ. In the 1990s, peasant preachers in China were claiming similar lineages, including one female fire-breather who insisted that she was Jesus's sister and led a cult called Eastern Lightning. Following in her mother's footsteps, Whitney, too, became a Christian.

Whitney's mother had fled an abusive relationship when she was pregnant with Whitney and remarried a small-town official. Whitney idolized her mom for this defiant act, rare in a society that forced women to accept their fate. Whitney clung to her mother because she was her only blood relative. She always spoke glowingly of her mother partially because she was worried that I, having been raised in the big city of Shanghai, would look down on her. I grew accustomed to Mrs. Duan's constant streams of quotations from the Bible.

Whitney's stepfather was a petty official in the local water department. Whenever her stepdad traveled, he packed a vial of explosively spicy chili sauce that he'd apply liberally to everything he ate. He brought a son to the relationship and the couple later had another boy, Whitney's half brother. Whitney would set up her stepbrother in the real estate business. Her half brother never worked and would live off Whitney until she disappeared.

Whitney grew up in a one-room dormitory in a big courtyard with other families in the water department near Weishan, a lakeside township near Shandong's southern border with Jiangsu. Whitney's father and mother were well-off compared to the farmers who lived nearby for the sole reason that they were paid their salaries in cash, and cash in the countryside was in short supply. Whereas my family counted on chicken once a year, Whitney's family dined on ducks, freshwater fish, eggs, and copious fresh vegetables.

The first time Whitney took the college entrance examination at seventeen, she failed. Her parents enrolled her in a vocational school for automobile mechanics and she spent a year learning to fix cars. Immersed each day in antifreeze and lubricants, her ungloved hands blistered and shed skin. They would remain puffy all her life. Despite her parents' entreaties for her to accept her fate, Whitney crammed to retake the exam, hitting the books in the early-morning hours and late into the night. She studied on a bench under a single lamp in the drafty hall of their dormitory throughout one winter, saddling herself with a lifetime of back pain.

Whitney didn't hate her humble roots, but she wanted out of the grimy compound she called home along with the surrounding countryside, denuded of trees, devoid of wildlife, and scored by foul-smelling irrigation ditches. Like me, she yearned to make her mark in China and for China.

In 1986, Whitney tested into the Nanjing Polytechnic Institute, a leading military university, in neighboring Jiangsu. She majored in computer science, graduated at the top of her class, and was offered a job at the school, a plum assignment in those days. She joined the Chinese Communist Party and became the assistant to the school's president.

Working for the president of a Chinese university gave Whitney a priceless education in how to deal with Chinese officials, a skill she'd hone to perfection. She learned how to alter her attitude, tone of voice, and language depending on her interlocutor. Nanjing Polytechnic was closely associated with the People's Liberation Army, so she also got a crash course in handling military officers.

Whitney sharpened her already fluent writing skills, authoring the president's speeches and learning how to channel his voice. Whitney littered those speeches with references to China's classics. Sometimes Chinese writing can get bogged down with literary allusions, but Whitney displayed a deep knowledge of Chinese literature without laying it on too thick.

After Whitney spent a year at the university, the school's president arranged for her to work as a deputy county chief in Shandong in charge of bringing in outside investment. The Party cultivated talented young men and women in this manner, giving them exposure to the bottom rung of government. Whitney spent a lot of time in Beijing, seeking out the many Shandong natives who worked in the Party bureaucracy, trying to cultivate the old-boy network to facilitate investment in the county.

Shandong taught Whitney a valuable lesson, similar to one that I learned in Hong Kong. She discovered that the only ones who truly succeeded in China were people with *guanxi*, connections into the system. Still, she didn't like the life of a deputy county chief. She was forced to drink so much that she broke out in hives. She was sexually harassed. And when the county chief was arrested and sentenced to jail on corruption charges, the backstabbing and rumormongering became intolerable.

That experience killed any desire on her part to work for the government. It planted deep inside her a visceral fear of the Chinese system and a commitment, as she put it, to ensure that "if you pulled my corpse out of my coffin and whipped it, you'd still find no dirt." She decided that a career in business was the way to go.

Whitney wrote to the university president in Nanjing requesting a transfer. She wanted to try her hand in a state-owned company. Business, she figured, offered her the best way to succeed. She promised herself, however, that in pursuing business she'd stay above reproach. In a dirty system, she believed she could keep herself, even her corpse, clean.

The president found her a position as the assistant to the CEO of a real estate development company run by China's military. At the time, the People's Liberation Army was into all sorts of businesses, including food production, pharmaceuticals, wineries, and weapons, all of which constituted a commercial empire worth billions of dollars. Courtesy of the PLA, Whitney got her first taste of the high life. She shopped for designer brands at the Wangfu Hotel in Beijing, a joint venture between Hong Kong's Peninsula Group and the Chinese army. She attended lavish dinners. Brick by brick, she constructed the façade of a high-powered deal maker with *guanxi*.

The corruption engendered by the PLA's businesses was legendary and was eroding China's ability to fight. I'd witnessed military corruption, too, when that firm I was assigned to liaise with on ChinaVest's behalf, Tait Asia, was approached by a Chinese naval officer offering the nation's battleships to smuggle beer. In 1996, Whitney set out on her own and founded a company, which in English she called Great Ocean. A year later, China's Party chief Jiang Zemin ordered the military to divest itself of its commercial holdings.

Great Ocean began with real estate projects in Tianjin. The Tianjin branch of the China Ocean Shipping Company staked Whitney her first $1 million, making a connection that would prove portentous later on. But after Whitney developed three projects and multiplied her net wealth, Tianjin began to feel small.

Whitney wanted a bigger canvas and, ninety miles to the northwest, Beijing beckoned. Like me, she yearned to do something remarkable in a country so full of opportunity. That untamed ambition, that wild desire to make something of our lives, was what drove us together and provided the underlying logic for our partnership. Whitney wrote her ambition into the Chinese name of her company—Tai Hong. Those two words came from a sentence written by the ancient Chinese historian Sima Qian, who observed that a human life could be as weighty as Mount Tai or as trifling as a feather. That was how she saw herself and ultimately me. We'd come from nothing, and if we ended up making nothing out of our lives, it wouldn't matter. So why not go for it all? That was her life's motto, and without that kind of attitude she'd never have been able to pull herself from the bottom of the pile to the top. Her hometown wasn't even a third-tier city. Her family was broken. In my opinion, her half brother and stepbrother were good-for-nothings. But, by God, she wasn't going to be as trifling as a feather; she and I were going to be as weighty at Mount Tai.

In 1999, Whitney moved to Beijing. She rented an office in the Oriental Plaza, the capital's flashiest business address, with the aim of projecting power, success, and credibility. She leveraged the relationships she'd made working for the army and began by selling IBM servers and other equipment to state-run telecom companies eager to expand their services. And she networked like mad, cadging invitations to exclusive functions with senior officials of the Chinese Communist Party.

Like Edward Tian at AsiaInfo, Whitney discovered that to unlock the door to success in China she needed two keys. One was political heft. In China, entrepreneurs only succeeded if they pandered to the interests of the Communist Party. Whether it be a shopkeeper in a corner store or a tech genius in China's Silicon Valley, everyone needed sponsors inside the system. The second requirement was the ability to execute once an opportunity arose. Only by possessing both keys would success be possible. That's what Whitney set out to do and how I entered the picture.

Whitney and I matched in many ways. When she told me her story of humble origins, I saw myself. We were both late to the marriage market, so that aligned us, too. And we both hungered for success.

Our union embodied on a deeply personal level the story of China's modernization. In the nineteenth century, Chinese scholar-officials had advocated the theory that Chinese learning should remain the core of China's march into the future while Western learning should be employed for practical use. The scholars called this *zhongxue wei ti, xixue wei yong.* Whitney epitomized Chinese learning, or *zhongxue,* and I stood for *xixue,* or Western education. I was coming from China's periphery both literally and metaphorically and joining Whitney at China's core.

Whitney invited me on a journey into China's heart. Each bend of the river carried us deeper. With each twist, we became more and more creatures of China's "system," a Chinese code word used to signify the country's unique amalgam of political and economic power that emanates from the highest levels of the Chinese Communist Party. While most of China's 1.4 billion people spend their lives under the spell of the system, we joined it and thrived inside it.

In the early summer of 2002, Whitney and I took a ten-day trip to the Canadian resort town of Banff. Whitney believed that traveling together was the best way to learn about a potential mate. For me, it was a way to exhibit my talents at navigating the Western world and show off my Western learning for "practical use." We complemented each other in another way. I was naturally curious; Whitney was more closed. She needed someone to pry her out of her comfort zone, to push her down inviting alleyways and, as it were, find a different way to the pool. She trusted me to be her guide. I arranged everything. I booked the train trip on the glass-ceilinged Rocky Mountaineer from Vancouver and our lodging at the Fairmont Chateau Lake Louise with a room overlooking the eponymous lake. We ate at the best restaurants and took in the raw beauty of the scenery. We explored together, saw deeper into each other, and, in a bubble all our own, basked in the moment.

Returning to Beijing, Whitney approached me and said that now that we were ready to move to the next stage in our relationship, she needed to get our union endorsed by a special friend. With that, another door opened and our lives would change again.

CHAPTER SIX

I WAS CURIOUS WHY I HAD TO OBTAIN ANOTHER stamp of approval. I'd already met Whitney's parents and Whitney had road-tested our relationship on our Banff getaway; did I really need someone else's blessing? So it was with a sense of apprehension that I readied for a dinner on a late-summer evening in 2002.

Whitney had settled on the trendy Cantonese restaurant, Yue Ting, in the basement of Beijing's Grand Hyatt hotel. The hotel was a testimony to China's idea of itself in the 2000s—somewhat garish and a little over-the-top. Custom-tailored plush chairs and sleek, ebony tables complemented the Italian marble flooring and gold fixtures. Among the clientele were representatives of the two Chinas that coexisted in Beijing. One was newly rich and comically flamboyant. Men who intentionally left the tags on their jacket sleeves to show off the brands. The other China, the official China, avoided flash to escape unwanted attention and potential jealousy.

Whitney and I arrived early to settle on the menu and inspect the private room she'd reserved. Whitney told me that our guest was an important elder whom she respected enormously. She told me that she'd only reveal the elder's identity after the meal. I had no idea who we were hosting. I only knew that it was going to impact our future.

Shortly before 6:30, we ascended the circular marble staircase to the Hyatt's lobby and headed to the front door to await our guest. We were dressed smartly; Whitney wore Chanel and I'd donned a suit. A chauffeured black BMW rolled up and out stepped a rather plain-looking middle-aged lady in a blue Max Mara outfit offset by a floral scarf. Whitney introduced her to me as Zhang Ayi, or "Auntie" Zhang, using the endearingly respectful Chinese appellation for an older woman.

Auntie Zhang had a welcoming smile that put me immediately at ease. Hand at her elbow, Whitney escorted her downstairs and into our private room. Auntie Zhang walked directly to the seat of honor, signaled by a napkin stuffed into a wineglass and arranged like a peacock fan.

As we dined on steamed grouper and stir-fried Chinese broccoli, Auntie Zhang peppered me with questions about my background and education, Shanghai, America, and Hong Kong, private equity, and PalmInfo. She played the role of an inquisitive elder. Whitney had told me nothing about her other than that she was a close friend and important to her. As the meal drew to a close, I still couldn't guess who she was.

Early into the banquet, I'd discounted the possibility that she was a high-ranking official or married to one. To my mind, those types belonged to a separate species. They moved differently than us commoners and spoke a peculiarly stilted form of Mandarin sprinkled with buzzwords like "the organization" (for the Communist Party). Conversations with them were the Chinese version of the inside-the-Beltway chatter you hear in Washington, D.C., who's up and who's down, what new policy is coming down the pike. These characters also never traveled alone, perpetually accompanied by obsequious assistants who'd be banished to tables outside private rooms while they dined within. Auntie Zhang had come to the Hyatt alone and displayed none of the idiosyncrasies of China's political elite.

In fact, Auntie Zhang seemed like one of us. Well-to-do, for sure, and self-confident, but within our genetic paradigm. She was approachable and comfortable in her skin. Still, there was something about her unassuming flair as well as the obvious deference Whitney displayed toward her that made her special in my eyes.

With the meal over, Whitney and I undertook the multistep dance of bidding a respected guest goodbye. We walked her upstairs to her waiting car. I opened the passenger door, placed my hand on top of the doorframe to make sure she didn't bump her head getting in, and then jogged around to tip her driver. Chauffeurs are important in China. Chatty drivers have been responsible for the downfall of many officials, so it's important to keep them happy. I rejoined Whitney at the entrance to the Hyatt where we stood at attention and waved. Auntie Zhang rolled down the window and smiled as the car eased into Beijing's nighttime traffic and disappeared.

I turned to Whitney and only then did I learn that Auntie Zhang was Zhang Beili, the wife of one of China's then vice-premiers, Wen Jiabao.* It was an open secret that Wen was going to succeed Zhu Rongji as China's next premier in 2003. Wen

* In China, a wife generally does not take her husband's name.

would soon become the head of China's government and the second most powerful man in the Chinese Communist Party. And Whitney was friends with his wife. I was floored.

Whitney had met Auntie Zhang in 2001, some two years after Whitney had arrived in Beijing. Auntie Zhang had just turned sixty and her husband was the vice-premier in charge of managing China's entry into the World Trade Organization. Whitney had been invited to a girls' night out that Auntie Zhang had also attended. That evening Whitney's magnetic personality had been on full display; she'd quoted from the classics and thoroughly charmed Auntie Zhang. The pair had exchanged cell-phone numbers and Auntie Zhang had told Whitney to call her "Auntie," a sign she was willing to consider a more personal relationship. Then Whitney did something few other Chinese would have done. She didn't contact Auntie Zhang.

Whitney knew that when cultivating someone powerful in China, the pursuer should never appear too eager. Other people would harass their targets and refuse to take a hint. But Whitney knew the psychology of China's elite. With so many people angling to profit from a connection with Auntie Zhang, Whitney needed to separate herself from the pack. She was a fantastic judge of character. She'd baited the hook with a smash performance during their first meeting. Now with her line in the water, she waited.

After a week, Auntie Zhang bit. She called Whitney and scolded her for not reaching out. "We had such a good talk," she said. "Why didn't you contact me? I've been thinking of you." Auntie Zhang suggested they meet again. This time the setting was more intimate: a quiet dinner for two.

Whitney was a master at teasing out the details of other

people's lives, a key competence in a world where forming relationships was crucial to success. Once she'd decided that Auntie Zhang was a target worthy of cultivation, Whitney set out to learn everything she could about her.

Whitney discovered why Auntie Zhang didn't exude the phoniness so common among the wives of other Chinese officials. For one, she wasn't a child of the red aristocracy. Her parents were commoners, so she hadn't grown up in the rarefied atmosphere of Beijing cared for by nannies, eating food from a dedicated supply chain, and attending elite schools as had the offspring of Party luminaries. In addition, Auntie Zhang had had her own career before her husband's rise forced her to take a backseat. And in that career, she'd become comfortable with people of all sorts.

Auntie Zhang was born in 1941 in the middle of World War II in Gansu Province, a poor region in northwest China. After China's Communist revolution in 1949, her family, originally from coastal Zhejiang Province, stayed in China's west. She attended college at Lanzhou University in Gansu's capital and majored in geology. She met Wen Jiabao in 1968 when she was a graduate student and Wen, after graduate studies in Beijing, had been dispatched from the capital to lead a geological survey team in Gansu.

Word has it that Auntie Zhang, who was Wen's senior by a year, pursued Wen. She was outgoing and liked to sing and dance and she won his heart by regularly surfacing at the door to his dormitory, offering to do his laundry. A serious-minded bookworm, Wen was attracted to her bubbly personality and love of adventure. She showed us a picture of the two of them deep in China's remote western mountains on a geological project. Auntie Zhang was smiling brightly; Wen's face was blank.

Soon into his stay in Gansu, Wen shifted his focus from geological work to politics, serving in Communist Party positions as he climbed the ladder of the province's geological bureau. Auntie Zhang became her husband's chief cheerleader and adviser. Her spirited disposition and willingness to take risks complemented his introverted, cautious nature.

The pair married and, in 1982, Wen was plucked from Gansu and brought to Beijing, where he served on the Party committee at the Ministry of Geology and Mineral Resources. After a stint as deputy minister of geology, in 1985 Wen got a huge promotion to deputy director of the General Office of the Central Committee of the Chinese Communist Party. The General Office is the main gatekeeper of all Party functions, somewhat akin to the office of the White House chief of staff. It handles the logistics of major Party meetings, puts together policy papers on key topics, and transmits Party decisions to stakeholders, such as the security services, government ministries, and state-owned enterprises.

The director of the Party's General Office is known colloquially as China's "chief eunuch," a throwback reference to China's imperial past when castrated males constituted the backbone of the administrative workforce inside the Forbidden City. In 1986, Wen became the "chief eunuch." He'd direct the General Office for the next seven years, serving not one but three "emperors": Communist Party general secretaries Hu Yaobang, Zhao Ziyang, and, finally, Jiang Zemin.

During normal times it would have been quite a feat to work for three Party chairmen, but during this period of political turbulence it was nothing short of herculean. Party elders purged Wen's first two bosses, Hu Yaobang and Zhao Ziyang, for failing to crack down on student demonstrators. After the army's assault on Tiananmen Square in 1989, hard-liners picked his third boss, Jiang Zemin. Still, Wen stayed put.

Wen's biggest test came on May 19, 1989, at 5:00 in the morning at the height of the massive protests around Tiananmen Square. He accompanied Party General Secretary Zhao Ziyang to the square for an impromptu meeting with student demonstrators who'd massed there by the thousands. In a rambling statement aired on China Central Television, Zhao promised the protesters that the Party would negotiate with them in good faith. He wasn't telling the truth. What Zhao neglected to say was Party elders had already decided to purge him and had mobilized China's military to clear the square. A day after Zhao visited Tiananmen, hard-line premier Li Peng declared martial law. Two weeks later, on the night of June 3, 1989, the People's Liberation Army opened fire on the protesters, and, by the morning of June 4, hundreds were dead. On Tiananmen Square, tanks flattened the Goddess of Democracy, a Statue of Liberty look-alike that art students had hoisted opposite the giant portrait of Chairman Mao. Zhao would spend the next fifteen years under house arrest until his death on January 17, 2005.

Following the crackdown, Party investigators weeded out thousands of officials who'd sided with Zhao's view of a more liberal future for China. But with counsel from Auntie Zhang, Wen avoided the purge. There did appear to be penance involved. For almost a decade after 1989 while he toiled at the heart of the Party bureaucracy, Wen was only photographed in Mao suits, wearing his loyalty to the Party literally on his sleeve. The first time Wen appeared in Western attire was 1998, after China's then premier

Zhu Rongji moved Wen from his Party post to a top government position as a deputy premier.

Wen's personality saved him. It's probably going too far to say that at heart he *was* a political eunuch. However, he was extraordinarily careful; he never insulted or threatened anyone. He managed up and avoided any association with political factions. More so than most officials, he stayed in his lane. To get to his position, he obviously had to have ambition, but it was a restrained type of ambition that didn't threaten his comrades at the Party's heights. When Zhu Rongji was termed out as premier in March 2003, Wen became a natural compromise candidate to replace him.

As premier, Wen cultivated a man-of-the-people image. When a massive earthquake rocked Sichuan Province in 2008, Wen sped to the scene wearing a rumpled jacket and track shoes. Chinese people took to calling him Grandpa Wen.

Wen's strong suit became a weakness. He did seem to possess a vision for a freer, more open China. After his old boss Zhao Ziyang was muzzled under house arrest, Wen was the only Chinese leader to continue to speak publicly about universal values, such as freedom and democracy. Still, Wen very much hewed to the rules of the Chinese power structure, which strictly limited the jurisdiction of the premier. Wen's job was to run the government. Only Hu Jintao, the Party general secretary, who outranked Wen, could push for political reform. And he never did.

My impression from observing Wen and speaking with Whitney, Auntie Zhang, and his children was that his views on democracy were aspirational. He talked about it, but he had no desire to upset the status quo and actually do the things necessary to make China a freer place. That understanding—that he might

speak up sometimes but would continue to play within the rules of the system—was a key reason why Wen got and stayed at the job.

Wen was too trusting of his family, especially of Auntie Zhang. He delegated far too many things to her and allowed his kids to profit off his name. He was interested in nothing but work. Unlike Zhu Rongji,who played the *erhu,* a Chinese string instrument, or Deng Xiaoping, who enjoyed bridge, he had no hobbies. He was a workaholic. He left everything else to Auntie Zhang.

Auntie Zhang loved being surrounded by people. She collected them. When she brought people in to see her husband, they snapped a photograph with him, then showed it around as a way to prove they had connections in Beijing. She never learned to put her guard up. Most officials and their family members had gatekeepers who'd screen people and suppress unflattering news. Auntie Zhang lacked that infrastructure. She had no off switch and no filter. That explained why her jewelry purchases became the subject of sensationalized exposés in the pages of Hong Kong's gossip magazines. Auntie Zhang was game—for anything.

CHAPTER SEVEN

WHAT REALLY INTRIGUED WHITNEY WAS THAT AUNTIE Zhang's support of her husband's career didn't stop her from pursuing her own. In Gansu Province, Auntie Zhang specialized in gemstones and would become a trailblazer in China's jewelry industry. When the couple moved to Beijing in 1983, Auntie Zhang opened the first showroom for gems in the Geological Museum of China, founded the Gem Minerals Research Office, started a magazine called *China Gems*, and helped establish China's first gem appraisal service. In 1992, while her husband toiled at the heart of the Party bureaucracy, she became head of the state-owned China Mineral and Gem Corporation, which sourced and sold gems throughout China. In that position, she began investing state money in jewelry start-ups just as China's economy was taking off and Chinese women began wearing jewelry again. Among the new firms was one called Beijing Diamond Jewelries Company, a retail chain that had access to the best stones. In 1997, as the firm's president and CEO, Auntie Zhang shepherded Beijing Diamond to a listing on the Shanghai Stock Exchange, earning herself a handsome payout in management shares and the nickname the Diamond Queen.

You'd be hard-pressed to say that Auntie Zhang was in it purely for the money. Beijing Diamond was among the first batch of state-own firms to list on the Shanghai exchange. She saw herself as creating a new industry in China. She, too, was seized by a desire to do something extraordinary.

In 1998, when Wen left his Party position and was promoted to vice-premier, Auntie Zhang transitioned from player to referee in the jewelry business, taking the helm of the National Gemstone Testing Center, China's main gem appraiser. Auntie told us that her reason for accepting that position was that she wanted to dispel any perception that she was somehow monetizing her relationship with her husband. Also, as an officer of a listed company, Auntie Zhang would have been required to reveal details about her personal wealth. She wanted to avoid that, too. It was a critical period for her husband because he was being groomed for higher office. Any real or perceived issue that could hinder his ascendance had to vanish. Still, Auntie Zhang's experience successfully founding an industry and listing a company had whetted her appetite for deals. Whitney was convinced Auntie Zhang could become the perfect partner in future ventures with her.

Whitney needed to know all the players in Auntie Zhang's life. She met the couple's two children—Wen Yunsong, known as Winston Wen, and Wen Ruchun, who went by Lily Chang. Like many offspring of the Party elite, both had earned graduate degrees in the United States. Winston Wen had an MBA from the Kellogg School of Management at Northwestern University, while sister Lily earned a similar degree at the University of Delaware.

Lily had a little-rich-kid disposition that mixed tantrums with silent treatments. She'd routinely scream at her parents and act like a spoiled brat. After graduating in 1998, Lily had reportedly worked at the ill-fated Wall Street firm Lehman Brothers, which collapsed during the financial crisis of 2008. Lily had also reportedly lived in Trump Place, the luxury apartment complex overlooking the Hudson River in Manhattan. Later, she joined Credit Suisse First Boston and then, back in Beijing, opened a consulting firm, Fullmark Consultants. The *New York Times* reported in 2013 that the investment bank J.P. Morgan paid Fullmark $1.8 million from 2006 to 2008 to help land Chinese clients. The *Times* also reported that in connection with this deal, the U.S. Securities and Exchange Commission had investigated J.P. Morgan for violating the Foreign Corrupt Practices Act, which bars US companies from giving anything of value to foreign officials or their family members to obtain an improper advantage in business.

Winston wasn't as obnoxious as his sister but was no less ambitious. He'd settled on private equity. In 2005, he founded New Horizon Capital with an investment from SBI Holdings, a division of the Japanese group SoftBank, and Temasek, the Singapore government's investment fund.

Singapore's state-owned investment funds were masters at cozying up to a group known as "the princelings," the sons (and daughters) of Communist Party bigwigs. Various firms associated with the Singaporean government invested money in Winston's firm as well as funds associated with the grandson of Party General Secretary Jiang Zemin, and others. Of all the peoples in the world, the Singaporeans knew how the game was played in China and profited considerably from that knowledge. Eventually, many other sons and daughters of Chinese leaders would follow

Winston into private equity and obtain capital from Singapore. Winston was an early adopter.

Whitney and I thought Winston was playing too aggressively. We were worried that he was cutting his contemporaries out of deals and making enemies. Winston's firm took stakes in companies shortly before they planned listings on stock exchanges across the world. Most of those deals were sure bets, as the businesses were already pretty mature; we're not talking angel investors here. There was a lot of money chasing these opportunities, but instead of sharing them, Winston seemed to be trying to dominate the field. He arranged for his father to visit those firms, essentially declaring to them, "If you let me in the door before everyone else, look at who I can deliver." We thought it was ill-advised and made him a target of jealous competitors.

As Whitney drew closer to Auntie Zhang, she felt more comfortable dispensing advice to her children. I remember Whitney telling Winston, "You can make a lot of money without getting all this attention. Why don't you make money behind the scenes?" But Winston, like my old colleague Feng Bo with his red Rolls-Royce, had become spellbound by the limelight. He liked being on the big stage. We disapproved.

Eventually, people and news reports, often purposely, didn't distinguish between the money Winton's firm made and his personal wealth. If his fund made half a billion on an investment, they'd say *he'd* made half a billion, when actually his share was a fraction of that. We told Auntie Zhang that he could've done even better operating in the shadows. He didn't listen.

The financial success of Wen Jiabao's wife and kids is summed up in the Chinese proverb: "When a man attains enlightenment [or in this case the premiership], even his pets ascend to heaven." That said, neither Whitney nor I believed that Premier Wen was fully aware until very late that his family members had become billionaires. I believed Wen's daughter charged foreign companies hefty fees for her connections. Winston was running New Horizon and Auntie Zhang was meeting with scores of people hawking opportunities. Meanwhile, each family member was collecting luxury cars. But the premier seemed to have little idea what it meant.

When Auntie Zhang came home with a fat rock on her finger, or a priceless jade bracelet, Wen would admire it with the eye of a geologist, not of a seasoned jeweler. Wen had never spent a day in a commercial enterprise. When he was a lowly official, he went to the government canteen and downed whatever food was put in front of him. At home, he ate whatever the cook prepared and had no conception of the cost. He'd never checked out an Hermès store. The only time he ever visited a mall he brought along an entourage. He had no idea that a handbag could cost $10,000 or more. There was something in him that recalled George H. W. Bush's 1992 visit to a grocery store and his puzzled reaction to a barcode scanner. The day-to-day lives of average people seemed a mystery to Premier Wen.

Others had a more jaundiced view: they rejected the notion that Wen had been snookered by his family and concluded he'd chosen not to act. In September 2007, according to documents released by Wikileaks, the head of the China operation of the Carlyle Group, a major American investment firm, told US diplomats that Wen was "disgusted with his family's activities, but is either unable or unwilling to curtail them." The businessman passed on a rumor that Wen had considered a divorce but was "constrained by the prominence of his position."

Whitney and I didn't buy it. We observed legitimate affection between Auntie and her husband, and our instincts told us that Wen just didn't dwell much on his wife's and children's business affairs. He had larger concerns and deep down really did seem to want China to become more open and democratic.

Soon after Wen was appointed premier in March 2003, the family moved into a courtyard home in the center of Beijing. There is no White House for China's president or US Naval Observatory residence for its second-in-command. In Beijing, the Party owns hundreds of properties that are doled out to senior Party officials who live in these homes until they die. The houses are often inherited by their children. This creates a headache for the Beijing mayor's office which needs to acquire more of the dwindling supply of courtyard homes to quarter China's political elite. During China's imperial days, when a senior official retired he and his family left the capital and brought their knowledge and connections back home. Now no one goes home. Winston and Lily were definitely not going back to Gansu.

As the Wens moved into their new home, Auntie Zhang opened a private office with Whitney on half a floor at the Oriental Plaza, a short drive from her residence. Whitney became Auntie Zhang's closest female companion, juggling her roles as friend, counselor, and confidante. I was amazed at Whitney's capacity to insinuate herself into Auntie Zhang's world. It was like one of those Chinese soap operas about life at the imperial court, where ladies-in-waiting vied for the attention of the empress. Hundreds of people wanted to get close to Auntie Zhang, but Whitney bested them all. It was a painstaking process of cultivation and of anticipating her needs, all based on Whitney's intimate knowledge of Auntie Zhang's life and family. Before Auntie Zhang realized she even required something, Whitney provided it. After she did that a few times, Auntie Zhang was hooked.

Whitney shared with me her plan to groom Auntie Zhang and others in the Party hierarchy. Navigating human relations in China was such an intricate affair at that level that Whitney needed someone she could trust absolutely with whom she could strategize. Every relationship came with its own calculations and its own dimensions. We pored over these issues together, gauging what our counterparties wanted, what motivated them, and how to get them to help our cause. "Should I approach her this way or that?" she'd asked me. "How do you think she's going to react?" I became the one person in the world with whom she could explore these issues. It brought us closer and heightened our intimacy; it was us against the world.

Serving Auntie Zhang at the center of power in China became Whitney's life. Every time Auntie needed her, Whitney was there. She submerged herself into Auntie Zhang's world and everything else fell away. Both of us became like this, catering to the whims of others. We were like the fish that clean the teeth of crocodiles.

At the time, Auntie Zhang was the most important piece on the chessboard of Whitney's professional life. Whitney aimed to be a master of the game in Beijing. There were potentially huge financial payoffs and an enormous boost in prestige. But there was also the mental challenge of figuring out how to work the system, solving the puzzle presented by Communist China as best as she could. Whitney was driven to embrace this challenge and she did it with a ferocity few in Beijing could match.

To make Auntie Zhang useful, Whitney had to deepen their relationship. Working with an interior designer, Whitney led the project to redecorate the Wens' new residence. The house on Dongjiaomin Alley was located to the east of the Forbidden City in the old Legation Quarter, a neighborhood that was developed in the 1860s after the Qing Dynasty lost the Opium War to the British and China was forced to allow Western diplomatic missions in Beijing. To me, it was always a bit ironic that the premier of Communist China was sleeping in the same bedroom that had been home to what the Party called "foreign imperialists."

The Wens' house was one of three residences on the alley, all occupied by Party officials. The houses stood behind a tall, slate-gray gate. Soldiers, manning the inside, communicated with the outside via a peephole straight out of *The Wizard of Oz*. The structure in which the Wens resided—a rambling two-story brick mansion—was the last house on the lane. A generous yard encircled the home. The front door opened to a large foyer and an expansive living room to the left and a dining room to the right. A wide wooden staircase cascaded down from the living quarters upstairs.

Whitney recommended that Auntie Zhang line the downstairs with Italian marble. It was the in thing in Beijing. She picked the fixtures—opting for gold over the more subdued hue of brushed nickel. Whitney even offered to arrange for the work. But that was impossible. A special department of the government was responsible for renovations due to security concerns. Auntie Zhang always complained about the poor workmanship and the high price.

I visited the house several times, once to celebrate the one hundredth day of the birth of Winston's son, a tradition in China. Although the house was big enough for three families, it was clear to me that some of its members chafed at living with multiple generations under one roof. Winston's wife, whom he'd met while studying in America, had long appeared to want to live separately from her in-laws, where she could be out from under the thumb of her mother-in-law, Auntie Zhang, and her tempestuous sister-in-law, Lily.

We thought Lily's love affairs were a headache for Auntie Zhang, and Whitney soon got involved. Lily initially was pursued by a fat-faced Chinese businessman named Xu Ming, a mogul from the seaside city of Dalian who had made his money in real estate and plastics and owned a Chinese professional soccer team. In 2005, *Forbes* magazine estimated his net worth at more than $1 billion. The pair went on a vacation together during which Xu Ming took a selfie with Lily. He began showing it around, claiming he was about to become the son-in-law of Premier Wen. That tacky move said a lot about Lily's taste in men.

Whitney argued that someone like Xu Ming, although fabulously wealthy, came with too much baggage. Xu belonged to a Party faction led by Dalian's former mayor Bo Xilai, who was the son of a Communist Party "immortal" named Bo Yibo. Rumors swirled that much of Xu's wealth was ill-gotten, and years later Xu would, indeed, be convicted of corruption and sentenced to prison. (He died unexpectedly at the age of forty-four in 2015, a year before he was to be released.) Then another admirer named Liu Chunhang emerged.

Liu was very much in my mold. He'd studied overseas, earned a PhD from Oxford University and an MBA from Harvard, and done stints at the consulting firm McKinsey & Company and the investment bank Morgan Stanley. Liu's parents were low-level government employees in Shanghai and, like mine, didn't belong to the red aristocracy. He, too, was a commoner.

Lily accepted her mother's advice to give him a chance. Liu's academic track record and CV gave her bragging rights. Whitney and I were amazed that Liu was interested in Lily. She was so petulant; we didn't see how he'd ever be happy. It seemed to me that once they married, Lily looked down on Liu's parents, who, as a result, rarely visited their son in Beijing. In China, a wife traditionally marries into the family of the husband even though she does not take his name, but Lily would have none of that.

Liu was willing to let his parents suffer these petty slights because of the opportunities presented by marriage to the daughter of China's premier. Years later, Whitney and Auntie Zhang would try to get Liu promoted to a vice-ministerial position, meaning he'd become a "high-ranking official" or a *gaogan*. That jump is the most important in any official's career. Not only does it promise a more generous pension and access to the best hospitals, best medical care, and best food; it also portends entrée into the halls of political power. However, Liu's promotion didn't materialize. Still, thanks to his marriage to Lily, he saw a China he never would have seen.

Whitney's close relationship with Auntie Zhang ruffled the feathers of her children, particularly Lily, who'd complain loudly that her mother favored Whitney over her. Whitney tried to head off a confrontation by accompanying Lily to fashion shows and other events. She directed me to buddy up with Lily's husband. But the bad blood remained.

Auntie Zhang's closest male friend was a burly former factory manager named Huang Xuhuai, who hailed from a small town on a bend in the Yangtze River. The pair met in 1992 when Huang was twenty-six and struggling financially and Auntie Zhang was fifty-one and just starting her career as a jewelry mogul. Huang followed Auntie Zhang to Beijing, tried to attach himself to her entourage, and, out of pure gumption, succeeded. Auntie Zhang got him a job in one of the diamond companies she managed. And then later, when Auntie Zhang moved into the Oriental Plaza with Whitney, Huang ensconced himself in a small office abutting Auntie Zhang's. His business card read: "Office Manager to Madame Wen Jiabao."

Naturally, wherever Auntie Zhang traveled, Huang would tag along. Although she never had any direct proof, Whitney had suspicions that Huang, despite his paunch and rusticated ways, was Auntie Zhang's paramour. We referred to him as Auntie's *mianshou*, a word from classical Chinese that means "the kept man of a noblewoman." In short, a gigolo. This wasn't a usual arrangement among the Party elite. Male officials had mistresses, sometimes by the dozen. But it was rare to hear of women keeping men. Many times, Whitney would wonder what in the world Auntie Zhang saw in Huang. But Auntie Zhang, we'd already learned, was special.

Like the mistresses who flocked around China's senior leadership, it seemed to us that Huang had put his whole being on a platter for Auntie Zhang. People of her elevated position didn't come upon these opportunities that often. There were always bodyguards, assistants, and drivers around, so it was difficult to indulge private desires. When someone like Huang happened along, apparently offering his soul, it was hard to resist. Besides, Auntie Zhang always had unpleasant tasks she needed done. Whitney was there to facilitate business and offer advice. But Auntie Zhang also required someone to do her dirty laundry, get people out of jail, or make people go away. Those, in our opinion, were Huang's strengths.

Auntie Zhang played many roles on China's stage. She was in part a puppet master. She exhibited almost total control over people like Huang. With Whitney, the relationship was also hierarchical, but there was more give-and-take. All of Auntie Zhang's ties were seasoned with a healthy dose of coldhearted calculation and manipulation but also genuine emotion. Whitney and I thought we knew how the game was played. We didn't fear her.

What Whitney did fear, however, was the Chinese state. From her early days in Shandong, she'd seen how a corruption investigation could violently upend the lives of people around her. Whitney was intent on maintaining an aura of incorruptibility as she played her high-stakes networking game among China's elite. As I've said, her mantra was: "If you pulled my corpse out of my coffin and whipped it, you'd still find no dirt." On one level she said this to assure people that doing business with her was a safe bet. On the other she was revealing subconsciously a worry that somewhere down the road she, too, would be raked over the coals of a Party-led probe.

From our early days together, friends and contacts in the system offered Whitney a fast-track government sinecure. She turned them down. "You could be one of China's leaders," one Party bigwig declared. Whitney wasn't interested. "I am never going back to that Shandong life," she told me after another senior Chinese official told Whitney that if she played her cards right, she could become China's first female premier.

Whitney was worried that hangers-on like Huang would bring calamity onto the Wens. He was too brash; he brandished his connections to the Wen clan like a weapon. One day, he got into a traffic accident on Chang'an Street, the main east–west boulevard that bisects the heart of Beijing. A police officer responded to the scene and Huang accosted him, causing a lot of embarrassment to the Wens. Whitney and I prided ourselves on being discreet. We didn't try to sell our access for a quick buck, and we kept a low profile; we were in it for the long haul. But not Huang. People like him were dangerous because they attracted too much heat.

Huang appeared to leverage the Wen name to enrich himself. According to reporting by the *New York Times*, in 2004, Deutsche Bank hired Huang as part of a plan to get Chinese government approval to invest in a midsize Chinese bank called Huaxia. Even though Huang had no experience in the financial sector, he was paid $2 million, the *Times* said, quoting bank documents. Deutsche Bank's application to buy Huaxia was approved. In 2006, according to the *Times*, Huang landed another $3 million from Deutsche Bank, although what he actually did for that batch of cash was unclear, and Deutsche Bank did not respond to specific questions when asked. Whitney and I didn't approve of this kind of activity. Whitney warned Auntie Zhang, but she seemed unwilling to rein Huang in.

I didn't realize it at the time, but my dinner with Auntie Zhang that summer evening in 2002 was a mixture of job interview and personal vetting. Whitney had determined that she could trust me, but Auntie Zhang's view was equally important. I wasn't only being considered as a potential match for Whitney. These two driven women were making a judgment on a potential partner. They didn't know exactly how we'd ultimately work together, but they needed to be convinced that I'd be a good fit. Was I husband material for Whitney? Toward the goal of achieving remarkable things, did I possess the necessary business acumen to complement Auntie Zhang's political heft and Whitney's networking flair? Finally, and most important, could I be trusted, completely and totally?

I was poised to enter a tight circle of people at the heart of power in the People's Republic of China. In addition to my expertise on financial matters, the quality that attracted them was that I was a blank slate. I was sufficiently Chinese, but I also had been educated overseas. I'd no baggage. I didn't know other people in officialdom and none of my family members were officials. I had no hidden agenda.

Still, Whitney was always playing three-dimensional chess. And, so far, Auntie Zhang was the most powerful piece on her board. Bringing me to an audience with Auntie Zhang wasn't simply a way to determine whether I'd cut it as a partner. It also signaled to Auntie Zhang how much Whitney valued their relationship. Just as Auntie Zhang treated Whitney as a surrogate daughter, so Whitney looked to Auntie Zhang as a mother figure. In introducing me before we'd gotten engaged, Whitney was giving Auntie Zhang veto power over the most intimate decision of her life. If I was going to be Whitney's husband, I needed Auntie Zhang's blessing. In China, at that level, trust is first and foremost. If Auntie Zhang felt that she couldn't trust me, my relationship with Whitney would have ended then and there.

Subconsciously, Whitney seemed to be modeling our relationship on that of the Wens. Auntie Zhang had pursued Wen Jiabao because he was serious minded and competent, someone in whose chariot she could ride as he headed off to glory. So, too, Whitney looked at me as a man, in a very patriarchal society, who could help a capable and ambitious woman, like her, realize her dreams. Whitney was impressed by how Auntie Zhang and Wen had been able to maintain such a close partnership for so many years, and at how Auntie Zhang had groomed and cultivated her husband until their relationship transcended a typical marriage to span politics and business. The Wens' humble roots resonated with Whitney, too. As did Auntie Zhang's garrulous personality. Like Whitney, Auntie Zhang was extremely talkative and could dominate a room. In Auntie Zhang and Wen Jiabao, Whitney saw a reflection of the life she wanted with me.

Whitney and Auntie Zhang were in an early stage of collaboration. Whitney had already brought in people with ideas to meet with Auntie Zhang. But they'd yet to settle on a way forward. With our dinner, Whitney was introducing Auntie Zhang to a prospective partner who'd help turn these inchoate dreams into a profitable reality. A few days after the Grand Hyatt banquet, Whitney reported back. "Auntie Zhang says you're not bad," she shared. I'd passed the test.

CHAPTER EIGHT

WHITNEY AND I WERE DUMBFOUNDED BY AUNTIE Zhang's energy and desire to remain actively engaged in the wider world. It wasn't really for the money; she'd already made a decent chunk in the diamond business and, given her husband's position as a top Party official, the rest of her life was going to be comfortably subsidized by the state.* Granted, she swapped cars frequently; the black BMW we saw at the Hyatt gave way to a seat-massage-equipped Lexus, which eventually was exchanged for a black Audi. But that was chump change. She also fancied jewelry, but she got more revved up by a good deal on a jade bracelet than in garlanding herself in sparkling baubles.

For Auntie Zhang, we concluded, it was the thrill of the chase. With Wen Jiabao poised to become China's premier, she wanted to carve out her own sphere of influence and not wither on the sidelines as an irrelevant appendage to her husband's career. From the start of her marriage, she and Wen had been on an equal footing, and she wasn't going to let that change. She kept her own

* In 2005, the Party paid out $12 million to each family of a former National Leader.

schedule and almost never accompanied him on trips around China or abroad. She told us that if the masses didn't see her with him, she'd have more freedom to do her own thing. She traveled frequently below the radar, although she didn't try to mask her identity, like her daughter had, with an alias. Auntie Zhang's struggle to forge her own way brought to mind Hillary Clinton's predicament when husband Bill won the White House. Auntie Zhang wanted her own space to live her life, not fade into the wallpaper like so many other wives of Party leaders. And to her, the ideal arena was business. It was a spellbinding game, particularly in an era in China when so much was changing and opportunities abounded. She relished being a player, meeting people, absorbing ideas, judging the prospects, and taking action. It didn't hurt that, given her connections, her failure rate was low.

Still, what she was involved in wasn't simply a rigged treasure hunt like it was for many other Party officials. Neither Wen nor Auntie Zhang were descended from the founders of Communist China. Those people had access to duty-free shopping concessions and, often, exclusive contracts that were licenses to print money. Auntie Zhang and Wen had worked their way up the Party ladder. They had to hustle. The wives of other Chinese leaders were also interested in dabbling in power games and being players. We called them the Taitai Bang, or the Gang of Wives. But few could compare to Auntie Zhang. She was a firecracker, happy-go-lucky and, with her experience in business, extremely capable and determined.

Auntie Zhang further distinguished herself from her peers, we believed, in that she kept her business activities secret from her husband. Other Chinese leaders took an active role in the financial affairs of their clan. Officials such as Jia Qinglin—who served on the Standing Committee of the Politburo, China's most powerful body, for a decade from 2002 to 2012—thought nothing of attending meals with his son-in-law, whom I knew well. Old Man Jia could always be counted on to strong-arm local officials into granting his son-in-law exclusive access to business opportunities. The Party's top dog, Jiang Zemin, dispatched emissaries to exert influence on behalf of his children and his grandkids, too. But Auntie Zhang conducted her business essentially without Wen's knowledge or implicit support. That sometimes made things difficult because even though she—and by extension we—operated under the halo of the nation's premier, we knew we could never count on Wen to actually get involved.

Whitney and Auntie Zhang had a verbal agreement that Auntie Zhang would get 30 percent of any profit from our joint enterprises and we and any other partners would share the remaining 70 percent. In theory, the Wens were responsible for putting up 30 percent of the capital as well, but they rarely did. In the few instances that they provided capital, it was always after the project was a sure bet. Auntie Zhang never took any risk, so we deducted their investment stake when we distributed the profits.

Nothing was on paper; it was all done on trust. The arrangement generally followed the "industry standard." Other families of high-ranking Party members extracted a similar percentage in exchange for their political influence. The template was always fungible and could be tweaked to accommodate investment opportunities as they arose.

Chinese officials, executives at state-owned companies, and

private businessmen who were close to the Party presented insiders like Auntie Zhang with opportunities all the time, but the deals weren't as sweet as those available to China's red aristocrats. The red aristocrats got access to monopoly businesses. An example would be the contract to provide a kind of mineral water, called Tibet 5100, on China's high-speed rail network. That reportedly was landed by relatives of Deng Xiaoping, who paid next to nothing for the rights to bottle the water in Tibet. From 2008 to 2010, the Ministry of Railways bought two hundred million bottles of the stuff. When the company listed on the Hong Kong Stock Exchange in 2011, its market capitalization was $1.5 billion. The Deng family never commented on reports that it was linked to the firm. Anyway, Auntie Zhang couldn't muster that kind of juice.

Our deals required more work. None were sure bets. You needed judgment on two levels. The first was basic due diligence. That was where I came in. I analyzed the industry and had a good sense of the market. I did the legwork, visiting the site and delving into the details. The second type of judgment was an ability to size up a proposal's political cost.

People trafficking in prospects always wanted something. To get a deal, would it be worth aligning ourselves with someone's political faction or personal network? Would it be worth owing someone a favor that he or she would eventually come to collect? That was Whitney's expertise and Auntie Zhang relied on her counsel as they conducted lengthy guesstimates of what potential partners would expect in exchange for providing us access to an opportunity.

As our relationship deepened, Whitney and I became far more than "white gloves," shielding Auntie Zhang's business activity from unwanted publicity. We became partners. We provided finance, direction, judgment, and, critically, execution. Auntie Zhang gave us political cover. We liked to say Auntie Zhang was our "air force" and we were the "infantry," slugging it out in the trenches. Still, there was a big difference between the Wens and other leading Communist clans. Auntie Zhang's air force might have had shock value on paper—thanks to its connection to the office of the nation's premier. But she couldn't rely on her husband to drop any bombs.

We turned the Grand Hyatt's Yue Ting Restaurant into our private canteen. Our backup was the Lei Garden, a Michelin-starred restaurant situated on glitzy Jinbao Street near the Beijing branch of the Hong Kong Jockey Club. Sea bass at $500 a pop was a favorite dish of ours, as was a $1,000 soup made out of fish maw, the air bladder of big fish.

Ministers and deputy ministers, presidents of state-owned enterprises, and entrepreneurs angled to get an invitation to our table. Together we scoured the landscape for opportunities, judging the characters of those who wanted to enter Auntie Zhang's circle, scrutinizing potential partners and candidates for vacancies at top government posts that her husband could fill.

Neither Whitney nor I felt much discomfort spending more than a thousand dollars on lunch. To me, it was just the cost of doing business in China in the 2000s. That's how things were done. A big element was the Chinese concept of "face." Everybody knew we were paying ridiculous prices for the soup, the fish, and even the veggies. And it was precisely that fact that gave our guest face. If I'd been buying lunch for my personal consumption, I would have looked at it as a value proposition. But I wasn't there for fun, I was there for business, and if I wanted to do business in Beijing, that's what lunch cost.

In the fall of 2002, a few months after I'd passed my test with Auntie Zhang, Whitney got a tip from a contact at the China Ocean Shipping Company. Whitney was friendly with people there; the firm had once given Great Ocean a loan. Whitney's contact said that COSCO wanted to sell a portion of its stake in Ping An Insurance Company, one of the few companies in China licensed to offer a full suite of financial and insurance services. COSCO had been one of three founding shareholders of Ping An in 1988 along with China Merchants Bank and the Shenzhen government.

The year 2002 had been a difficult one for COSCO's shipping business. It faced a cash crunch and so its CEO, Wei Jiafu, wanted to sell a small part of COSCO's stake in Ping An to dress up the firm's balance sheet. Whitney approached Wei and expressed interest in buying those shares.

Wei wasn't averse to selling some of COSCO's stake to Whitney and by extension the Wen family. He didn't have any specific demands at the time, but for an executive at a state-run firm, getting on the good side of the premier's family might serve his purposes later on. The halo of Premier Wen put us on the inside track to buy a piece of COSCO's stake. Wei wanted to sell 3 percent of Ping An; we figured we could buy 1 percent of the company and thought Auntie Zhang would be interested in the remaining 2 percent. As this was going to be our first transaction with Auntie Zhang, and a one-shot investment to boot, it didn't follow the seventy-thirty template. Besides, we lacked the capital to take more than one-third of the allotment.

It wasn't a sweetheart deal. We were offered the shares at 10 percent above their net asset value, which had been determined by an accounting firm. Similar sales at a similar valuation were being negotiated at the time and not all went through. The American investment bank Goldman Sachs, which had bought 10 percent of Ping An for $35 million in 1993, had tried to sell its stake at about the same time but found no takers. (Instead, Goldman dumped its shares in a little-known firm named Alibaba, which ended up as the biggest online shopping site in the world. If Goldman had held on to those shares, it could have made, literally, tens of billions of dollars.)

Whitney traveled to Ping An's headquarters in Shenzhen and met with Ma Mingzhe, Ping An's CEO and founder, to assess the deal. If Auntie Zhang agreed to go in with us, we and the Wens would be on track to become major shareholders in the company. Ma revealed, not inadvertently, that the Hongkong and Shanghai Banking Corporation was planning to buy a significant chunk of Ping An's stock. HSBC was a major brand in the financial world and not known for risky investments. We told Auntie Zhang that we thought the Ping An deal was a low-risk, stable-return type of play.

Auntie Zhang wasn't particularly keen; Lily was against it. Lily didn't expect Ping An to be particularly profitable, although it seemed to us that her prophecy was made more because she was envious of Whitney's relationship with her mother than from any knowledge of Ping An's business. Nonetheless, Auntie Zhang was spooked.

Whitney worked on Auntie Zhang. She explained our rationale. Insurance licenses were a hot commodity at the time in China and insurance of all types was an up-and-coming business. We stressed the fact that a big player like HSBC wouldn't put money in the company if it thought the investment was sketchy. What's more, because Ping An wasn't listed on any stock exchange, we were insulated from market swings unrelated to the company's performance. It was normal in China at the time to borrow money to buy assets and we both would have to borrow to buy COSCO's Ping An shares. After days of debate, Whitney told Auntie Zhang that if the Wen family wasn't interested, we'd be going forward anyway. At that point, Auntie Zhang tapped the table. She held the checkbook in the Wen family. "We're in," she said.

In December 2002, Whitney agreed in theory to purchase 3 percent of Ping An from COSCO for $36 million. Under the terms of our deal, the Wen family would take two-thirds of those shares and Great Ocean would get the remainder. Still, we both faced a big challenge; neither of us had the money to buy the shares.

It's hard to exaggerate just how much we needed capital in those days. This was a problem common to every entrepreneur in China. Given the multitude of investment opportunities during the boom-boom days of China's economic rise, all of us were leveraged to the hilt. It was a sign of how crazy the Chinese market was and how much enthusiasm about China's future coursed through society and the financial world. Everybody was laying maximum bets, and because of that, everyone was short of cash. Of course, many bets didn't pan out. Two-thirds of the people on China's one hundred wealthiest list would be replaced every year due to poor business decisions, criminality, and/or politically motivated prosecutions, or because they'd mistakenly aligned themselves with a Party faction that had lost its pull.

Anyone running a sizable business was bound to be violating

some type of law, whether it be environmental, tax, or labor. So while the returns could be lofty, you were always vulnerable. When the Chinese government passes a law it invariably makes it retroactive, so events that occurred years ago that had been unregulated could become crimes today.

Nonetheless, those challenges made no dent in the consensus that everything in China was pointing up. The 2000s were a decade of non-stop, double-digit growth, of huge ambition and tremendous success, of one of the greatest accumulations of wealth in history. If you weren't fully leveraged, you were falling behind. If you weren't fully leveraged, you were stupid.

Whitney had continued to make a decent profit of some $2 million a year selling IBM mainframe equipment to China's telecommunications companies, but we were still short of cash. In fact, so short that even after Whitney and I moved in together to an upscale apartment in the Oriental Plaza in 2003, we continued to mooch from my parents: $100,000 here, $200,000 there, just to tide us over. My folks, who'd made a small killing in the Shanghai real estate market, were astonished. When we first met, Whitney was being chauffeured around in an S600 Mercedes, the top of the line. Then Audi came out with a model sporting a six-liter W12 engine and she had to have that. We were living together in an outrageously expensive apartment and driving a car that in China cost five times what it would cost overseas. We were buying the most expensive things. And yet we were going to my parents for spare change. "Maybe you should tone down your lifestyle," my mother suggested. She and my father had grown up in a poor country. My dad was the child of parents who weren't trusted by the state. My parents had scrimped and saved and kept their heads down. Frugality and hard work had allowed them to join the middle class. They couldn't understand the new world that I'd entered where the logic of the system compelled us to spend like sailors on shore leave.

By my logic and Whitney's, the accoutrements of a high-end lifestyle served our business interests. If you wanted to go for the maximum deal in China, you couldn't seem weak. Who'd run with you then? No one. Putting on airs was part of the game.

Whitney's conspicuous consumption also had a deeply psychological dimension. She carried a chip on her shoulder because of her humble background. At some level she always worried about being looked down upon. She was on a crusade to "show 'em." Whitney's cars, jewelry, and, later on, artwork weren't just about consumption. They were about fortifying herself against the world, standing as a rampart against other people's sneers.

When Whitney got wind that a license plate number "Beijing A 8027" was for sale, she bought it for $200,000 so she could hang it on the Audi. Whitney had to work on Beijing's chief of police to get permission to use the plates on her car.

License plates were a huge status symbol in China. There were many different license plates on the streets of Beijing. There were military plates from the different services. There were plates from Party headquarters in Zhongnanhai. There were black plates for foreigners. The plates constituted a language of their own. And with Beijing's streets constantly jammed, having high-status plates was a must. With the right plates, you could cruise down the bus-only lane, drive on sidewalks, make an illegal U-turn, run a red light, and park in a no-parking zone near a favored restaurant.

In a nation finely attuned to status, a vehicle with an "A 8027" turned heads. The "A" meant we came from Beijing's urban core. The 80 meant that the car belonged to someone of a minister's rank or higher. And 027 was a low number, which implied that we were connected in some way to the State Council, China's cabinet. That's why Whitney needed the police chief to sign off. It looked like our Audi belonged to a high-ranking official. In the West, if you have money, you can buy vanity plates. Not in China. You need *guanxi*.

We sought status in other ways. At one point we went on a worldwide tour to find a jade bracelet to fit Whitney's thicker than average wrists. Eventually, she found one for half a million dollars. Artwork, too, had become a sign of success for Chinese entrepreneurs, so Whitney directed me to start attending auctions. In 2004, we put in the winning bids for two antique paintings, including a Song Dynasty depiction of songbirds, for nearly $1 million. And like almost everything in China in those days, their values rose. The jewelry jumped tenfold and someone offered us ten times what we paid for the paintings. But we didn't really acquire these things to realize gains. We locked them in a wardrobe-size antique safe that I purchased from Austria. It had drawers for some thirty watches and shelves for antiques and a whole walk-in section for paintings.

For us, owning all this stuff was a talking point to prove to people in our inner circle that we, too, belonged at the apex of Chinese society and were beyond the contempt of those of more noble birth. Indeed, in our lives, everything had to be top-of-the-line. The car she drove, the jewelry she wore, the office where she worked, all of it became part of our personae, a reflection of who we were.

We agreed with the Wens that we'd each find our own financing to buy the Ping An stock. Whitney secured a bridge loan of about $12 million from a pharmaceutical company. Once we had the shares in hand, we used them as collateral to secure a bank loan to repay the pharmaceutical firm. The Wens' shares were purchased with the help of a Chinese businessman who fronted Auntie Zhang the cash.

After helping Auntie Zhang buy the shares, the businessman gave her some of the stock but held a portion for himself. The businessman assured Auntie Zhang that he'd give her the rest of those shares later, but he never did. The fact that Auntie Zhang was incapable of relieving him of those shares, which ultimately ballooned in value to tens of millions of dollars, spoke to the relative weakness of the Wen clan.

Wen Jiabao was in theory number two in the Party hierarchy, but his lack of Communist lineage and his somewhat passive disposition made him less of a player than others at his level. Wen's comrades at the Party's heights routinely marshaled the entire judicial system of the nation for their personal benefit, employing corruption and other criminal probes to dispose of political opponents. Wen either couldn't or wouldn't engage in that kind of chicanery. No one in the family had thought to inform its most powerful member, Wen Jiabao, what was going on with Ping An or any other deals. When things went south or when people like the Hong Kong financier stole millions from his wife, Wen couldn't be relied on to step in.

Whitney, Auntie Zhang, and I determined that all of our combined shares would be held in Great Ocean's name to avoid public scrutiny of the Wen family. I also took a seat on Ping An's

My father, Shen Jiang, stands on the far left of this photograph taken with his father, Shen Rong, and his siblings. The picture was taken soon after China's revolution, during the initial good days before the Communists seized my grandfather's house and shut down his law office.

(Courtesy of the author)

Here I am in Hong Kong soon after my parents and I moved there. This picture was taken in the living room of my maternal grandfather's apartment, where three families squeezed into a 750-square-foot space. We slept in the living room.

(Courtesy of the author)

This photograph is of the Queen's College annual swim meet held at the pool in Victoria Park, Hong Kong, across the road from my high school. I'm fifteen and I won it. The man presenting me the award is Henry Fok, a businessman who in the 1950s made a fortune breaking the trade embargo against Communist China.

(Courtesy of the author)

This is a classic Chinese-style portrait of Whitney with her parents—her mother, Li Baozhen, and her stepfather, Duan Xiangxi. Whitney's mother fled her biological father when she was still pregnant with Whitney.

(Courtesy of the author)

Whitney had this photograph taken of her on Tiananmen Square in the late 1990s. Just by her pose, you can tell she's carefree, confident, and, with her brightly colored frock, ahead of her time.

(Courtesy of the author)

This picture of me—on the left—was taken after I'd graduated from the University of Wisconsin and had returned to Hong Kong to take a job as a stockbroker. Competitive drinking was part of life in Hong Kong during those go-go years. Most of the others in the picture came from the United States, seeking their fortunes in the Far East.

(Courtesy of the author)

Whitney and I took this picture during a trip to Switzerland with Auntie Zhang in 2004. Lake Geneva is behind us.

(Courtesy of the author)

We took this picture in Inner Mongolia, in northern China, on a river rafting trip when Ariston was about five. *(Courtesy of the author)*

A relatively early photograph of the Wen family, including China's premier, Wen Jiabao; his wife, Zhang Beili (whom we called Auntie Zhang); their son, Winston Wen; and their daughter, Wen Ruchun. Given Wen's Mao jacket, the picture was probably taken when Wen was still working in the General Office of the Chinese Communist Party. *(Courtesy of the author)*

This picture of Premier Wen Jiabao was taken in 2008, after a deadly earthquake in Sichuan Province. Wen was viewed as a hardworking man of the people. After news broke of his family's wealth, he was much criticized but seemed, to us, not entirely aware of what had been going on. *(Reuters/Alamy)*

This picture depicts the initial public offering of Ping An Insurance Company on the Shanghai Stock Exchange. Ma Mingzhe, far right, is banging the gong. Ping An's listing on the Shanghai exchange meant a windfall for Whitney and me worth hundreds of millions of dollars. *(AP Photo)*

We are in Paris in June 2011 doing a vertical tasting of Château Lafite Rothschild, starting with a 1900 and ending with a 1990. The wines alone that night ran to more than $100,000. On the left, David Li Botan is sitting with his wife, Jia Qiang. I'm on the right with Whitney and developer Xu Jiayin and his wife, Ding Yumei. My French friend François is sitting across from me on the left. *(Courtesy of François Audouze)*

Whitney wanted a Rolls, so we purchased a similar model for an enormous markup due to hefty import taxes. I felt it was ostentatious, but, like most of the purchases we made during those years, the car was meant to establish a certain status, which the system required to do business at the highest levels.

(China Photos/Getty Images)

Chinese mega-artist Zeng Fanzhi stands between two of his paintings. Whitney bought the painting on the left, *Praying Hands*, for about $5 million. She outbid a major European art collector and businessman. These purchases were meant to signal we had the resources to make the biggest deals happen.

(Dan Kitwood/Getty Images)

This photograph of Beijing Capital International Airport shows the northern part of the airfield, which we built to handle cargo. Over the course of several years, our firm developed 6 million square feet of warehouses, cargo terminals, and offices.

(Courtesy of Airport City Development Co., Ltd.)

This is the library at Tsinghua University that Whitney and I built with a $10 million donation. It has become the most popular library on campus and students have to go online to reserve a study cubicle.

(Enrico Cano)

Here I am voting as a member of the Chinese People's Political Consultative Conference. I was a member of this group for a decade. We voted every year, but the votes didn't mean anything. We voted yes to all proposals. Most of us used membership on the conference to network.

(Courtesy of the author)

This is the Genesis development project, the capstone of Whitney's and my career in Beijing. On the right is the residence and the hotel; in the center is one of the office towers. This project allowed us to exercise our creativity to the fullest in leaving behind something stunning in China's capital. *(Courtesy of KPF)*

This is a picture looking into the lobby of the Genesis office building. Whitney disappeared from this entrance on September 5, 2017. *(Courtesy of KPF)*

Our friend Sun Zhengcai was destined to be China's number one or two political official starting in 2022. But his rise was derailed by a corruption investigation that clearly benefited Party boss Xi Jinping. Here, Sun is in court. He was sentenced to life.

(Imaginechina via AP Images)

I'd once participated in Communist Party–organized protests against democracy in Hong Kong. But here I am marching for freedom and democracy in Hong Kong on June 9, 2019. *(Courtesy of the author)*

Ariston painted this portrait of Whitney during the summer of 2017 in Beijing, just weeks before she disappeared. *(Courtesy of the author)*

CHAPTER NINE

ALTHOUGH WHITNEY AND I HAD BEEN LIVING TOgether since late summer of 2002, we hadn't gotten married. We changed that on January 17, 2004, when we formally registered as a couple in Hong Kong. Whitney held off on the wedding ceremony, wanting to be certain of the longevity of the marriage before we went public. But after a year she went into planning mode.

For my part, I hadn't pressed for a wedding ceremony *or* for the marriage. Whitney in those days had a bigger say in our relationship than I had and I allowed myself to be carried along by her enthusiasm.

Whitney knew the Four Seasons chain was building a hotel in Hong Kong and that it was scheduled to open in the fall of 2005. She booked our reception for October 2005, twenty-one months after we were legally wed, and spared no expense. She interviewed scores of wedding planners, florists, and chefs and pored over the portfolios of photographers as she assembled a crack team. She had us take dancing lessons and, for music, booked what seemed like a full orchestra. For her bridal gown, Whitney flew to designer Vera Wang's studio in New York to have it measured and made. I wore a black tuxedo by Tom Ford. Whitney also spent days on her parents' wardrobe, wrapping their provincialism in sartorial finery.

On a Saturday evening in October 2005, a month after the hotel opened, we held our wedding banquet. Auntie Zhang traveled down from Beijing, in her role as Whitney's surrogate mom. This ruffled the feathers of Whitney's birth mother, who at one point lashed out at her daughter for doting on Auntie Zhang. "I'm your real mother!" she exclaimed.

My parents were there along with classmates from Queen's College and an executive MBA program that I'd been attending in Hong Kong. In all, about two hundred people were there.

Whitney and I had decided against a function in Beijing because we wanted to avoid issues about whom to invite, who'd sit next to whom, who'd be a bridesmaid or best man, which table would be closest to ours. We were loath to reveal our connections to other invitees and we didn't want our invitees to be uncomfortable in exposing their relationship with us. In the West, a wedding such as ours would have been an event, a chance for people to see and be seen. But in China, where information is tightly held and fear permeates the system, we had to be careful. In China, connections constitute the foundation of life; we didn't want to divulge ours to potential competitors or the public at large.

The Hong Kong ceremony came at one of the happier times in our marriage. Whitney had put in a lot of effort to help turn me into someone who could prosper in the Chinese system. And we'd settled into a productive groove.

The reception was splashy and meticulously choreographed

to portray us as a perfect couple, superior in every way. But after the extravaganza, we opted against a honeymoon. We had much to do in Beijing.

The work we were doing together was fascinating. Whitney and I were in the middle of a project that would become one of the capstones of our careers. Its genesis mixes the serendipity, luck, connections, and hard work that defined our lives in China at the time.

I've written before that we were intent on using our *guanxi* to do something extraordinary in China. And the key to doing that was land. People had learned that Whitney was close with Auntie Zhang, so we were often presented deals. We spent weeks on a wild goose chase for projects in Whitney's home province of Shandong. In Rizhao, a grubby city on the coast of the Yellow Sea, we were met by the mayor, who offered us a piece of a half-finished container port. At a partially completed power plant, government officials drank so much with us that one participant tumbled facedown into a ditch.

Whitney was keen to invest, figuring that her roots in Shandong would ensure success. But I noted that lots of places were developing container ports and power plants. Competition was cutthroat and margins were slim; I figured it would be a race to the bottom, so I convinced her to hold off.

Back in Beijing we'd been trying to secure a piece of land to build high-end housing. In 2001, Whitney had started cultivating a man named Sun Zhengcai, who was then Party secretary of the Shunyi District in the northeast corner of the capital. Like Whitney, Sun hailed from the Shandong countryside. Sun was a natural leader; he had the gift of gab. With arching eyebrows and a steady gaze, Sun wasn't particularly handsome but exuded an affable self-confidence that came from making it on his own. His parents were farmers, not members of the red aristocracy. He'd climbed up the Party ladder due to hard work and smarts.

After college in Shandong, Sun did graduate work in Beijing. Unlike many Chinese officials who handed their homework assignments to subordinates, he actually wrote his own master's thesis. Following his graduation in 1997, the Party assigned him to a position as Party secretary at a research institute attached to the Ministry of Agriculture. From there, he moved to the top government position in the Shunyi District in Beijing. In February 2002, he became Shunyi's Party chief, a more powerful post.

Sun arrived in Shunyi just as China was opening the real estate sector to private investment and the district was transitioning from vegetable plots and fruit orchards to a bedroom community of the capital. Abutting the Beijing Capital International Airport, Shunyi became a favored location for gated communities, initially accommodating expatriate businessmen and diplomats on fat housing allowances, followed soon by nouveau riche Chinese.

As government chief and later Communist Party secretary in Shunyi, Sun doled out real estate projects to people he needed as allies. He gave Whitney and me a piece of land because of our connections to the Wens. He also approved land sales to relatives of Zeng Qinghong, China's onetime vice-president and a close ally of Party secretary and China's president Jiang Zemin. Later on, when Sun was purged in a high-profile corruption case, the Party accused him of accepting bribes. I don't think this was the case. It was more like barter. Sun allotted land parcels as favors to people who in turn facilitated his rise. In May 2002, Sun was promoted out of Shunyi to a position as the secretary-general of the Beijing municipal Party committee—a vice-ministerial position. He'd entered the ranks of the *gaogan*.

Whitney and I were impressed by Sun's resourcefulness and ability to plot his way forward. Whitney believed that Sun had unlimited potential and tried to stay close to him. In addition to the chunk of land, Sun helped Whitney get approval to attach our vanity plates to her Audi.

Secretary-general of the capital's Party committee is a challenging job. Your clients are national-level institutions such as the ministries of defense, state security, commerce, and foreign affairs. They have demands and you have to keep them happy. On the plus side, you have unfettered access to the levers of power. While the job was high pressure, it could also be high reward.

Sun didn't lack for ambition or self-regard. In a relatively short period, he'd gone from what was essentially a dead-end academic position at the Ministry of Agriculture, to managing a district with more than 1 million people, to playing a central role in China's capital.

By early 2003, we hadn't developed the Shunyi parcel, so we had to surrender our rights to it under a new rule that said developers needed to move faster to develop their plots. Outsiders believed that the real estate business in China was a license to print money. They were ignorant of the challenges that made it so risky. It was highly regulated and policy changes came in unpredictable waves.

Even though Sun had already moved on from Shunyi, we had an entrée into the district and were always included on the invite list for functions held by the local government. At Shunyi's

Spring Festival party in 2003, something transpired that set us to thinking. Normally, these were anodyne affairs: the district chief or Party secretary said a few words; people raised a toast, feasted on scores of dishes, and headed home through the late-winter chill. But this time the district chief, a crusty local named Li Ping, veered from the script. Directing his comments to representatives from the Beijing airport, which abutted his district, Li warned darkly that if the airport "busts over our redline," he'd block its plan to expand. "You have to come to me first," Li said, his face reddened with drink.

This was a wild time in China with government bureaus vying with one another for land, resources, and licenses—all of which, given China's breakneck growth, meant money. Competing state-owned phone companies ripped out one another's lines, even though, technically, they were all owned by the state. Bureaucrats deployed thugs to battle other thugs over the rights to develop property. Rival bus manufacturers sent gangs across provincial lines to kidnap their foes. It was no secret that Shunyi's district government hated the neighboring airport and was committed to hindering its expansion plans. Whitney and I wondered whether we might have a role in hashing out a truce.

Whitney pieced together the backstory. Two years earlier, in July 2001, the International Olympic Committee had awarded China the 2008 Olympics, sparking redevelopment projects throughout the capital. Long-dormant plans suddenly became viable as Beijing vied with New York, Paris, and London to build its own architectural icons, among them the monumental, $700 million headquarters for China Central Television, the largest and most expensive media headquarters in the world.

Beijing's airport was a natural for redevelopment, as it would be the gateway to the Games. Renowned British architect Norman Foster was engaged to design a dazzling steel and glass-sheathed terminal topped with a roof that evoked the scales of a dragon. In addition to developing the new passenger terminal, the government also approved plans to expand the airport's cargo business. Airports don't only move people, they move stuff, and Beijing's cargo-handling capabilities were in desperate need of upgrading.

The Ministry of Land and Resources approved a plan that brought the airport logistics hub up to Shunyi's redline. Shunyi countered by getting the go-ahead to lay an expressway along that border, thus fencing the airport in. Whitney learned that the Shunyi government was planning to place warehouses on the other side of the expressway as well, creating a competing logistics zone. She came up with an idea: Why not shelve the highway and combine the airport's cargo zone with that of Shunyi to create a massive and far more efficient center for moving products into and out of China? This would be an air cargo center with forklifts buzzing here and there, bonded warehouses, export and import processing centers, and quarantine capabilities along with tight security. Obviously, to realize this vision we'd have to convince the airport and Shunyi to end their war.

We set out to get to know the main players: Shunyi's chief, Li Ping, and the general manager of the airport, Li Peiying, who despite sharing the same last name weren't related.* We needed to figure out what might motivate them to work with each other and us.

* There are 91 million people surnamed Li in China.

Li Peiying was a legend at the airport. He'd started as a beat cop at the facility and became the chief of the airport police before moving into the executive suite. Dressed every day in a dark blue suit, two sizes too big, and a white shirt, Peiying walked with a pronounced limp due to a fall earlier in life. But the infirmity hadn't slowed him down. He was a can-do guy who ended up running not only the Beijing airport but also a corporation that owned thirty-six other airports around China.

Peiying crisscrossed China in a private plane, cutting in front of international airliners as he took off from Beijing. "Boss Li is ready to fly," went the call from the control tower as his jet maneuvered around wide-bodies to the front of the runway.

Peiying had a high opinion of himself. He magnified his legend by refusing an invitation to dine with the chief of police of Beijing, not necessarily a wise move. Still, as a leader of some forty thousand employees, Peiying maintained a man-of-the-people air. He was beloved at the airport for raising salaries and running it like a real business.

Peiying made the arrangements for all of China's Party poohbahs flying into Beijing. Each time a political heavyweight landed, Peiying would be in the room. He used this face time to great advantage. As the top honcho at so many airports, Peiying controlled access to monopoly businesses. He sliced them like cake, doling them out to the relatives of top government officials. He helped the family of China's president Jiang Zemin secure a license to sell duty-free products in Beijing via a firm called Sunrise. This was a model for the type of business the red aristocracy liked. Sunrise shared the duty-free business at the Beijing airport with a state-owned firm, China Duty Free Group. These duopolies were an emblem of China's economy, with a red family controlling one firm and a state-run entity controlling the other.

Peiying oversaw massive changes at the airport—the construction of the new terminal and new runways along with an express subway system connecting the airport to downtown Beijing. He was what the airport needed at the time—a strong leader with a vision. But as was often the case in China, once you monopolized power during the day, there was no check on you at night. Peiying had a gambling habit. In fourteen trips to the old Portuguese colony of Macao, a spit of land off China's southern underbelly, he reportedly lost $6 million of state money playing baccarat. He flew to the US territory of Saipan in the western Pacific and gambled for three straight days without sleeping. He'd run afoul of the government later on, proving that the ones who fall in China are usually the most capable. But when I first encountered him, he was at the top of his game.

We had something Peiying wanted—access to the Wens. For years, Peiying had been stuck at a director general's level in the government hierarchy. He had his heart set on moving up a notch to vice-minister. Prestige was one factor. If he made vice-minister, Peiying would outrank all of China's other airport chiefs. Promotion to vice-minister would also mean that Peiying would enter the ranks of the *gaogan*. So Peiying was motivated to work with us, meet Auntie Zhang, and strike a deal with Shunyi.

Unlike Peiying, Shunyi's chief, Li Ping, didn't crave a promotion. Barely five-six with a belly known as a *laobandu*, or a boss's pot, Li, day in and day out, donned the uniform of Communist officialdom: blue slacks and a white shirt, long sleeves in the winter, short sleeves in the summer. While Peiying loved to head downtown to dine with Auntie Zhang or munch on sushi at the boxy Kunlun Hotel in the upscale Chaoyang District, getting Li Ping to even leave Shunyi was a trial. To him, downtown Beijing was foreign territory. I can count on one hand the number of occasions he ventured into the city to eat with us. The only times he did so willingly were when he was summoned directly by Auntie Zhang.

At heart, Li Ping was a peasant from the days when Shunyi was a rural backwater. In his home district, he felt safe. With just a call, the Shunyi police would clear the road for him or his guests. Everyone respected him; he was the man.

In Shunyi, Li was famed for his hospitality. He was especially proud of his ability to drink. We were all very precise regarding our capacity for alcohol and Li's hovered around eight hundred milliliters, a tad less than a quart, and that's of 106 proof Moutai. He was a pro at getting his adversaries to down more than he did—an important skill in the Chinese bureaucracy, where wining and dining occupied center stage.

Li Ping's interests differed from those of Peiying. He was a product of Shunyi, had spent his whole career there, and would retire there. His relatives were scattered throughout the district's bureaucracy. He wanted to cement a legacy that would garner him respect in his golden years as a local worthy, a *tuhuangdi* or "dirt emperor" in the parlance of the day. He wanted a triumph that he could boast about. When we later wrangled approval for the first airport-based open port in China, for example, Li Ping had a great sense of achievement. "We're the first," he thundered at the banquet held to celebrate the event. Li was eager to make things happen in his district, the grander the better.

Whitney proposed the idea of forming a joint venture, called Airport City Logistics Park, that would include a stake for the airport, the Shunyi District, and Whitney's firm, Great Ocean. We offered to take 40 percent, with the airport getting 45 percent, and the remaining 15 percent going to Shunyi. Believing that the deal would establish a relationship with the premier's family, Li Peiying agreed that the airport would take less than half of the venture. Under that arrangement, he'd be named chairman, with me as the CEO.

Whitney never needed to say that the Wens were interested in investing. She let Auntie Zhang's body language and attitude toward us do the talking. At meals with both Lis, Auntie Zhang praised Whitney and me and made generic comments to the effect that we should "all cooperate and build mutual trust." Anyone within China's system would intrinsically understand the message and know why she was dining with them and why she'd brought us along.

Our ownership proposal ensured that none of the individual state shareholders controlled more than half of the project. That was decisive. If a state-owned company had dominated the venture, it never would have gotten off the ground. Our idea was so novel and needed the blessing of so many ministries that no state-owned firm would have wanted to take it on. The ministries and offices concerned with customs, quarantine, transportation, aviation, infrastructure, state planning, and state assets all had a say. We needed to lobby all of them. Keeping our two state-owned partners each below half meant that on the big decisions Whitney and I would have substantial flexibility and would cast the deciding vote.

At a meal to celebrate the signing of the venture, Li Ping rose to give another toast. This time his threats had been replaced by praise. "The airport and the district government would never have signed a treaty if it hadn't had been for you," he said, pointing to Whitney and me. "Yours was the soft tissue that connected us."

We were able to play that role because of Auntie Zhang but also because we had a vision. Nobody else could have pulled this off, Li Ping said. We came in with money, know-how, and political backing. We brought with us things that no state-owned enterprise, no purely private entrepreneur, and no foreign company could deliver. With a truce agreed upon, the hard work began.

Combining the airport's and Shunyi's land gave us a parcel of more than two square miles. We drew up plans to build 11 million square feet of warehousing and seven miles of roads and piping. Factories sat on the land along with three villages. We first had to clear out the workers and the residents before anything could happen.

I had no idea what I was doing. I'd never built anything before, much less a logistics hub at a big urban airport that needed a strict delineation between tariff-free imports and those subject to tax. There were security concerns as well. I reached out to airports around Asia and the world. I traveled to Frankfurt, Seoul, Amsterdam, Hong Kong, and other facilities seeking guidance. I considered the possibility of bringing in a foreign partner with experience in this industry. I dropped that idea when several offered very little capital for a very big stake.

I needed to learn everything from scratch. How tall should the warehouses be? What is the ideal distance between columns to allow a forklift to maneuver? What's the height of a loading dock?

The width of the roads? I had a huge dream in front of me, but in the winter of 2004, a whole year after we'd come up with the scheme, we still hadn't broken ground. And building wouldn't even be the hardest part. Far more torturous was getting the approvals.

To construct Beijing's Airport City, we needed seven different ministries to sign off on almost anything we planned. And within these ministries there were layers upon layers of authorizations. In all, we needed 150 different chops, Chinese seals that are used in lieu of a signature, and every one was a story. It took three years just to start construction and even after that there were roadblocks aplenty. I stationed people outside the offices of officials from whom we needed a stamp. I sent people to hospitals to get chops from bedridden bureaucrats. My employees waited for months trying to curry favor with officials, bringing them fine teas, doing their errands, taking them to saunas, looking after their wives and kids. One of my employees accompanied so many people to so many bathhouses that his skin started peeling off.

Friends at the Shunyi government laughed at me. There is no way that a representative from a state-owned firm would go through this rigmarole, they observed, just to get a project moving. In state offices, everyone is punching the clock, they said. Nobody really cares whether the project flies or not. But not us; for Whitney and me, this was an entrepreneurial endeavor. This was our big chance.

To make the most of it, I had to get on my hands and knees in front of these guys no matter their rank. For sure, it was dehumanizing. And other than a faint halo, the Wens provided little else. Auntie Zhang, Whitney, and I went out from time to time with a minister or vice-minister to lobby for help, but Auntie

Zhang would never issue orders. She acted more like a character witness, vouching for our competence. This differed from the family of China's then president, Jiang Zemin. His representatives demanded obedience. But because her husband was in the dark about the family business, Auntie Zhang couldn't afford to be so bold. She let people read between the lines.

Throughout the airport project, I, like all businessmen in China, paid extremely close attention to the macroeconomic policies and the political whims of the central government. Every time we requested an approval, our application had to show how the project aligned with the shifting political and economic priorities of the Chinese Communist Party.

Often, these things are very subjective. But they illustrate how every major aspect of the economy was controlled by the state, despite all the talk about capitalism in China. Any project of significance in China needed the approval of an organization called the National Development and Reform Commission, which had bureaus at all levels of the government: in the major cities, all thirty-two provinces, and Beijing. No matter if a company was state owned or private, if it wanted to do something big it needed the support of the commission. To construct our logistics hub, we required approvals from these commissions at all levels. And we needed an endorsement from the State Council, the country's highest government body.

The National Development and Reform Commission was responsible for China's Five-Year Plan, a throwback to the days when China's economy was planned and prices for everything were set by the state. Even though China had undertaken significant economic reforms, those Five-Year Plans remained important. And each level of China's government—including the cabinet, provinces, cities, and counties—all issued their own Five-Year Plans, aligning them with the national blueprint. As the CEO of a joint venture involved in a big infrastructure project, I needed to show, in my applications to these many layers, how my project adhered to the spirit of the latest plan. There was a formula to writing these submissions. You always began with what we applicants called "a hat," which was a nod to all the Five-Year Plans of the various organizations that had a say in your project, and a disquisition on how the project fit into their goals.

Another challenge for us was getting permission from China's General Administration of Customs, which managed imports and exports. For many years, customs duties constituted the bulk of China's revenue, so the ministry had outsize influence within the Party and government. Customs was in charge of erecting regulatory barriers designed to protect Chinese companies from foreign competition. And we were asking for approval to build a comprehensive tariff-free zone, a distinction that, at the time in China, had only been granted to two seaports and no other airport.

Getting approval for this zone was hugely important to the profitability of our scheme. If ours could become the first airport to attain tariff-free status we'd soak up pent-up demand. A lot of businesses would be interested in setting up in our zone. Think aircraft maintenance. If you have a tax-free zone, all spare parts, engines, and even the plane could be flown into the zone without paying tariffs. The work would be completed in the zone and the plane would depart tax-free. Think warehousing, too. Businesses don't want to pay tariffs on all of their imported inventory at once. They could use our bonded warehouses to store their stuff and pay the tariffs only when they needed to bring their goods into China.

In the past in China, different customs zones had been established for single purposes, one for soybeans and another for computers. But in the comprehensive tariff-free zone that we were planning, all kinds of products could flow through the zone in either direction. And as China subsidized most of its exports, once manufacturers shipped goods into our hub, they could immediately apply for money from the state well before the goods reached customers overseas. We needed to create a narrative to justify this breakthrough.

We prepared a report linking our project with the reforms of China's customs authority that followed China's 2001 accession to the Word Trade Organization. Our relations with the Wen family also came into play because we required the blessing from other ministries in the central government as well. All of these applications demanded considerable creativity on our part.

Initially, I hired the CEO of a company that ChinaVest had invested in to manage the project. His firm had developed warehouses on the southeastern edge of the capital, so I thought he knew the business and had connections within Customs and other ministries. I set him up with a driver, a receptionist, and an accountant. Each time I visited the office, he was all smiles. He'd shoot up from his desk and bow and scrape. But he couldn't get anything done, so I let him go.

In some ways, China was little different from the rest of the world. Money, sex, and power drove people. Whitney and I could provide access to power, so we needed to offer less money and arrange for less sex. We rarely gave cash. Instead, we doled out presents: a set of golf clubs for $10,000 here, a $15,000 watch there. On one trip to Hong Kong we bought half a dozen identical watches from the Carlson Watch Shop in Hong Kong's Central shopping district. This was pocket change to the people who accepted them. It wasn't so much a bribe as a sign of our affection.

Like Auntie Zhang did with her clan, Whitney controlled the purse strings in our family, and that didn't change after we married. While I was responsible for filling most of the positions in our company, the one executive she insisted on hiring directly was our chief financial officer. He had to be her man.

When we started our partnership, Whitney had far more capital than I, so it was somehow natural that the money should be in her name. But as time passed and our business grew, the money issue became a delicate one. Each time I made a purchase, I had to speak with her about it and send the bill to the CFO's office. She used money as a way to control our relationship. On my side, I was so caught up with the issue of face that I found it difficult to address the matter directly. I didn't believe that I should have to ask her to let me have equal control of our finances. I wanted her to cede that authority willingly. I didn't want to plead. We'd bicker about this issue from time to time, but it never got resolved.

We wined and dined our contacts in hotels around Beijing. To avoid notice, we chose venues like the frumpy Beijing Hotel just off Tiananmen Square. It provided the requisite privacy and the restaurant staff knew the drill. The top floor of the hotel was divided into private dining rooms. On any given night, three or four ministers and a handful of vice-ministers would be feted on this floor. The hotel employed two full-time coordinators to stagger the guests, the dishes, and the checks to avoid anyone running into anyone else. Who was hosting whom was a closely held secret in a system where information was at a premium. The whole enterprise worked like clockwork.

But even when we thought we'd smoothed things over with the bigwigs, we'd still confront problems at lower levels. Section chiefs, bureau chiefs, and division chiefs ran their departments like personal fiefdoms. They could give you a thousand reasons why an approval had been held up. They'd never refuse outright; they'd just tell you to wait. They wielded so much power that they were known throughout the Chinese system as the Bureau Chief Gang or the Chuzhang Bang. One such bureau chief was Kuang Xin. People called him Grandpa Kuang.

CHAPTER TEN

A TALL, BONY BUREAUCRAT WHO WAS PROUD OF HIS full mane of thick black hair, Grandpa Kuang served as the director of the airport construction bureau of the Civil Aviation Administration and later in a similar position at the National Development and Reform Commission, the department that generated the Five-Year Plan. He was pretty low on China's bureaucratic totem pole. At the Civil Aviation Administration, he didn't even have his own office; he shared it with two subordinates. Nonetheless, he was a powerhouse.

China was undergoing an airport construction boom. When Whitney and I started the logistics hub, China had 120 airports. By the time we sold it, there were 180. Kuang's bureau was responsible for approving each project. It wasn't unusual for provincial deputy governors, who qualified as *gaogan* and far outranked Grandpa Kuang in the Party hierarchy, to travel to Beijing to plead with him personally to certify their plans. Kuang made these supplicants line up outside his office, where they'd busy themselves playing video games on their phones. Kuang had his office arranged so that he faced the wall on the right side of the door.

When he finally granted these officials an audience, he didn't bother to turn around to face them. He'd simply balance his chair on two legs and offer them a dead-fish handshake over his right shoulder. He didn't even say hello.

Officials began calling Kuang, who was only in his mid-forties, Grandpa due to his influence. In the West, they might've dubbed him something like Big Daddy. But in China, grandfathers are higher on the social hierarchy than fathers, so people called him Gramps.

Kuang fancied himself an intellectual. I took him out to dinner a few times and invariably he'd throw out a few sentences from classical Chinese poetry, to which I'd always respond with a shit-eating grin, declaring, "Director Kuang's level of culture is very high!" He knew I was buttering him up, but he'd heard others say the same thing so many times that he actually started to believe it.

We needed Kuang's approval because we wanted to increase the size of the airport expansion project. As I've written, Shunyi District had originally planned an expressway along the airport's border. We needed to scrap the expressway to combine the zones in Shunyi and the airport into one. We wanted things configured so that when cargo came off planes, a truck would be able to move the goods into bonded warehouses without leaving the airport's grounds.

Whitney and I twisted ourselves into knots catering to Kuang's whims. At meals, I plied him with expensive dishes. I offered him bottles of ten-year-old Moutai. Whitney discussed Chinese literary figures with him and, like me, praised Kuang's knowledge of Chinese poetry. We'd go to the theater together and afterward Whitney and I would pretend to be interested in his take on the show. We both encouraged Kuang's self-regard. I worked on Kuang's emerging appreciation of red wine. Wine was just beginning to gain a foothold in China, so Kuang was anxious to appear au courant. His comments were unpolished, but I'd praise them anyway. After months of schmoozing, Grandpa Kuang approved our plans. In the end, however, he alienated too many people above his pay grade. In December 2009, state-run media reported that he was being prosecuted for corruption. He was sentenced to ten years in jail.

We played a similar game with a vast array of bureaucrats. Each approval was obtained through connections. Each connection meant an investment in a personal relationship, which meant an awful lot of effort and even more Moutai. Forging personal ties and establishing *guanxi* was the most difficult part. *Guanxi* wasn't a contractual relationship per se: it was a human-to-human connection, built painstakingly over time. You had to show genuine concern for the person. The tough part was that I had so many relationships that needed managing, but I also had a project on my back with a deadline. I had to squeeze all of these interactions into a pipe, and the diameter of the pipe was time. Obviously, I had to delegate, but the more I got directly involved in relationship building the more approvals we received.

In addition to Kuang, we also needed approvals from the Chinese Customs bureau and from the General Administration of Quality Supervision, Inspection and Quarantine. But even when we obtained them at the national level, we still required the cooperation of officers on the ground. In fact, it often didn't matter if the minister was on board. His underlings could always scotch the deal. They'd raise a bunch of totally legitimate, execution-level issues that sounded reasonable. Because the minister didn't concern himself with minutiae, he'd just say, "sort it out as soon as you can." In that way, control of the project leaked from the top of the bureaucracy to the bottom.

One particularly tough nut was the chief of Chinese Customs at the airport. Fat, in his mid-fifties, and so bald that his head resembled a khaki-colored cue ball, Du Pingfa saw the project as an opportunity to leave a legacy behind. Previously, the airport's expansion had been carried out randomly and Chinese Customs found itself spread out across the facility with its various dorms, warehouses, and offices separated by almost a mile. Our project promised Customs a centralized location.

In exchange for his cooperation, Chief Du had some needs. He demanded we build Customs a new office building, providing four hundred thousand square feet of space for his three-hundred-man workforce. He also pressed for an indoor gym with regulation-size basketball and badminton courts, outdoor tennis courts with a high-end surface, a two-hundred-seat theater, a dormitory with four-star-equivalent rooms, a generous banquet hall with private rooms for senior officials, a karaoke bar, and a grand lobby with an atrium two stories high. Chief Du hashed this out with me over dinner one night. "If you don't give this to us," he said with a big grin, "we're not going to let you build." All of our political backing couldn't move him. In the end, his demands added $50 million to the cost of the project, and that didn't even take into account the cost of the land.

Obviously, when one part of the bureaucracy makes a killing, other parts smell blood, too. The quarantine department demanded two hundred thousand square feet of office space. They didn't get the theater or the indoor gym, but they did cadge tennis courts, a big restaurant, and rooms at the standard of a four-star hotel. The Quarantine guys never let me forget it. "You owe us," one of their senior officials told me whenever we met. "We were never as greedy as Customs."

We started the airport project with an initial investment of $30 million. Whitney and I put up $12 million. Auntie Zhang promised to pay $4 million, but she didn't put down any capital. We also took out loans. And this is where our association with state-owned players came in handy.

Having airport boss Li Peiying as the chairman of our joint venture gave us access to a huge pool of capital. The Beijing Capital International Airport Group opened up a line of credit for our project. Banks approved loans for us at an interest rate set for state-owned enterprises, which was at least two points lower than the rate set for private ventures. China's economic system had always been geared to benefit state-run firms over private ones. Even at the height of China's short-lived capitalist experiment in the early 2000s, the rules were skewed toward state firms. We couldn't have pulled off the project without them.

Li Peiying was all in. He used his muscle and charisma to make sure his underlings supported our work. With Li as our greatest ally, and with our muleheaded moxie, we finally broke ground on June 29, 2006, more than three years after Whitney had hatched the plan. At that point, we expanded the venture's capital by another $30 million.

Then, just months into construction, our first crisis hit.

Most of the employees at the airport loved Li Peiying, but he'd ruffled feathers as he hectored and strong-armed his staff to get things done. As the head of almost forty airports, he was a target. He'd beaten out many officials to get the top job. Lots of competitors hankered after his post.

The state-owned bureaucracy had a cardinal rule. Under the regulations set by the state-owned Assets Supervision and Administration Commission, which was responsible for all of China's state-owned companies, each firm was supposed to generate a 6 percent return on equity every year. Smart SOE bosses hit the target because they understood that if they came in too low, they'd get sacked, but if their return was too high, foes would angle to get their jobs. Li Peiying violated that cardinal rule. He'd made his position a plum assignment because he'd done too good a job.

Add to that Li's gambling habit, which left him open to allegations of corruption. Enemies constantly wrote reports to the Party's Discipline Inspection Committee ratting him out. Finally, in late 2006, the allegations proved too much and Li Peiying vanished into the maw of a Communist Party investigation.

Li went incommunicado for months. On January 26, 2007, the Civil Aviation Administration announced that Peiying was no longer the general manager of the Beijing Capital International Airport Group, but bizarrely he retained his position as chairman of our joint venture. That meant we still needed his signature to move our project along. But we couldn't find him. And no official authority would tell us where he was.

Without Li's signature, we couldn't draw on the loans that we'd already secured from our banks. All of us involved in the project began guessing about the implications of his disappearance. The vultures began to circle. Contractors lined up for money. The joint venture had poured hundreds of millions of dollars into this venture and was on the hook for millions more and suddenly our bank account was down to $150,000. Forget about the contractors, I couldn't even make payroll for my staff. I woke up in the middle of the night in cold sweats wondering how I was going to make it through. My hair fell out in clumps, never to return. Whitney was hard on me. "What are we going to do if it fails?" she asked.

To make things worse, at about this time we needed to demolish some buildings to make way for warehouses. The accepted narrative—at least in the West—is that avaricious developers in China run roughshod over tenants' rights. And that does happen. But what also happens is that people learn of your plans to develop a section of town and buy out the existing owners with the goal of extorting a handsome inducement to leave.

Several buildings were sitting in the middle of our construction site, but their owners had refused to let us level them. The owners were connected with officials from the Shunyi District government. So even though the Shunyi government was our joint-venture partner, the locals were playing both sides against each other, waiting for a fat payoff. But I couldn't make that payoff. Since our venture involved a state-owned enterprise, our books were monitored by the State-owned Assets Supervision and Administration Commission. I couldn't hand over a few million to the building's owner to get him to disappear even if I'd wanted to. Right in the middle of all this, in November 2006, Li Ping, Shunyi's district chief, was transferred, severing a key connection to the local government.

Then, at our office, I began to discover bookkeeping discrepancies. It appeared that our construction manager was pilfering from the joint venture. Although I lacked absolute proof, one day I came unannounced into his office and accused him of embezzling funds. "You're stealing from a state-owned enterprise. That's like stealing from the state," I said. "You can deny it, but I will give my proof to the cops and then you all can sort it out." He cleared out the same day. You need to play the cards you're dealt. I was learning how to be a boss in China.

It must have been the swimmer in me; I just kept paddling. I didn't know when or whether I was going to reach the other side of the pool. But I saw no other way. I kept wining and dining the people I needed. Many days I'd go through one bottle of Moutai at lunch and another at dinner—my liver be damned—in a desperate attempt to delay payments, smooth relations, or procure a loan. We stumbled along. Two breakthroughs saved us.

On March 1, 2007, Ping An listed on the Shanghai Stock Exchange, opening up the possibility that we could sell our shares and use more of our own capital to save the airport project. Under the rules, we couldn't trade for six months. During that time Ping An's share price surged as high as eighty times, bringing the value of our 1 percent of the company to almost $1 billion. I found a buyer who agreed to purchase our shares at forty times our initial investment, once the blackout period ended. That meant a profit of more than $450 million. But Whitney refused. She thought Ping An's stock price wouldn't stop rising. She and I had fundamentally different perceptions about risk. She never saw a potential downside to holding assets, but I'd lived through the Asian Financial Crisis of 2007. She and the rest of her generation of Chinese entrepreneurs had never experienced a downturn. If there was a down cycle, it was always followed by a V-shaped recovery and a huge bounce back. I, however, wanted to limit our downside risk.

Six months after Ping An listed on the Shanghai Stock Exchange, I convinced Whitney that we needed to sell. We cleared a profit of over $300 million, about twenty-six times our initial investment. Auntie Zhang's stake was worth double that of ours with a potential profit above $600 million. But she didn't sell. Worried that so much of her family's fortune was technically owned by Great Ocean, Auntie Zhang decided instead to transfer the name on the stock from Whitney's company to that of Wen Jiabao's mother. That move would prove to be a fateful mistake.

The Ping An sale allowed us to keep the airport project afloat. We injected another $40 million of our private money into the joint venture to make sure construction continued. Our friends thought we were crazy to use our own funds to help a state enterprise when at that time most private entrepreneurs were using state money to benefit themselves. Suffice it to say, Whitney didn't agree to subsidize the project willingly.

Still, after Li Ping's departure, I needed a new way into the Shunyi government. I found one in, of all places, Los Angeles.

In April 2008, I hosted a group of officials from Shunyi and the airport on a "study tour" to the United States. Such junkets were common in those days and an essential part of doing business in China. There was always a little study—we planned to visit a few airport logistics hubs and to attend an industry conference—but the main goal for me was bonding, and for my guests it was the prospect of a pleasure-packed excursion to the USA. Our first stop was Los Angeles, but everyone was really looking forward to Las Vegas.

On the trip was a deputy district leader named Li Yousheng. Li had three stents in his heart and was under the care of a prominent cardiologist at Beijing's 301 Hospital, China's version of America's Walter Reed National Military Medical Center. Li's doctor had cleared him for travel.

Arriving in LA, we checked into the Peninsula hotel on Santa Monica Boulevard in Beverly Hills and tucked into a big meal. The guys were itching to go out, so I found them a local casino, and they spent all night playing blackjack. Nobody, including Li Yousheng, slept.

The next morning at breakfast, Li complained of chest pains. I brought him to the UCLA Medical Center and got him in to see a cardiologist. A blood test revealed elevated enzyme levels. The doctor strongly recommended that Li stay for observation. But the rest of the gang had headed off to Vegas and Li wanted to join them. He called his doctor in Beijing. "We know you've always had elevated enzymes," the doctor said. "Americans are too cautious. If you were in Beijing, you'd be released." The American cardiologist didn't agree, but Li insisted on leaving. We went back to the hotel for lunch and then planned to catch up to the group in Vegas.

After we ate, Li and I walked through the Peninsula's lobby. As he rounded a bouquet of flowers in the middle of the hall, Li collapsed in a heap. Foam collected around his mouth. I fumbled with my cell phone and called 911 but then decided on bundling him into a taxi to get him to the hospital faster. *What if he dies in the car?* I thought as the cab took a wrong turn.

Finally, back at the UCLA Medical Center, we were rushed from the ER to an operating room. A team of surgeons went at Li for seven hours, performing a triple bypass. By the end of the operation, the whole delegation had returned to LA and was camping out in the hospital's waiting room.

When our group was allowed into the ICU, we found Li hallucinating that he was back in China. "You are against the Chinese Communist Party," he shouted at invisible foes, tubes running into and out of his body. "Mafia! Mafia! I am going to destroy you! I am going to beat you all up!"

It was 2008 and prior to our trip Li's responsibilities had included helping with the build-out for the upcoming Summer Olympics. Specifically, he was involved in relocating people to make space for new construction. Many of them had been unwilling to move and Li had led teams into neighborhoods to roust people from their homes. *Wow,* I thought to myself as Li hollered at the imaginary villagers. *This guy is really devoted to the Party.*

After a day, Li regained consciousness. Then a new round of worries set in. Under the rules then in place to limit the profligacy of these trips, Party officials were allowed only ten days on overseas "study tours." In China, after a seven-hour bypass, a patient would be hospitalized for months. But we learned how different the US system was from China's. The doctors told Li they'd discharge him within three days and he could return to Beijing in a week. No one on the delegation believed this would actually happen. "If he can do it, I will down a bottle of Moutai in one go," one of the officials vowed. On the third day, Li was standing up and shaking the surgeon's hand. I moved Li to the nearby W Hotel and for the next few days he held court from a lawn chair by its pool, ogling girls in bikinis. Within a week, we were flying back to Beijing.

I hadn't known Li very well even though he was important to the success of the project. He ran the district's planning and land department, and the airport project impacted both. Although, like the district chief, Li Ping, Li Yousheng was a local and had relatives scattered throughout Shunyi's bureaucracy, he was from a different faction. From the start of the project, he'd always been cool to our plans.

Taking him to America was my way of trying to break the ice. We needed his help on several fronts, including demolishing villages to make way for more warehouses. He was integral to what we wanted to do. Still, I never imagined how much saving his life would change things.

The moment we returned to Beijing, we received a huge welcome from the whole district. Following that, each time I went into any government office, the first thing the leading official would declare was, "You are the benefactor of Shunyi!" Every meeting, every gathering, someone from Shunyi would mention Li Yousheng's story.

Li saw me as his white knight. He was fifty then. Whenever I sat down to a meal with him, he placed me in the seat of honor. And for his whole gang, I became the guy. Li's circle viewed me as the defender of Shunyi because I'd rescued a "big brother," as his colleagues called him, from certain death in an alien land. And I'd given him "a new engine"—or at least a repaired heart—to boot. The negotiations over the project shifted. Discussions changed from "what are you going to do for me?" to "how do we solve this together?" It gave my staff far more space to maneuver. Li Ping's departure became a distant memory.

Li Yousheng began inviting me to lunch with officials whose help I required. He tried to solve our problems on the spot. His message to his Party comrades was: "Let's get this done." And then he was promoted to executive district chief, which made things move even more smoothly. We'd become part of the Shunyi family.

Li's case allowed me to come into my own and taught me what was required to make the project a success. Whitney ran interference for me from the top down. But I also needed to work hard to get things moving from the ground up. Saving Li's life was proof that it was on me to build one-on-one relationships not with just Li but with a whole slew of middle-aged chain-smoking heavy drinkers who'd rarely left Shunyi.

I began showing up more at government offices in the district for meals. The routine was the same each time. I entered the dark, dank government offices a little after quitting time at 5:00. The staff had all gone home. The rooms were empty. I'd walk up stairs and down dark corridors illuminated by buzzing fluorescent lights. I'd push open a door and there, behind a haze of cigarette smoke, were my contacts, digging into a box of fruit from Shunyi's orchards. We'd sit around and talk about nothing.

Being together with them for the sake of being together demonstrated that I was part of their group. I had to reacquaint myself with this kind of relationship. It was as if I were a boy back in Shanghai with my arms draped around my friends' shoulders, gathering with people for no reason other than to bond with them, and doing it on a daily basis. The whole idea was to reinforce the sense of belonging.

This was critical in a system where the rules regarding what was legal and what was proscribed were full of vast areas of gray, and every time you wanted to accomplish anything you had to wade into the gray. In the West, laws are generally clear and courts are independent, so you know where the lines are. But in China, the rules were intentionally fuzzy, constantly changing, and always backdated. And the courts functioned as a tool of Party control. So that's why building this sense of belonging was so crucial. To convince someone to venture into the gray zone with you, you first had to convince him or her to trust you. Only then could you take the leap together. To do that the two of you would research each other's background, like Whitney had with Auntie Zhang. You'd talk to former colleagues and you'd spend hours cultivating each other so you could understand who each other really was. Auntie Zhang could vouch for Whitney and me on a macro level. But on the local level, it was up to me.

After an hour of chitchat, fruit, and cigarettes, we'd walk across the government compound to its canteen and file into a private dining room. There we'd find a dozen dishes arrayed on a table. There was so much food that we'd be lucky if we could down a quarter of it. Halfway into the meal the chef would come out and we'd either ask him to rustle up something special or cap the meal with noodles or dumplings.

The whole affair was lubricated with bottles of aged Moutai. As it had when I was in Hong Kong, the alcohol stripped away my natural reserve, and it brought me and these men closer. By the end of the evening, there I'd be holding hands with a fifty-something bureaucrat, cracking off-color jokes, and slapping him on the back.

I began to feel increasingly comfortable in this environment, talking about random topics like tea and fruit. I knew they were beginning to accept me, too, when one observed, "You don't really seem like someone from Shanghai." That was high praise. Northerners thought people from Shanghai were stingy, unmanly, and sneaky—in a word, Westernized.

I shed the paraphernalia that'd been imposed by Whitney to make me into a new man. Under her tutelage, I'd girded myself with the armor of a Chinese business executive. Glasses, Zegna suits, no flashy colors. But as the locals grew to accept me in backwater Shunyi, how I looked didn't matter that much anymore. I started dressing casually. I rediscovered the love of style that I'd developed with my friend Steven in Hong Kong. I added flair to my wardrobe. My new friends in Shunyi joked about it, but if I'd dressed like they did, they'd have thought it strange anyway.

I spent about $300,000 on Li Yousheng's medical expenses. A few years later, the Shunyi District government reimbursed me for about half. The money didn't matter. The goodwill that experience bought was priceless.

In late spring of 2008, the airport finally acknowledged that the ex–general manager Li Peiying was under investigation. He'd been held for a year and a half without charges. That announcement opened the way for the appointment of a new airport general manager who could sign for the joint venture's loans. After saving a life, reaping the Ping An windfall, and regaining access to funding, I looked forward to shifting the project to a higher gear.

CHAPTER ELEVEN

WHITNEY AND I HADN'T YET HAD CHILDREN, BUT that wasn't for lack of trying. After our Four Seasons wedding reception in the fall of 2005, Whitney's parents began campaigning for a grandchild. In particular, they wanted a grandson. Being from Shandong, they were more traditional than my parents and me. We weren't very concerned about gender. But Whitney's parents insisted on a boy. Whitney and I were in our late thirties, so getting pregnant had its challenges. In 2007, we began investigating in vitro fertilization.

In Beijing, we found a military hospital that was reputed to be a national leader in IVF. Whitney went there for a couple of cycles, but my seed could find no purchase. Like many Chinese, we quickly lost faith in the medical system at home, so we looked overseas. We started in Hong Kong and, through Whitney's banker, were introduced to the premier IVF doctor in Hong Kong. He had a two-year waiting list. Whitney paid to cut the line. We spent a year with that doctor with no results. We then turned our attention to New York.

We were marching on a well-worn path. China would not

relax its one-child policy until 2013, so couples of means often ventured overseas to have a second child, undergo sex-selective abortions, which were illegal in China, or give birth to their child in another country so he or she could obtain a foreign passport.

In New York, we found a leading reproductive endocrinologist. He had a waiting list, too. Instead of a payoff, we used connections. One of Premier Wen's former staff members contacted China's top diplomat at the Chinese consulate in New York, who reached out to the doctor's office and secured us an appointment.

We went to New York near the end of 2007. At the doctor's office, it was all very civilized. His staff pointed out beds that had been reserved by the world's elite. A bed for the wife of a media mogul, and a bed for a princess from a royal family.

Whitney had taken time off from Great Ocean to make our dream of having a child come true. At first she stayed in a New York hotel, then we rented a place, and finally we bought an apartment near the hospital. Whitney knew she couldn't commute from New York to Beijing, so she stayed put. She brought her mother and stepfather over to help. Each morning Whitney went in for blood tests and received shots depending on her hormone levels.

Whitney brought the mind-set of a successful Chinese businesswoman to the project of getting pregnant in New York. She didn't trust that she'd get good care unless she had a special connection with her doctor, so she cultivated the doctor's entire family. His son was an aspiring artist. We attended his shows in New York, and Whitney leaned on him to accept the gift of an expensive painting. We took the whole family out for dinner numerous times. This was Whitney's mode of operation; this was what she knew how to do. This is how she could guarantee good medical care in China. She figured New York couldn't be much different and that human nature was the same the world over.

Our doctor reacted politely. Clearly, he had many appreciative patients. After all, he was giving the gift of life. But he was thoroughly professional and never let the generosity of his clients affect the quality of his service. The culture clash continued throughout Whitney's stay in New York. I doubt anyone in his family had ever seen anything quite like Whitney before.

Sometimes Whitney's tradecraft embarrassed me. Most of the time, however, I just felt a little awkward. In the West, the way she did things seemed out of place. We'd already paid handsomely for the chance to have a child. She didn't need to do this extra stuff. But some understanding was also in order. Whitney was the product of an environment that emphasized personal relations. Without those ties, nothing would get done, especially in the critical area of medicine. In China, if a doctor didn't accept your "red envelope" stuffed with cash, you immediately grew concerned.

Whitney's broken English made it more difficult for her to express herself and to understand how things worked in the West. She'd try her hand at a few sentences and then rely on me to translate the rest. I found myself shifting away from word-for-word interpretation, modifying her meaning to make it more culturally apt.

After just two cycles, we succeeded in fertilizing not one but four eggs. We implanted three in her womb and froze the fourth. One of the eggs took; we learned that it was going to be a boy.

Whitney worked to control the process. She set the delivery date to ensure that our son would be born a Taurus. He already was going to be born in the Year of the Ox, according to the

Chinese zodiac, but Whitney wanted to magnify the boy's bull-like tendencies.

The first time I saw my son was on April 21, 2009, in a delivery room of a New York hospital. I'd seen images of newborns and was expecting something as wrinkled as an old man and hairless as an egg. Then out came this baby boy in a smoothly executed C-section. And he had a full head of hair and didn't look like a prune. Chinese put great stock in nicknames and it was my job to give one to our newest arrival. Even minutes into this world, I was impressed by how good he looked. I named him Junjun or Little Handsome; it stuck.

When it came to selecting Junjun's given names in English and Chinese both Whitney and I chose ones that reflected our dreams for him. For his English name, I picked Ariston, derived from the Greek *áristos,* meaning "excellence." For his Chinese name, Whitney settled on Jian-kun, two words taken from one of our favorite Chinese poems. *Jian* and *kun* stress the necessity of continued efforts to become, well, as weighty as Mount Tai.

Some of our friends felt that these names formed too heavy a burden for our son to shoulder. But neither Whitney nor I belonged to that superstitious group of Chinese who called their children Smelly Mutt or Dog's Balls to avoid the wrath of jealous ghosts. We figured Ariston could handle the gravitas of a big name.

Whitney had embraced the mission of having a child and had taken a lot of needles from Beijing to Hong Kong to New York. That day in the maternity ward, she and I looked forward to seeing Ariston grow into a young man in a China that offered even more opportunity than we ourselves had found.

While Whitney had been trying to get pregnant, I'd been studying how to raise a child amid wealth. Ariston's upbringing was going to be very different from ours. Whitney and I were born poor. But Ariston came into this world with a silver, even a platinum, spoon in his mouth. In the lives of the children of China's nouveau riche, there'd been frequent horror stories. I knew the son of one of China's richest men whose family sent him 20,000 British pounds a month for living expenses in London, while his friends plied him with prostitutes. When a young kid has that kind of money, parasites attach themselves pretending to be friends. I didn't want to put my son in a situation like that where he'd spend his whole life not knowing whom to trust, including his spouse, always wondering, *Is she with me because of my money?*

I started reading books and taking courses on wealth management and family legacy. I attended seminars in Switzerland, at the Stanford Graduate School of Business, and at Harvard University. I sought out families in the United States, Europe, and Asia. I waded through the three-volume history of the Rothschild clan—an endeavor that stunned the family's thirtysomething scion, Alexandre. "You actually read it?" he asked. In the United States, I interviewed the Guggenheim family. I met the family that owned Fiat and, also, a Bavarian prince who traced his roots back to the second century. I learned much from Jay Hughes, the author of *Family Wealth: Keeping It in the Family*. The messages I received were similar. Whitney and I needed to build a family story and a value set. We needed non-physical things—a belief system—to bind us together. One of the most successful families I came across was Indonesian; their secret, they said, lay in the fact that the family's matriarch had founded her own religion. Money will dissipate, I learned, if we aren't united by intangible things. I committed myself early to letting Ariston feel my love. I never really felt that from my parents, even though they sacrificed so much for me. I decided love would be the glue that bound Ariston and me. And I promised myself that I'd try to teach Ariston to achieve by embracing success, not fearing failure.

As I studied the subject, wealthy friends began to send their children to me for advice about how to live and, from time to time, I arranged talks with leading experts on family legacy, family values, and charitable work. I sensed that many nouveau riche Chinese thirsted for knowledge about how to hold on to their newfound wealth. At the same time, they also confronted a yawning moral vacuum in a society that had destroyed traditional Chinese values, tossed aside Communist communitarian norms, and was focused solely on the pursuit of lucre. I established the Tsinghua Kaifeng Family Heritage Center at Tsinghua University to help wealthy Chinese families think strategically about how to use their resources to benefit society.

One of China's richest men, a real estate mogul named Xu Jiayin, directed his wife and son to attend one of the seminars that I'd arranged. At one lecture, I saw his son dozing with his mouth open like a Venus flytrap. *He was at a nightclub until four in the morning,* I thought.

Another participant was a young man named Ling Gu, who was the son of Ling Jihua, a senior official in the Chinese Communist Party. Ling Gu was in his mid-twenties when we met. He shared my interest in fast cars and we spent a couple afternoons taking sports cars for a spin around Beijing's racetrack. Our relationship was close enough that he called me Big Brother Shum.

I advised Ling Gu on investments and encouraged his studious side. He was particularly interested in the history of Skull and Bones, the Yale University secret society. Ling Gu organized a reading group with other members of the red aristocracy modeled on Skull and Bones. He looked at his group as a fraternity of sorts, a brotherhood, a place where the sons and daughters of the red aristocracy could gather to discuss the hot topics of the day. Instead of partying and chasing women, he wanted a group that would bond over ideas. He formed a book club. I suggested a few titles; the members only met a few times. Ling had worked for the government in a low-level job in Shandong Province to get a sense of how the other half lived. He gave me hope that at least some of the privileged in the younger generation were interested in more than parties, girls, and booze. Later on, I'd be shocked to learn how he died.

Whitney brought Ariston back to China in the summer of 2009 when he was a few months old. We'd moved from the Oriental Plaza to the Palm Springs apartment complex on the east side of Beijing. Her return to China found me a changed man. The first phase of the airport project was nearing completion. When work began in June 2006, I knew nothing about such things. I didn't even know what a proper construction site looked like. The one that stretched out in front of me then was a mess, equipment scattered willy-nilly. I thought that was the way it should be. I didn't realize poor management was to blame. But I'd learned.

I'd been through the wringer and come out the other side. I'd lost the airport GM, my friend Li Peiying, to a corruption investigation. Shunyi chief Li Ping had left, too. But my team and I had rallied. I'd saved a life and won some karma, and now warehouses and office buildings were rising where there was once only mud.

I'd grown enormously, thanks to Whitney. She'd taught me how to act and prosper within the Chinese system. She'd helped me learn the rules of the road. As I evolved, I gained self-confidence. I rediscovered the avant-garde styles of my youth. I dropped glasses in favor of contact lenses. In fact, Whitney and I went to Hong Kong and scheduled LASIK surgery on the same day back to back, not the brightest move, as we were basically the blind leading the blind all the way back to the hotel. I no longer worried about being "an old head on young shoulders." I was becoming myself.

Cashing out our Ping An shares in 2007 gave Whitney and me access to a kind of wealth we'd only read about in books. We'd made another killing in June 2006 when we'd participated in the listing of the Bank of China on the Hong Kong Stock Exchange. Bank officials had needed Whitney's help to fast-track the bank's IPO approval process at the State Council. In exchange for her support there, we were given the opportunity to buy about 3 million shares as the bank was preparing to list. On the first day of trading, June 1, 2006, the stock price went up 15 percent. We sold several days later. We participated in several more IPOs like that one. The money rolled in.

I started buying things without looking at the price tag, setting aside the skill I'd honed twenty years earlier while clothes shopping with my pal Steven in Hong Kong. I acquired cars—a Lamborghini and a Ferrari. I even lent them out to friends, such as the twentysomething Ling Gu. At the University of Wisconsin, my interest in wine had been piqued by that first tasting menu at the Everest restaurant. Finally, I'd enough money to begin my own wine collection. Today I have several thousand bottles in storage on two continents. Whitney continued to control the purse strings. I sent my bills to her finance guy. It upset me that we hadn't come to a better arrangement about our money, but, as before, I procrastinated and thought we'd be able to deal with it later. That day would never come.

It wasn't just *us* who were spending big. All around us in the mid-2000s, China's nouveau riche were opening their wallets. "Crazy rich Asians" in the cities along China's eastern seaboard were powering a consumption boom. In the 1990s, China's well-off bought knock-offs. In the 2000s, we bought the real thing—LV, Prada, Gucci, and Armani. No one had spent real money for so long in China that once we had some extra, we went wild, embracing a splurge mind-set. We were like cavemen who'd finally made it out of the cave. Emerging from our hovels, we'd no idea what to buy, so we fixed on the brightest stars and the most famous brands and bought those, often at inflated prices. In wine it was Château Lafite. In cars it was Rolls-Royce. As Chinese lavished money on these luxuries, their prices skyrocketed worldwide.

Whitney and I were pretty floored by our windfalls. Still, when we completed the Ping An sale, I was so deep into the airport project that it wasn't like all of a sudden a financial load had been lifted off my shoulders. Our sense of our worth definitely jumped a peg, but I wasn't particularly euphoric. I'd been sucked into a project that demanded 24/7 attention. I was too busy dealing with the headaches of managing a company and getting something done.

More than me, the payout seemed to really change Whitney. She'd always been a big spender, but after the Ping An sale, her consumption hit a new level. We traveled the world on the lookout for expensive things to buy. We went on a hunt for a colored diamond. At the House of Abram shop at the Mandarin Oriental in Hong Kong, Whitney dropped $15 million on a pink one. Then we scoured every major diamond dealer in New York City for a yellow one.

I had my sports cars and wine, but Whitney always had a larger appetite. She had this deep desire to show the largeness of her life to people around her, a desire that grew as her wealth increased. She needed to convince people that she was bigger than they were, better than they were, superior in every way. She flaunted her riches to prove to those around her that she could cruise through all of the difficulties blocking her and that she'd left Shandong behind. Although we'd once agreed to stay out of the limelight, the temptation was too much for her. Even in our choice of cars.

I thought we didn't need the Rolls-Royce. There weren't many around Beijing at the time and I worried that it would attract unnecessary attention. But she insisted, so we bought one—a Phantom in Salamanca Blue.

While Whitney collected things to show how far she'd come from her humble background, I acquired my expensive toys mostly out of curiosity. From my youth, whether it involved finding a new alley to the pool or leaving Hong Kong for Wisconsin, I'd always been adventurous. I wasn't interested in simply making money for money's sake. Instead, I used it to try new things. I wanted to know what owning a Ferrari felt like, so I bought one. *What kind of mental state will that put me in,* I wondered, *owning a car most men only dream of?* And once I owned one and found out what it was like, I ticked that box and moved on.

Sometimes the conspicuous consumption left me feeling a bit idiotic. For my fortieth birthday, Whitney gave me a custom-made Swiss timepiece worth half a million Euros that took two years to make. The watch was from a series crafted by watchmaker F.P. Journe. I received the seventh in the series; from all accounts, Russian leader Vladimir Putin got the second.

Because of our association with the Wens, we'd previously been careful not to display our wealth. We'd amassed collectibles that we showed to close contacts, but we didn't parade our riches like some others in our class. We didn't mingle with other businessmen or -women. We didn't want rumors circulating about us and we weren't in the market for partners. But that, too, changed once we made the Ping An sale, and Whitney was seized with a desire to extend herself and her influence.

Whitney began hobnobbing with painters such as Zeng Fanzhi, who was the brightest star on the Chinese modern art scene. Zeng was always surrounded by an entourage that included Beijing's beautiful people, writers, critics, fellow artists, dealers, and Western elites. Whitney became one of Zeng's patrons. She wrote the introduction to a catalogue for one of Zeng's exhibitions. Everybody who read it was blown away by the way she used words.

Whitney competed fiercely to buy Zeng's paintings. One of her rivals was the French billionaire François Pinault, owner of the Gucci Group and one of the world's most prominent collectors of modern art. Pinault had an assistant whose job was to shadow Zeng and take pictures of paintings that he was working on. Pinault would offer to buy them even before Zeng had finished the works.

Whitney and Pinault got into a bidding war over one painting that Zeng titled *Praying Hands*. "I'm a Christian," Whitney told Zeng. "I'm very devout. This painting speaks to me. Don't sell it to Pinault." Zeng agreed. Whitney always found a way to win. And, because she'd been Zeng's patron, she got a good deal. She bought the painting for $5 million, which for a big painting by Zeng Fanzhi was a cut-rate price.

The Ping An deal was basically a fluke and proved a theory I—and others—had that wealthy people aren't so much brilliant as lucky. We bought the stock not sure that it would go up and unaware that the company was planning an IPO. I was ready to dump our shares once the stock hit four times what we paid for it, but regulations didn't allow it. We only garnered such a big return because we weren't able to sell when I'd wanted.

For us, the Ping An sale was the first of two enormous financial triumphs, and chance played a major role in both. We'd viewed Ping An as a safe investment. Granted, we got access to the shares because of our connections, but that happens in thousands of deals across the world. All of those transactions involve a certain amount of influence peddling. Ours was the Chinese variety. It wasn't influence peddling through an official; it was influence peddling through an official's wife. It wasn't particularly defensible, but it was how the Chinese system worked.

Whitney taught me that if you wanted to do big things in China, you had to work within the system. If you wanted to participate in China's rise, this was the only way to go. It was an inference drawn by every Chinese but also by foreigners and multinational corporations.

There's a simplistic argument made these days that all of China's rich are morally compromised. But if that's the case, everyone who did business with, invested in, and engaged with China at that time was "morally compromised," and that involves a large number of people, governments, and corporations from all over the world and even the people who held shares in those companies and filled their homes with made-in-China products, too. What the majority actually believed, I'd counter, was that China's system was dovetailing with that of the West and that as time passed it would become more transparent and more open as private enterprise grew to dominate the economy. That process has been aborted by the Chinese Communist Party and it probably was never in the cards anyway, but back then we didn't know that. I take full responsibility for all of the things that Whitney and I did together and will accept the burdens that come with those decisions. But living it, as we did, I've come to understand that things were far more complex than another person might suppose, viewing it from afar. Life isn't perfect. I will march on.

After the Ping An deal, COSCO's CEO, Wei Jiafu, tried to leverage his relationship with Whitney and Auntie Zhang to secure a promotion to minister of transport. When we took him to dinner with Auntie Zhang, he regaled us with stories about opening new routes, buying a port in Greece, and getting an award from US Senator (and later Secretary of State) John Kerry for saving the Port of Boston. Still, in the end, there was no quid pro quo for the opportunity he'd given us to purchase those shares. Wei never made it to minister. The China Ocean Shipping Company ran aground during the financial meltdown of 2008 and Wei retired from COSCO in 2013.

That didn't stop other members of his family from trying to use the deal to their advantage. Wei's daughter who was living in California with her American husband asked us for a $500,000 loan. Whitney was upset that she felt entitled to our money. We'd bought Ping An's shares at the market price, she observed. Just because COSCO sold it to us didn't mean we owed Wei or the rest of his family anything. We never gave Wei's daughter the loan. We believed it wouldn't be repaid.

The Ping An investment was the biggest deal that the Wen family would ever participate in. Its success solidified our relationship with Auntie Zhang. We became something like honorary members of the clan. Our interests became even more aligned and we became even more indispensable to Auntie Zhang.

Auntie Zhang's interactions with Whitney grew closer and more trusting. She had Whitney send me to Hong Kong on shopping trips to buy personal items for the premier. Auntie Zhang gave Whitney tips on spicing up our love life. Whitney hinted that the Wens should become our role models. Approaching seventy, Auntie Zhang was still lusting for life, and Premier Wen appeared eager to keep pace.

Keen on anticipating the family's needs, Whitney and I took it upon ourselves to clean up Premier Wen's disheveled look. We bought him suits and ties. We chuckled when we saw him sporting them in public. Whitney and Auntie Zhang made plans for Whitney to put her formidable writing skills to use ghostwriting Wen's memoirs after he retired. Still, our relationship with Auntie Zhang was never one of equals. Whitney and I focused on being one step ahead of her to determine and satisfy her desires before she had time to realize what they were.

The Ping An deal also boosted Auntie Zhang's sway within her family. She'd always ruled the clan, doling out jobs and business opportunities to her children and relatives and advising her husband. But the success of the Ping An stock deal confirmed Auntie Zhang's judgment and gave her a fortune—worth hundreds of millions of dollars—that she could wield.

CHAPTER TWELVE

LABORING TO MAKE THE AIRPORT PROJECT HAPPEN was hard work, but it also gave Whitney and me a sense of optimism, not just about ourselves, but about China. We were building something big in our homeland. Even though we were entrepreneurs, we were operating deep within the belly of the Communist Chinese system and we were making headway.

We had the impression that China was evolving in a positive direction. We saw how capitalists like us were becoming essential to its modernization. Entrepreneurs were creating most of the new jobs and much of the wealth. Sure, we read the criticism of the Party in the Western press. But we felt like we were living in a different country than the one depicted in the *Washington Post* or the *New York Times*. Whitney and I were convinced things were improving. Today was better than yesterday and this year was better than last year. The official Chinese defense was "Look how far we have come." And we agreed. You could argue that China's march into modernity needed to be even more rapid, but the country was definitely on the march. And it wasn't just people like Whitney and me in the upper crust who felt this way. The whole society shared our optimism. We all sensed that we were heading ineluctably toward a more open, freer society.

As early as July 1, 2001, the Party had officially changed its policy on capitalists when then Party boss Jiang Zemin made a speech that welcomed all leading Chinese, including entrepreneurs, into the Party's ranks. Even though Jiang wrapped this announcement in Party-speak, calling it the "Three Represents," that word salad couldn't mask the momentous nature of this change. Communist China's founder, Mao Zedong, had relegated capitalists like those in my father's family to the bottom rung of society. Deng Xiaoping had given them a leg up by acknowledging that with economic reforms a small group would "get rich first." Now, a generation later, Jiang Zemin was inviting entrepreneurs to join the Party and enter at least the margins of political power. It was enough to make you dizzy.

Even high up in the Party, the elite seemed to be preparing mentally for a change. In 2004, Chen Shui-bian was reelected as the president of Taiwan, the island of 23 million people that the Communists have long claimed belongs to China. In 2000, Chen had become the first opposition candidate to be elected Taiwan's president, ending five decades of one-party rule by the Nationalist Party. Taiwan's democratization process shook Communist Party bigwigs because they saw in it a potential road map for mainland China and thus a threat to the Party's monopoly on power. After his reelection, Chen announced that it was time to go after the riches of Taiwan's Nationalist Party. When the Nationalists ran the island, they'd treated its economy as their party's piggy bank. After the vote in Taiwan in March 2004, I was invited to a dinner with Deng Lin, Deng Xiaoping's eldest daughter. A painter,

Deng Lin had made a small fortune selling her mediocre works to rich Hong Kong businessmen eager to ingratiate themselves with her clan. Deng Lin steered the conversation to Taiwan. "We need to increase Party dues to build up the Party's funds," she declared. "Then we need to take the assets of the state-owned firms and turn them into Party-owned firms." In the future, when the Chinese Communist Party faced an election like the one that had just transpired in Taiwan, she said, "at least we'll have a big nest egg to fall back on." *Is that how people are thinking at the top?* I wondered. Were they actually considering the possibility that the Chinese Communist Party would one day have to share power with a real opposition party? Obviously, Deng Lin wasn't a person of political consequence in China's political universe. However, her worries reflected elite opinion. A lot was up for grabs in China and her concerns were signs of the time.

Other government officials seemed more supportive of China's peaceful evolution toward capitalism and a more pluralistic political system. In private conversations, they shared with us their view that the nation's economy would inevitably become more open. They seemed to understand that state-owned enterprises couldn't survive in the long term because of their inherent inefficiencies. One of the most senior officials who expressed these beliefs was Wang Qishan.

For decades, Wang Qishan stood at the center of China's economic reforms. Wang was a longtime follower of Zhu Rongji, the reformist-minded architect of China's economic boom from 1993 to 2003. In 1996, when Zhu was first vice-premier in Beijing, Wang led one of China's biggest financial institutions and teamed with Henry Paulson, then the CEO of Goldman Sachs and later

US Treasury secretary, to list shares from China Telecom on the New York Stock Exchange as part of an American-backed effort to modernize China's moribund financial system and its network of state-owned businesses. Paulson and others interpreted Wang's and Zhu's moves as a way to privatize China's economy. But actually, the Party's goal, apropos of Deng Lin's worries, was to save the state-owned sector so that it could remain the economic pillar of the Party's continued rule. This was one of the many instances where Westerners thought they were helping China evolve toward a more pluralistic society with a freer market when in reality the Party was actually employing Western financial techniques to strengthen its rule.

Shortly after the listing, Zhu appointed Wang to be executive vice-governor of Guangdong Province. There he partnered again with Goldman Sachs to successfully manage the largest bankruptcy restructuring in Chinese Communist history, making Goldman a lot of money and saving Guangdong Enterprises.

Whitney met Wang at a dinner hosted at the Beijing Hotel by Auntie Zhang in 2006 while he was mayor of Beijing. By this time, Whitney had drawn even closer to Auntie Zhang, who'd matured into her dual roles as the emissary of her husband, Premier Wen Jiabao, and as a businesswoman in her own right. Auntie Zhang didn't like going out with her children and refused to be escorted in public by Huang, her apparent "friend with benefits." That would really be a scandal. So, Whitney accompanied her everywhere.

Although Wang Qishan was Beijing's mayor, he was in line for a promotion to vice-premier under Premier Wen. Naturally, he sought avenues to improve those chances. Mingling with Auntie Zhang and Whitney furthered his chances of getting a promotion.

After the meal, Wang invited Whitney to visit him at the mayor's office. Later, after he became vice-premier in 2008, their meetings moved to Party headquarters at Zhongnanhai. It became a regular thing. Every two or three weeks, Wang summoned Whitney and her chauffeur would take her across town. Whitney and Wang would spend several hours drinking tea and discussing politics.

Wang appreciated Whitney's cleverness. To hear Whitney tell it, the pair discussed everything from world history, to political thought, to the direction of politics in China and the world. Wang didn't rely on Whitney for counsel, like some of the other officials did. Instead, he probed her for details about Wen Jiabao, who was technically his boss.

Inside that tight circle of people near the height of power in patriarchal China, there were very few women other than flight attendants or waitresses. Whitney was a rare bird. She held no official position, but coming as she did with the seal of approval from Auntie Zhang, she was in high demand as someone of substance, a conduit for juicy gossip, and a wellspring of inside information. What's more, although Wang was married, he had no children. Just as Auntie Zhang slipped naturally into the role of a surrogate mother to Whitney, so Wang fussed over Whitney like a kindly uncle. For Wang Qishan, getting close to Whitney served multiple purposes.

The same was true for Whitney. No sooner had Wen become premier in 2003 than we began discussing what would happen when he retired in ten years. Whitney saw the need to broaden our web of connections so we could add pieces on her chessboard. Wang Qishan fit the bill.

Whitney found that Wang's views on China's trajectory aligned with her own. Wang predicted that China's state-owned enterprises would one day be sold off and advised Whitney to put aside capital so that when the time came we could invest. We should get our bullets ready, he told her, so that when it was time to pull the trigger we'd have ammunition to burn. Wang described the Chinese economic system as a giant game of musical chairs. At a certain point, he predicted, the music would stop and the Party would be forced to accept large-scale privatization. We'd need to be prepared.

Wang also shared some of the paranoid delusions particular to China's ruling elite. He was, for example, a huge fan of a 2007 best seller, *Currency Wars*, written by a financial pundit named Song Hongbing. Song claimed that international, and particularly American, financial markets were controlled by a clique of Jewish bankers who used currency manipulation to enrich themselves by first lending money in US dollars to developing nations and then shorting those countries' currencies. Song's book mixed the disdain, suspicion, and awe of the United States held by many of China's leaders. Wang Qishan, at least, should've known better; he'd worked closely with Westerners for decades.

A master networker, Whitney didn't stop at Wang Qishan in her pursuit of new contacts to eventually replace the Wens. Her prized prospect was Sun Zhengcai, the former Party boss in Shunyi. Sun had doled out a plot of land to Whitney and me in the early 2000s, although we didn't develop it. He'd helped Whitney get approval to hang those vanity plates on her Audi.

Sun's career had taken off since he'd left Shunyi in 2002 to become secretary-general of the Party committee of Beijing.

Whitney was deeply involved in securing Sun promotions, especially while Wen was premier. In December 2006, Wen backed Sun's promotion to minister of agriculture, making him, at forty-three, one of the two youngest ministers in China.

Getting Sun a minister's position was hard work. To become a minister in China you need an unwavering advocate on the Standing Committee of the Politburo and you need to make sure that none of the other members opposes your rise. Whitney and Auntie Zhang ensured that Wen sponsored Sun. At the same time, Sun had to work on other members to make sure no one blocked him. Remember that Sun had handed out parcels of land in Shunyi to relatives of China's vice-president Zeng Qinghong. Zeng was close to former Party chief Jiang Zemin. Both extended families knew Sun as a good guy. He called in those chips. He did that on his own.

Throughout the process, Whitney provided guidance. She was particularly forceful with Auntie Zhang. She thought Sun's promotion would be good not just for us, but also for the long-term security of the Wen family. Wen Jiabao never had a network of loyalists who'd protect his family's legacy and guarantee its continued influence after he exited the political stage. Sun represented a chance to change that, to leave behind a flag. Sun's jump to minister at such a tender age put him in the running to be the future leader of all China. And who'd got him there? Whitney and Auntie Zhang, with the help of Wen Jiabao.

This trajectory was confirmed in 2009 when Sun, at age forty-six, left the Ministry of Agriculture to become Party secretary of Jilin Province in northeast China. All pretenders to China's throne needed time out in the provinces, running a mini-empire, before they took on the grand task of running all of China themselves. This was to be Sun's moment.

In China, officials never reveal their ambitions in public. Biding one's time is a key tenant of Sun Tzu's *Art of War*. But behind closed doors, Sun moved aggressively. He paid special attention to one contender, an official named Hu Chunhua, whose CV mirrored that of Sun. Like Sun, Hu came from humble origins, having been born in 1963 into a family of farmers in Hubei Province. Hu was not quite six months older than Sun.

Both Sun and Hu seemed to be riding a rocket ship to the top. Both made it onto the Party's Central Committee in 2007 and were the two youngest members that session. Both became Party secretaries of provinces in 2009. Both entered the Politburo in 2012. Hu was a product of the Party's Youth League faction and a protégé of Party boss Hu Jintao. For that reason, he was known as Little Hu. It was clear that he and Sun were being groomed for the two top spots that would open up in 2022; the only question seemed to be who would land the top job, as Party general secretary, and would play second fiddle, as China's premier.

During his many trips to the capital, Sun sought Whitney out. He was obsessed with Hu's meteoric rise. Late at night, Whitney and Sun would meet at a teahouse on the east side of Beijing to discuss how Sun could beat out Hu for the top spot.

The life of an ambitious official involved constant dining out. On many evenings in Beijing, Sun would attend three dinners. One at 5:00 featured subordinates, people who had requests or needed favors. They'd agree to an early meal because they understood that Sun was busy and had other things to do. A second dinner at 6:30 was reserved for his superiors or political equals.

Important political business was transacted in these gatherings. The third dinner at 8:00 was with people with whom he felt more comfortable. By the time he arrived there, he'd already be reasonably drunk, so he'd want an environment where he could drop his guard. His hosts consented to a time well past Chinese dinnertime because they knew he was on the make. Around 10:00, after the final meal, Sun would text Whitney and they'd meet in a private room at the teahouse and linger past midnight.

Seeing Whitney at that late hour underscored how much Sun valued their ties. It showed that they were so friendly that they could dispense with the formalities of a meal and focus on the content of their communication: how to help Sun move his pieces on China's political chessboard. Whitney noticed how tense Sun was, how worried he became at one point when he fell several months behind Hu in promotions, and how intent he was on catching up.

On a trip to Manhattan, after Sun's promotion to Jilin Province, Whitney and I stopped by Zilli, an upscale French menswear store on the ground floor of the Four Seasons Hotel in midtown. There we bought Sun a pair of fancy fur-lined boots. Jilin was famed for its cold winters and we wanted Sun to know we were thinking of him.

We were always doing things like this; we had an internal checklist of those who needed to be thrown chum. Every trip abroad was a chance to find a bauble for one of our contacts, to deepen the connection and show we cared. Back in the early days of our relationship, Whitney had criticized me for letting my mind idle. But I'd changed, adopting her view that we needed to keep our eyes on the prize, seeking opportunities to serve our masters in the Chinese Communist Party.

Sun's feet barely had time to freeze in Jilin. Even though he was technically based there, he spent almost half of his time in Beijing, meeting with Whitney and other supporters. Whitney would often take him out with Auntie Zhang. Each time, Whitney was doing Sun a favor. Auntie treasured the evenings, too, because Sun invariably came with information that would be useful to her husband. It seemed to me that, among her many roles, Auntie Zhang served Premier Wen like an intelligence officer.

In November 2012, Sun along with Hu ascended to the Politburo, becoming two of the twenty-five most powerful officials in China. Soon after, Sun was appointed Party chief of Chongqing, China's World War II–era capital, while Hu got the top Party post in Guangdong. Their stars were rising.

Whitney wasn't simply content to cultivate China's rooks, knights, kings, and queens. Pawns were important, too, and she actively worked on the aides to China's powerful. Called *mishu* or "secretaries" in Chinese, assistants control access to their bosses, shape their agendas, and can sway key decisions. Along with the Gang of Wives and the Bureau Chiefs Gang, the Assistants Gang—or Mishu Bang—constitutes a third pillar of power in China.

Whitney had a natural affinity for the assistants. After all, she'd started her career as the assistant to a university president. Granted, he wasn't at the apex of power in China, but the relationship was similar. Whitney taught her charges how to manage up.

Whitney's relationship was so close with Zhou Liang, one of Wang Qishan's assistants, that he called her Big Sister. Whitney spent hours on the phone advising Zhou how to deepen his relationship with his boss. She'd query Wang Qishan about Zhou and then feed Zhou tips about how to better do his job. Often those calls happened when Zhou was pulling an all-nighter as the overnight assistant monitoring international developments. Whitney and I would come home from dinner at 9:00 and she'd spend the next three hours on the phone with Zhou describing how Wang saw him, where he was weak, what he needed to improve, and what promotion he should pursue. Sometimes the calls went on so long that I'd fall asleep and Whitney would move the conversation to the living room until the wee hours of the night.

In exchange, Zhou assisted us on the airport project. At several junctures, Whitney induced him to call an assistant at the Ministry of Transport to inquire about an approval we required. Zhou didn't need to say that Wang Qishan wanted it issued; he just needed to raise the subject. The other side would necessarily react as if Wang had a direct interest in the project. Calls like these didn't help us burst through all the barricades, but they gave us a running start by bringing the imprimatur of another top government official to our side. Whitney rewarded Zhou for his assistance, using her connections to the Wen family and elsewhere to help Zhou secure a position on the graft-busting Central Commission for Discipline Inspection.

Zhou wasn't the only pawn in Whitney's arsenal. She nurtured the career of Song Zhe, who from 2002 to 2007 served as one of three assistants to Premier Wen. Song was a minister counselor in the Chinese embassy in Britain in 2000 when Auntie Zhang, Whitney, and I traveled there. Song showed us around and told us that he "missed Beijing." That hint was a sign that Song was angling for a promotion. With Whitney's encouragement, Auntie Zhang arranged to have Song transferred back to the capital to work in Wen's office as the assistant in charge of managing the foreign affairs portfolio for the premier. Whitney was useful to Song because she obtained firsthand information on Wen's views of him and advised him on how to better serve his boss. Song returned the favors; it was he who arranged the appointment with the fertility specialist in New York. In 2008 in part because of Whitney's lobbying and Auntie Zhang's support, Song was appointed China's ambassador to the European Union, and after that he became the Foreign Ministry's chief representative in Hong Kong. While in Hong Kong, Song made vice-minister rank, becoming a *gaogan*.

The success of Whitney's contacts reinforced our sense that the opportunities in the new China were going to be endless as we worked hard to install allies in positions up and down the Party's pecking order. I began to entertain broader ambitions than simply building a logistics hub for one of the world's major airports. I started to consider the possibility of competing for other projects in China and overseas. I was also inspired to look beyond business to consider the prospect of using China's entrepreneurial class as a force for wider changes. While embryonic, my thinking—and that of other capitalists—began to focus on how to work within the system to shape China's future.

In 2003, I'd been introduced to the Aspen Institute by the consultant, author, and businessman Joshua Cooper Ramo, whom I'd met for lunch at the Grand Hyatt hotel in Beijing. Ramo was at work on a paper that he'd publish the next year called "The Beijing Consensus," which argued that China's mix of an authoritarian political system, meritocratic government, and semi-free market economy constituted a new model for development around the world. Ramo would soon go to work for Kissinger Associates, the firm started by former secretary of state Henry Kissinger, which made its money doing a foreigners version of Whitney's *guanxi* business in China.

With its many seminars and fellowships, the Aspen Institute was, at least to me, a stimulating place. From my earliest days, I've been a curious person, seeking out new intellectual experiences and ideas, and Aspen allowed me to fully exercise that muscle. It encouraged self-improvement, a trait I've embraced since my days in Shanghai reading the texts of Chinese philosopher Nan Huai-Chin, who argued that self-reflection was key to a full life.

I became a Crown Fellow at the Institute in 2005. Over five days in Colorado that summer with about twenty other people, I read and discussed philosophical texts while moderators challenged us to think about our lives. It was the first time since the failure of PalmInfo that I'd had the chance to reflect. This time, however, I did so from a position of strength. My team in Beijing was well on its way to securing approvals to build the airport logistics hub. I was full of optimism. The crisis sparked by Li Peiying's arrest was still in the future.

The Aspen experience inspired me to look beyond my career. If you have everything, what do you strive for next? Promoting social responsibility? Aspiring to a position in politics? One participant I met at Aspen was an eye surgeon who spent half the year volunteering in developing countries. Another told a story about an American named John Oldham who'd graduated from Columbia Law School in 1983. Tragically, John perished in the downing by Soviet fighters of Korean Air Lines flight 007 in September of that year. Oldham had been on his way to Beijing for a year at Peking University's faculty of law to teach and study. Following his death, his friends and family took up donations and created a scholarship in his name that each year brings a Chinese legal scholar to the United States and sends an American counterpart to China. This story gave me an idea.

Relations between China and the United States at the time were in a trough. I thought that China wasn't as bad as Americans tended to think. They just needed to better understand the average Chinese citizen's perspective. One of the moderators of our session was the Harvard philosophy professor Michael Sandel. I broached the idea with him of setting up scholarships at Harvard to support graduate students studying any aspect of China—from history to archaeology to sociology to political science. Sandel jumped on the idea. With a donation of a few million dollars and the advent of the Shum Scholarship in 2004, Whitney and I became two of the first Chinese entrepreneurs to donate to Harvard University.

At Aspen, I learned how people with money had always participated in the political process. China's system was the outlier in that sense, denying its capitalist class a say in the direction of the country. But those of us who identified as capitalists wanted a voice. We wanted protection for our property, our investments, and other rights. We wanted, if not an independent judiciary, at least a fair one where judgments were made on the basis of law and not on the whims of the local Party boss. We craved predictability in government policies because only then could we invest with confidence. Whitney, who was a Christian, also wanted more religious freedom. At the very least, she wanted the Chinese government to acknowledge that a Chinese person could love God and love China at the same time.

These goals led us and many others in China to donate to worthy causes. Charities in China were in their infancy and there was a horrifying amount of fraud. So Whitney and I established our own vehicle for giving, awarding scholarships to kids from poorer regions so they could attend Tsinghua University, one of China's great institutions of higher learning, which was built in 1911 as Tsinghua College with US government funds. We established our own think tank, the Kaifeng Foundation, to focus on promoting China's non-governmental sector and building a civil society, including independent charities, research institutions, and human rights organizations that the Chinese Communist Party had shuttered when it seized power in 1949. Kaifeng officially launched in March 2007, the same month Ping An Insurance listed on the Shanghai Stock Exchange, vastly increasing our wealth. Backed financially by Whitney's Great Ocean, Kaifeng was the first private research institute approved by China's central government.

Our relationship with Tsinghua University was sometimes testy. In funding the underprivileged students, I structured the scholarships to cover more than books and tuition. I remembered how hard it was for me not to have any spare change in my pocket when I first went to school in Hong Kong. I wanted to give the kids walking-around money so that they'd have a social life and wouldn't feel like second-class students. The two biggest issues for students from poor families were that despite their academic achievements, they often possessed low self-esteem and were socially awkward. If not dealt with, those issues would hinder their progress. Whitney and I met with them and shared our experiences. We organized outings for them, as well.

Tsinghua wasn't accustomed to donors being so involved in

the lives of its students. The university balked because on a per student basis our scholarships were the most generous at the school. This debate at Tsinghua led to a broader discussion about philanthropy.

The school's Communist Party secretary was Chen Xi, a Tsinghua graduate who'd studied for two years at Stanford University in the early 1990s. Every university in China is run by the Chinese Communist Party and all universities, just like all K–12 schools, have Party secretaries who are usually far more powerful than school presidents, deans, or principals. The same is true for China's political system, where the Party general secretary outranks the premier; in China's schools, state-owned enterprises, and research institutions, Party secretaries call the shots.

Chen had been on the faculty at Tsinghua for twenty years. Appointed Party secretary in 2002, he had strong backing within the Party. He was close to Xi Jinping, then a rising star in the Party's firmament. In fact, when Chen and Xi attended Tsinghua as students in the late 1970s he was Xi's bunkmate. When Xi was assigned a position as governor of Fujian Province in 1999, he'd asked Chen to be his deputy, but Chen demurred. Chen was loyal to Xi but not that loyal. He was a big fish in Beijing; why would he want to exchange that to become a deputy governor in a faraway province?

Chen was tall, with bookish good looks and a compelling charm he could turn on to great effect. As Tsinghua's Party boss, he rallied students easily and was gifted at coming up with slogans. "Be ambitious, enter the mainstream, climb the big stage, do great things, choose the right goal, persevere," was how he began a speech to students in October 2005. Chen's central message was to encourage Tsinghua's students to enter the Party system and serve the state.

Under his leadership, Tsinghua became the most prestigious university in China and a political heavyweight. In the mid-2000s, all seven members of the Standing Committee of the Politburo were graduates, a fact that Chen never let anyone forget. Chen encouraged students to study military technology, especially rocket science, and join China's military-industrial complex. He played a leading role in the Thousand Talents Program, a Chinese government effort to entice leading scientists, both Chinese and foreign, to move to China to teach and conduct cutting-edge research. Having studied for two years in California, he was particularly intent on bringing talent from the USA. He told Whitney and me how he used former teachers and relatives to entice Chinese from the United States. Tsinghua had a vast network of alumni and Chen wielded it to benefit both the school and the country.

Because Tsinghua was under the control of the central government, it was limited in what it could pay the prominent scientists it lured from abroad. So Chen tapped rich alumni and businesses to subsidize their pay. Chen loved to talk about his successes. When we invited him downtown to dine with Auntie Zhang, he'd spend ninety minutes of a two-hour meal boasting about how he'd been "grabbing geniuses," as he liked to put it, from around the world.

Whitney also tried to leverage Tsinghua's alumni network. In 2008, she entered a PhD program at Tsinghua that Chen had established to groom future leaders. Whitney's class list read like a who's who of up-and-coming officials: a trusted assistant of Xi Jinping; the son of then Party General Secretary Hu Jintao;

director generals; vice-ministers; a Party secretary from a city of 1.3 million people. Whitney undertook this challenge as part of her never-ending search for more connections. Sure, we had the Wen family, but they wouldn't be around forever. And the Tsinghua alumni network was one of the best in China.

Whitney's course was modeled after the Kennedy School's executive program on public policy at Harvard University. Classes were held four days a month. Whitney wrote her thesis on China's stock market. She was one of the few participants who actually produced her own thesis; the others entrusted their assistants with the job. She was the star of the class and her classmates elected her class president. Throughout the course, her fellow students encouraged Whitney to get out of business and into politics. But she held fast to the vow she'd made years before in Shandong.

Chen was committed to turning Tsinghua back into a complete university with humanities departments to complement its specialization in physics, engineering, and math. During Mao's time, when China copied the Soviet model, it had become a technical school, churning out engineers and physicists. In the late 2000s, Chen got word of the discovery of a collection of ancient Chinese texts written in ink on strips of bamboo. Leveraging the Tsinghua alumni network, Chen convinced a wealthy entrepreneur to buy the strips at auction and donate them to Tsinghua. The strips constituted one of the most important discoveries of ancient Chinese and included essays that had been referenced by ancient writers but long considered lost.

Chen took Whitney and me to view the texts, located in a quarantined laboratory on campus. He assured us that we were only the third group of outsiders to have seen them, after then Party chief Hu Jintao and his predecessor Jiang Zemin.

Chen recruited us in his mission to bring the humanities back to Tsinghua. Our donations allowed him to lure professors from across China and the West. We funded the Chinese literature department and in 2007, the year we sold our Ping An stock, we donated $10 million to build a 180,000-square-foot library, complete with a rooftop garden and barbecue to encourage free-flowing academic debate. We completed that project in 2011 in time for Tsinghua's centenary celebrations. We had great faith in Tsinghua and were proud of our charity initiatives there.

China seemed to believe in us, too. In 2007, Sun Zhengcai, while serving as minister of agriculture, arranged for me to join the Beijing municipal branch of the Chinese People's Political Consultative Conference. The CPPCC, as it is known, was part of a bureaucratic architecture called the United Front Work Department that has been used by the Chinese Communist Party to control non-Party elements both inside and outside China—from minorities, like Tibetans, to the religious faithful, entrepreneurs, and overseas Chinese. I was listed as a representative from Hong Kong and Macao, one of about fifty from those two territories who'd been invited to join the Beijing municipal chapter.

The Beijing chapter was only one rung below the national level. The conference was basically a networking platform, like the Rotary Club in the United States, and membership was a sign that the Party saw you as a potentially useful agent of the Party's influence. We met several times a year and were taken on field trips to different provinces where the locals would push us to invest. During an annual week-long meeting in Beijing, the authorities would shut down roads for our buses and house us in five-star hotels. Authorities would dole out cash to us for plane tickets, which seemed silly to me considering that the net worth of most of us Hong Kong entrepreneurial types averaged north of $10 million. Anyway, few took the conference seriously. Members from Hong Kong often failed to show up.

I was amazed by certain things during my time at the conference. One was the brownnosing way in which people from Hong Kong addressed Chinese officials. Living in Beijing and working with mainland Chinese daily, I knew this was unnecessary. But it was the way rich people from Hong Kong believed they needed to act. It showed their superficial understanding of China, even though they were next-door neighbors. From a different perspective, it was yet another sign of how Party officials had taught the rest of the world to afford them and their country special treatment.

Other developments were more encouraging. Some of the issues being aired in our smaller meetings and even in public fora at the CPPCC were intriguing. A few bolder, mainland Chinese members of the conference advocated experimenting with democracy inside the Party by letting Party members choose between multiple candidates for top Party posts. Complaints were aired about pollution—a product of China's headlong rush to modernize. The conference began to bring in more businessmen and -women like me who were interested in these kinds of issues and not simply in using the CPPCC as a way to make connections or cut deals. We began to get a sense that perhaps the CPPCC was becoming relevant and one day could begin to operate like a second chamber of the legislature alongside the National People's Congress, which was technically in charge of promulgating China's laws.

This push from inside the CPPCC was reflected in society at large. From the early 2000s on, hundreds of other entrepreneurs also began to back NGOs and educational institutions, like we had. Private money went into muckraking media such as *Caijing* magazine. People began organizing civic associations. To call it an explosion of civic-mindedness wouldn't be an exaggeration. Entrepreneurs waded into areas that had traditionally been taboo. At our Kaifeng think tank, we hired as our director the political philosopher Yu Keping, who was well known for his 2006 book, *Democracy Is a Good Thing.* We saw Yu as a trustworthy academic pushing reasonable political reforms from inside the system.

We worked with think tanks overseas to help educate Chinese scholars about how democracies functioned and how they set foreign policy. When Premier Wen Jiabao visited Britain in 2004, we organized a trip for scholars from the Chinese Academy of Social Sciences at the same time. I went along and attended meetings at 10 Downing Street, the Bank of England, and the Upper House of Parliament. In 2006, we funded a delegation led by Romano Prodi, former president of the European Commission, to come to China for an off-the-record dialogue on foreign policy with Chinese counterparts. Foreign relations had always been a third rail in China, but we relied on Wen's assistant Song Zhe for guidance. We tried not to cross any redlines. We truly believed in the promise of China. We were all in.

CHAPTER THIRTEEN

IN RETROSPECT, THE DISAPPEARANCE OF AIRPORT manager Li Peiying in 2006 and his subsequent arrest on corruption charges should have raised alarm bells that broader changes were afoot. I ignored them, partially because I was so busy dealing with the fallout of his arrest and trying to keep the airport project afloat.

But with the benefit of hindsight, it's clear that Li's downfall came about not simply because he was addicted to gambling and lost millions at the baccarat table. Startled at the liberal tendencies of my fellow capitalists, the Chinese Communist Party, starting in the mid 2000s, moved to weaken the moneyed class, uproot the sprouts of civil society that we'd planted, and reassert the Party's ideological and economic control of Chinese society. As part of this effort, the Party sought to bolster state-owned enterprises to the detriment of private firms.

After Li disappeared into the custody of the Party, the authorities appointed a new general manager. When Peiying was the boss, he'd made all the decisions. Once he said yes, his department chiefs would fall in line. For sure, he had to yell, threaten, and cajole, but he got the job done. Li's replacement was a creature of a new system. Things became bureaucratized. One-man rule was over, replaced by "collective decision-making." We started having to deal not simply with the GM but with his underlings. We were told that we needed to go through committees. So while my work was eased in Shunyi thanks to the man I saved, it grew more challenging at the airport, our other partner.

The new GM sent senior members of his staff to our company to exert more control over the joint venture. Five people used to participate in our joint-venture board meetings. Now two dozen officials from the airport alone showed up. And they all had differing opinions. It complicated the management structure. Before, I'd made most of the decisions. Now, I had all these people coming in and their loyalty wasn't to the joint venture—it was to the airport.

People began to question why we, as private entrepreneurs, had won the right to develop the logistics hub. No matter that no one but us would have been able to arrange the shotgun marriage between Shunyi and the airport. All that history was forgotten. Now it was: Who are these capitalists trying to privatize part of what should have been a state-owned facility? This type of attitude wasn't confined to our project; it infected the entire economy. "State-owned enterprises march forward, private firms retreat" became the new buzzwords, signaling a shift at the top of the Party. State-owned firms began to carry out forced mergers with successful private companies. Entrepreneurs had been the engines of China's growth, but we were never trusted. Ever since it had seized power in 1949, the Chinese Communist Party had used elements of society when it needed them and discarded them when it was done.

China's bureaucracy was changing. In the past, local leaders would rise through the ranks. Li Peiying had worked his way up in the airport. Li Ping came from Shunyi. But it was hard for the central government to control these officials because of their roots in the community. As part of a campaign to centralize power, the Party began to parachute officials in from other regions. China's state-run press agitated against what it called "dirt emperors," local bigwigs who disregarded directives from Beijing. But the new brand of official created new problems because these characters arrived with the intention of staying for only a few years before moving out and up. They searched for quick wins to justify a promotion. For sure, the old system had its drawbacks. There was corruption, and dirt emperors often would run a locality like their private fiefdom. But the local officials also understood their communities and knew what was needed and what wasn't. Many had feelings for the place because they didn't want to be cursed when they left power and retired nearby. They worked for the benefit of family and lifelong friends in the locality. They were willing to focus on long-term, legacy projects. And because of their ties to the community, they could get things done.

Whitney and I had also viewed the airport project as a long-term investment. After we completed the first phase of the project, we didn't want to build and sell. We wanted to build and grow. And we wanted to take our model to other airports. I was thinking we'd develop airport cities across China and then in other parts of the world. I'd attended the Airport Cities World Conference in Hong Kong in 2004 and in 2010 we'd hosted the conference in

Beijing. We'd traveled to Chengdu, Guangzhou, Shenzhen, and throughout China to pitch our vision of a mixture of logistics, manufacturing, commercial, and residential development near their airports. We'd generated significant interest.

But the changes, subtle at first but then unrelenting, prompted me to reconsider. As the going got tougher in Beijing, as opposition to our ideas grew within the airport bureaucracy, my views shifted. I came to believe that in China a long-term business model wouldn't work. I began to understand what some of my entrepreneur friends had been telling me all along: the smart way to do business in China was to build something, sell it, take money off the table, and go back in. If you invest $1 and you make $10, you take $7 out and reinvest $3. But if you keep $10 in, chances are you'll lose it all.

The Communist Party seemed increasingly threatened by entrepreneurs. A segment of society with means was getting more independent. Entrepreneurs like us were pushing for more freedom, more free speech, and in a direction that was less under the Party's control. The Party was very uncomfortable with us wading into waters that it controlled.

Take foreign policy. In 2006, we'd brought the delegation from the European Union to China to discuss EU–China relations. During the meetings, Wen Jiabao's assistant Song Zhe received a call on the premier's hotline. A voice on the other end asked, "Do you know Desmond Shum?" "Yes," Song replied. "Do you know he's a Hong Kong resident, not a mainland Chinese?" the voice asked. "Yes," Song Zhe said. The phone went dead. Song concluded that the security services were paying close attention to our activities. He advised us to limit the scope of our charity work to less controversial topics; we dropped foreign policy initiatives as an area for our endeavors.

The Party had other ways to push people like us back into line. Whereas we'd once dared to think that we could constitute an independent force, the Party made it clear that we were still just cogs in its machine, little screws in a big system designed to perpetuate the Party's rule. Men like Jack Ma, the founder of Alibaba, or Pony Ma, the CEO of the other Internet giant, Tencent, might have untold wealth on paper, but they were compelled to serve the Party. Soon the Party would be passing laws such as national security legislation that obligated all companies in China, if directed, to spy for the state.

The negative changes began to accelerate in 2008 during the second administration of Party chief Hu Jintao and Premier Wen Jiabao. A main catalyst was the global financial crisis. The crisis validated a belief inside the Party about the superiority of China's political and economic system to that of the West.

The Chinese government responded to the crisis with a massive stimulus that was far more effective than anything tried in the West. The Chinese government distributed this stimulus via the state-owned sector, which was ordered to put the money to use. Instead of trying to convince entrepreneurs to invest, the Party directed state-owned firms to pour money into infrastructure. The Party's control over the state-owned enterprises enabled it to combat the global recession. The difficulties faced by capitalist countries, especially the United States, strengthened the hard-line argument that peaceful evolution into a more open society and economy would be a recipe for disaster for the Party and for China. China, they contended, needed to redouble its efforts to battle Western ideas because those ideas would only weaken China. Private entrepreneurs, who had saved China's economy just a few years before, were now painted as a fifth column of Western influence. Control needed to be reasserted over us and over our capital.

At the airport, our joint venture had never had a Party committee. We'd had a few Party members, of course, but we didn't grant the Party a say in what we did. But starting in 2008, we were required to establish a Party committee. Once we had a Party committee, we had to give weight to its opinions. Its presence muddled management decisions.

The Party forced these changes on joint ventures and private firms all over China. It dismayed me. We'd believed that China was moving in a good direction. We saw that China's government had been strengthening and there was a growing push to separate the Party from the state. People were advocating reforms and a slightly freer press. No one wanted to overthrow the Party. We just wanted a more open system. We were giving the Party a gentle nudge. But after 2008, it was clear that the Party's leaders viewed even a gentle nudge with alarm. We'd thought our wealth could foster social change. We were wrong. It was one of the saddest things I'd ever experienced.

Thinking back on it, I've concluded that the retrenchment was inevitable. Sure, analysts can come up with all sorts of reasons why the Party regressed. The Arab Spring and the Color Revolutions sweeping across the Middle East in the 2010s scared China's leaders. The Great Recession that rocked the US economy in 2008 helped convince Communist officials that China's system was superior and gave them the self-confidence to become more assertive on the global stage. The US Navy had suddenly woken up to the fact that China was building islands out of nothing in the South China Sea and began to push back, further galvanizing an already strong anti-American sentiment within the Party.

But to me the most convincing argument for the Party's dictatorial lurch remains the nature of the Chinese Communist Party. The Party has an almost animal instinct toward repression and control. It's one of the foundational tenets of a Leninist system. Anytime the Party can afford to swing toward repression, it will.

When Deng Xiaoping took over the mantle of leadership in China in the late 1970s, the state was effectively bankrupt. The economic changes Deng ushered in were driven not by any belief in the tenets of free-market capitalism but by necessity. To survive, the Party needed to loosen its grip on the economy. Even under Jiang Zemin in the 1990s, China's state-owned firms were losing buckets of money, so private entrepreneurs like Whitney and me were still crucial to keep the economy afloat and unemployment down. But after the first term of Hu Jintao and Wen Jiabao ended in 2008–2009, and decades of double-digit growth, state-run firms stabilized and the Party no longer needed the private sector like it had in the past. Beijing also reformed its tax system so the central government took a bigger piece of the pie. With these developments, it was no longer essential for the Party to relax control over the economy and thus over society. Capitalists became more of a political threat because we were no longer required as an economic savior. The Party could again tighten its grip.

The Li Peiying case started me thinking that perhaps it'd be a good idea to unload the airport project. After vanishing for almost two years, Li Peiying surfaced in the custody of the state. He was charged with bribery and embezzlement of as much as $15 million, and in February 2009 he was found guilty and sentenced to death. After losing an appeal and despite returning most of the money, Li was executed on August 7, 2009.

Li Peiying's fatal mistake was speaking too much. Generally, if you're arrested for corruption in China, you're supposed to shut up. The Chinese Communist Party functions like the Mafia; it has its own code of *omertà*. But, I was told, Li Peiying revealed all his dealings with senior Chinese officials. The people handling the investigation didn't know what to do with his testimony since it touched the Party's highest levels, including the family of China's former Party chief and president Jiang Zemin. Li also lacked the blood connections into the system that could have spared his life. Just a month before Li took a bullet to the back of the head in August 2009, another official, Chen Tonghai, the former chairman of the China Petroleum and Chemical Corporation, was convicted of corruption involving $28 million—almost twice Li's alleged haul. Except Chen wasn't executed. His father, Chen Weida, had been a major underground Communist leader in prerevolutionary Shanghai and had held leadership positions after 1949. We were told that Chen's mother appealed directly to Jiang Zemin, who was also active in the underground Party before the war, for leniency. This vastly different treatment of two corrupt officials was a telltale sign of how things were being run. Red aristocrats got a prison sentence; commoners got a bullet in the head.

In 2010, Whitney and I finished the first phase of the airport project, redeveloping 5 million square feet. We had originally planned to spend years completing the project, ultimately tripling its size. We were in an enviable position. We still held a lot of land for new warehouses. Those warehouses had unfettered access to the runway. We thought we could build out the rest of the project as the volume of cargo at the airport increased.

But as part of the fallout of Peiying's execution, not only did we have to deal with a new GM, but Customs swapped its top guy at the airport three times and some of our allies in Shunyi retired as well. As the bureaucracy turned hostile to private business, and as I saw how I'd need to do even more drinking and schmoozing to build ever more relationships just to remake the wheel, I decided to get out.

In 2010, we opened negotiations with several companies to sell our stake. Two of the firms were Chinese state-owned enterprises. The third was Prologis, an international real estate investment trust that was one of the firms that had presented me with a lowball offer at the start of the airport odyssey. Whitney and I argued over the deal because I had no intention of selling to the state-owned enterprises while Whitney, by contrast, thought she'd have more influence over the negotiation process with the state-run firms. I yearned for the transparency of a commercial transaction because if you did a deal with a state-owned enterprise, the Chinese government could always come after you in a few years, make a spurious allegation that you'd received an inflated price (and therefore stolen national assets), and have you tossed in jail. Ultimately, the deal Whitney sought didn't go through, although the presence of two Chinese suitors did assist in moving the Prologis deal forward. In January 2011, Prologis bought out our share of the joint venture, giving us a profit of close to $200 million.

For me, the airport was a priceless education in how the

Chinese system operated. One of my friends joked that just finishing the first phase, I'd already attained Buddhahood.

After Whitney and I sold our stake, I began to lobby her to do two things. First, we needed to diversify our risk by investing overseas. I knew the history of the Chinese Communist Party and how, after the 1949 Communist revolution, the Party had thought nothing of confiscating property, including my grandfather's house, his law firm, and the land that had belonged to my family. The Party only began to tolerate private property in 1979, but what the Party gives it can take away.

Thousands of rich Chinese were putting money abroad. I argued that we should follow them. Whitney reluctantly agreed to throw me a bone by letting me open an office in London to explore investments in luxury brands, Belgian chocolates, French crystal, and Italian cashmere. But she wasn't serious. The lion's share of our money stayed in China.

Second, I argued that we should start competing for projects in China on the open market and end our reliance on connections and backdoor *guanxi* deals. China was instituting public auctions of land; the process was becoming more transparent. Successful firms, like SOHO China, were operating and prospering in this space, winning contracts on the basis of their bids, not on their connections. Let's go compete against those firms, I suggested. At Great Ocean, we'd put together a great team. I believed we could win.

Whitney didn't agree. The open market scared her. She'd never done it before. She had enormous faith in her *guanxi* network to boost our business. She wanted to continue to play chess on the Chinese chessboard according to the old rules. If our firm succeeded on a level playing field against other businesses, what would that mean for her? She saw her role as always giving Great Ocean the inside track. But what if Great Ocean didn't need the inside track and could win the race without her?

With Wang Qishan, Sun Zhengcai, and other ministers, vice-ministers, and assistants in her Rolodex, Whitney had faith that we'd be able to find a new guardian inside the Party whom we could serve. And she was always looking for someone new. In 2008, Auntie Zhang arranged a meal with an up-and-coming Chinese official named Xi Jinping. He'd just been appointed China's vice-president. Auntie Zhang brought Whitney along as a second pair of eyes and ears to take the measure of this rising star. I stayed at home. At a dinner such as this, everyone needed to have a purpose. I was not a necessary participant in this exercise to build another relationship.

Xi brought his second wife, Peng Liyuan, a glamorous singer from the People's Liberation Army who specialized in syrupy patriotic ballads, somewhat akin in star power wattage to American country music phenom Dolly Parton. Xi was the son of the Communist revolutionary Xi Zhongxun, a member of China's red aristocracy. Xi's father had been a prominent ally of Deng Xiaoping and was one of the key figures in masterminding the Special Economic Zones in the 1980s that lay the foundation for China's export boom.

Xi Jinping had spent seventeen years working at various government and Party posts in Fujian Province. Although he'd been there when a massive smuggling scandal had unfolded, he hadn't been implicated. Xi had also held top Party posts in Zhejiang Province, one of the engines of China's private economy.

In 2007, Xi Jinping got his big break in an affair that revealed much about China's political system. A year earlier the Party secretary of Shanghai, Chen Liangyu, had been removed from his post as part of a corruption investigation involving the misuse of hundreds of millions of dollars from the city's public pension fund. Chen's downfall really wasn't about corruption, however. It was a political hit job masquerading as a criminal case. It came because Chen refused to swear allegiance to China's then Party chief, Hu Jintao. Chen had been a major player in what was known as the Shanghai Gang, led by Hu's predecessor Jiang Zemin. When Hu had taken over from Jiang in 2002 as Party chief, Jiang had declined to relinquish all of his Party posts, staying on as the chairman of the Central Military Commission for an additional two years. Jiang had also packed the Standing Committee of the Politburo with his cronies; for several years, Jiang's men held five of its nine seats, preventing Hu from doing anything without Jiang's approval. So, in 2006, when Hu's loyalists saw an opportunity to take down Chen Liangyu, a prominent Jiang loyalist, they struck.

When Chen was forced from office in September 2006, he was replaced by Shanghai's mayor, Han Zheng. Han had only been in office for several months, Auntie Zhang told us, before it was discovered that one of his family members had stashed more than $20 million in a bank account in Australia. The Party couldn't purge Han, too, because it would've been bad for the stability of the leading financial center of China to have both its Party secretary *and* its mayor ousted in swift succession. Auntie Zhang told us that Han Zheng was allowed to return to his old post as mayor while Xi Jinping was appointed Shanghai's Party chief. Han Zheng, too, would be forgiven his sins; he joined the Politburo's Standing Committee in 2017 and was appointed a vice-premier, showing that in China political alignment and loyalty trump everything else.

Xi's move to Shanghai proved fortuitous, if not decisive, in his rise to the top. It allowed him time to get close to Jiang Zemin and by the end of 2007, with Jiang's backing and Hu Jintao's consent, Xi had joined the Politburo and moved to Beijing. By then it was clear that he was one of two officials, the other being a Peking University graduate named Li Keqiang, who were vying to replace Hu Jintao as the next general secretary of the Chinese Communist Party when Hu was scheduled to be termed out in 2012.

What amazed Whitney is that throughout the meal with Xi he let his wife do the talking. He sat looking a bit uncomfortable, occasionally cracking an awkward smile. Whitney said she didn't click with either Xi or Peng. There were no ripples across the table. Whitney had always been good at finding a landing spot, especially with the wives of senior officials. But Peng didn't provide one. Xi was already slotted for greatness and he and his wife were guarded.

Whitney and I had used our contacts in Zhejiang and Fujian provinces to try to determine why the Party had picked Xi to run China. The consensus among many of our friends and contacts was that he wasn't even borderline talented. Mao Zedong's former assistant Li Rui, who was close to Xi's father, recalled meeting Xi a few years earlier and complained that he wasn't educated. Regardless, Xi Jinping would prove to be a savvy and cold-blooded political infighter and become China's most powerful Party boss in a generation.

The general consensus in our social circle was that Xi would follow the established rules in China. Whitney was confident that we'd be able to keep playing the *guanxi* game under the leadership of Xi Jinping just as we had when the Party was run by Hu Jintao.

This disagreement between Whitney and me over diversifying our risk and competing in the open market grew with time. I concluded that Whitney had a deep sense of insecurity about branching out. She feared that if we stopped relying on her connections to win contracts in China, she'd become irrelevant and that I might become too independent.

Because of these concerns, she sought more control over what I said and did at the exact moment when I believed she should be loosening her grip. At the beginning of our relationship, I'd suppressed my desire to break free and tried to learn at Whitney's feet. But the more I succeeded in life, the more I wanted to make my own rules. Once we'd made it in Beijing, I naturally thought we could take on the rest of China and the world. Whitney resisted, and because the money was in her name I had to go along. I did so unwillingly.

CHAPTER FOURTEEN

WITH SO MANY OPPORTUNITIES TO DO EXTRAORDINARY things in China, Whitney wanted us to double down on *her* way by continuing to insinuate ourselves into the upper echelons of the Party and cultivate even more members of the red aristocracy. One such member was Li Botan, who went by the English name David. He was the son-in-law of Jia Qinglin, a member of the Politburo's Standing Committee.

From 2003 to 2013, Old Man Jia chaired the Chinese People's Consultative Conference and, by extension, the Party's United Front Work Department, which led the Party's efforts to control all non-Communist elements of society, such as minorities, religious groups, and entrepreneurs. As I've noted earlier, I'd been given a seat on the CPPCC's municipal branch in Beijing, thanks to Sun Zhengcai.

With his slicked-back hair, pudgy cheeks, and expansive belly, David's father-in-law was a jolly, sociable character with an easy smile. His purported corruption was also the stuff of legend. While serving in the early 1990s as the vice-governor, governor, and then Party secretary of Fujian Province, located north of Hong Kong and opposite Taiwan, Old Man Jia was rumored to have abetted a massive smuggling enterprise. This was smuggling on an epic scale, involving thousands of foreign cars, billions of foreign cigarettes, tons of foreign beer, and more than one-sixth of China's oil imports, all flowing into China through naval ports on Fujian's coast.

Old Man Jia's wife (and David's mother-in-law), Lin Youfang, served as the president of Fujian Province's largest state-owned import-export firm throughout the smuggling escapade. I was told that after the scandal broke in 1999, Lin Youfang, once a leading light on the Party's social circuit, was so afraid that she and her husband would get caught up in the investigation that she had a breakdown, lost the ability to speak, and spent years hospitalized in Beijing. Still, neither Lin nor Jia was ever prosecuted, evidence that in China it wasn't what you might have done, but who you knew.

Party General Secretary Jiang Zemin had known Old Man Jia ever since the pair had worked together at the Ministry of Machine-Building Industry in the 1960s. Jiang not only ensured that the family was protected, he even promoted Old Man Jia.

Jiang brought Old Man Jia to Beijing in 1996 as vice-mayor of the city. Next year, Jia became mayor. In 2002, Jia was elevated to his position as one of nine members of the Politburo's Standing Committee. After Jiang retired from the Standing Committee in 2007, Old Man Jia stayed on for another term as a representative of Jiang's political faction. Jia would serve until 2012. So clearly it was still worth it to Whitney to cultivate his son-in-law, David Li.

David was six feet tall, with the patented paunch of a successful Chinese businessman. He dressed smartly but casually. He liked to hang out with Beijing's in crowd, fraternizing with artists, singers, directors, and the sons and daughters of China's red aristocracy.

David had made a fortune apparently by leveraging his father-in-law's connections. He owned large stakes in numerous firms, mostly via his holding company, Zhaode Investment Company, based in Beijing. In December 2009, David opened "The Moutai Club." At the time it seemed like everyone with money wanted to own a private club and they sprouted like weeds across Beijing, Shanghai, and Guangzhou. Discretion was one goal; in a private establishment, you could cut political and business deals and nobody would know whom you were meeting and they wouldn't be able to listen in. Also, Communist Party royalty were shy about flaunting their riches in public but enjoyed doing so among trusted friends. A private club allowed them to be ostentatious behind closed doors. And finally, in many cases, the best thing about a private club was that you could open the club on state-owned property, harnessing a government-owned asset for personal gain. Talk about low overhead.

David situated his club on a tree-lined street in downtown Beijing near the Forbidden City in a traditional courtyard house that apparently belonged to the Beijing city government, an arrangement seemingly eased by the fact that Old Man Jia had once served as mayor and Party secretary of Beijing.

Walking into The Moutai Club, you encountered an exquisite table—over twenty feet in diameter—made from the trunk of a yellow flowering pear tree, one of the most valuable woods in China and practically extinct. On the table's surface, patterns in the wood's rippled grain resembled ghosts dancing in a golden tableau. Behind the table, a spacious entryway led to a courtyard and private dining rooms. Decorated with priceless antiques, or at least good fakes, the club was redolent of the type of Oriental sophistication that David and those around him cultivated.

David's big selling point was his back channel to the Kweichou Moutai Company, the distiller of Moutai, the drink of choice among China's business elite. David even had a seat on the company board. This connection was forged with the apparent assistance of Old Man Jia, who, as head of the Party's United Front Work Department, had tentacles deep into all of the areas in China where minorities, like Tibetans and Uighurs, predominated. Moutai was distilled in Guizhou Province, the home of the Miao ethnic minority, a hill tribe that inhabits the mountains of southwestern China and has offshoots in Vietnam, Laos, and Cambodia.*

David told me that he had a lock on one-third of the ten-year-old Moutai that the firm released each year. Most aged Moutai sold in China barely contained a drop of genuinely old liquor. David had access to the real stuff.

Moutai was China's national drink. Everybody who was anybody bought special vintages to show off. There was a vintage for the People's Liberation Army, for the State Council, and for the police. Some bottles went for $125,000 or more. The posturing by Moutai connoisseurs recalled the same snobbery and one-upmanship exhibited by aficionados of fine wine. "You bring a '82 Lafite and I'll counter with a '69." It was no different with Moutai.

David sold his ten-year-old Moutai in red bottles. We called them "red hair," or *hong mao*, a play on the word "Moutai." Those

* In the West, the Miao are known as the Hmong.

in our circle never touched Moutai from regular stores. The counterfeiting industry in China faked everything: Moutai in particular. Chinese moonshiners got so good at bottling imitation Moutai that normal Chinese would travel overseas to buy their Moutai believing that foreign stores could be relied on to stock the genuine hooch.

Those who wanted access to David's precious crop of "red hair" had to join The Moutai Club. Membership cost tens of thousands of dollars. But in the same way that obtaining a Beijing vanity plate required adroit use of connections, money alone wouldn't guarantee a spot in The Moutai Club. David had to vet you and, given the necessity that the applicant be someone of importance, membership soon became one of the most sought after in Beijing. Some of the top tycoons in China were on the board. There was Liu Changle, the chairman of Phoenix Satellite Television, a technically private media empire based in Hong Kong that churned out pro-Beijing propaganda. Also, Kong Dan, the chairman of the CITIC Group, China's biggest state-owned conglomerate, and Jack Ma, the founder of tech giant Alibaba. I walked into the club once and met a fresh-faced boy who introduced himself as Alvin. Only later would I learn that he was Alvin Jiang, the grandson of Party boss Jiang Zemin. Alvin would go on to found a billion-dollar private equity business in his twenties.

After running the club for eighteen months, David broached with me the idea of creating a wine club spin-off. Always interested in cozying up to power, Whitney encouraged me to cultivate David. Whitney and I agreed to be angel investors in the wine club scheme. I shared my knowledge with David about wines. Most of the time I just buttered him up. David would rave about a particular vintage. Regardless of its quality, I nodded like a bobblehead as David praised its body, tannins, and terroir.

David and I started looking for a location for the wine club. One day we took a stroll in Beijing's Beihai Park across the street from the north gate of Zhongnanhai, the headquarters of the Chinese Communist Party. We were mulling the idea of "borrowing" a building in the park and were poking around to see if it was suitable for renovation. Yet another example of repurposing state assets for private use.

As we circled the facility, David noticed someone striding toward us. Sporting wire-rimmed glasses and a dark blue suit with no tie, he had the air of a Chinese official. "My God," David said as the man approached. "It's Minister Meng." Meng Jianzhu was the minister of public security, China's top cop, and he was out for a postprandial stroll. We fled the scene like two school kids. "No wine club here," David muttered as we scurried away. No one wanted to cross paths with Minister Meng.

I loaned my management team to David so he could draw up a business plan. Like many of the red aristocrats, he didn't have a good staff. He didn't really need one. He made his money wielding connections to get access to inside deals or hawking stuff he obtained because of who he was. He used Old Man Jia to obtain Moutai and he had a guaranteed market for it. For a time, David's investment company's biggest asset was the Friendship Store building, a landmark on Jianguomenwai Street on Beijing's east side. It was rumored that David had obtained that building when, thanks to his father-in-law, he arranged for its original owner to be released from prison. Once out of jail, the businessman transferred the building to David Li. David's firm also won the exclusive contract to sell ads on the ubiquitous bus stops around Beijing. That was a license to print money. Later on, David would invest in electric car technology, taking a piece of a US firm called Canoo.

While David wasn't a red aristocrat by birth, he'd married into the aristocracy and adopted some of its quirks. He kept his thick salt-and-pepper hair cropped close in a crew cut, a throwback to the Party's military roots. When you entered his office, he'd offer you tea and a cigar. The cigar had to be Cuban in a cynical nod toward world revolution. The tea was invariably aged *pu'er* from Yunnan Province to reflect the cultural authenticity he craved. Indoors, David wore black cotton slippers with white soles and white socks, mirroring the tradition of the men in the *hutong* alleys of Old Beijing. The faddish footwear contained a question. Decoded, it said: "Our ancestors wore these shoes in Ancient China. Did yours?"

In the spring of 2011, Whitney suggested that we take David Li and his wife, Jia Qiang, to Europe to give them a crash course in wine. He liked the idea and invited two other prospective wine club investors and their wives along for the ride. The first was Xu Jiayin, the CEO of the Evergrande Group, China's biggest property developer, whose son had snoozed through the seminars that I'd arranged on family wealth. The second was Yu Guoxiang, a foul-mouthed construction company mogul nicknamed Little Ningbo because he was both short and from Ningbo, a port city south of Shanghai. We were all considering investing $5 million each to build the club's wine collection and get the club going.

I didn't know whether David and his wife, Jia Qiang, had been to Europe before but his daughter, Jasmine, certainly had. In November 2009, Jasmine, decked out in a floor-length Carolina

Herrera gown, made the scene at the Hôtel de Crillon's annual debutante ball in Paris. A photograph of the fresh-faced debutante landed in *Paris Vogue*. Jasmine would later attend Stanford University and then be identified in the Panama Papers as the sole shareholder of two offshore investment entities that were registered in the British Virgin Islands and specialized in investments and consulting. Seems like the apple hadn't fallen far from Old Man Jia's tree.

The first order of business on our European junket was transportation. By this time, Whitney had grown accustomed to flying in private jets and she and I had already joined a waiting list to buy a $43 million Gulfstream G500. We suggested a jet. David agreed but added that for convenience's sake, maybe we should take three. In June of 2011, we—four couples—departed for Paris.

We'd planned to travel in the three jets, but at the last minute the other men decided they wanted to play cards. We still took the other two jets; they just followed empty. Face played a role here. "If you have a private jet, well, I've got to have one, too." Also, being Chinese, you never knew, maybe a business opportunity would arise and one of us would have to rush back early to cut a deal.

On board, as our wives chatted and sampled sushi, we played *doudizhu*, or Fight the Landlord, a popular Chinese card game with its roots in Communist China's brutal land reform campaign of the early 1950s. Through multiple rounds of bidding, the first person to shed all his cards—and "kill the landlord"—wins. I was amazed at the stakes. I'm not an accomplished gambler and I was a reluctant participant. I dropped $100,000 on that leg. I was more embarrassed than concerned. Losing money to men like these could actually turn out to be good for business. Who doesn't welcome a willing sucker? I knew they'd always invite me back, providing me with an opening to deepen a personal connection.

At the card table, the conversation turned toward business. Yu Guoxiang had apparently tangled with the law several times before. He'd reportedly "lent" a Zhejiang Province official $500,000 to win a $1.2 billion contract to build an expressway around the city of Hangzhou. That official was ultimately sentenced to life in prison for corruption. Published reports and US diplomatic cables also linked Yu to a questionable loan from Shanghai's state-managed pension fund in 2003 that enabled him to buy Shanghai's Jing'an Hilton hotel for $150 million.

Toasting Yu and his run-ins with the law, David declared that "in today's China jail is the modern version of the Whampoa Military Academy. A Chinese businessman who hasn't been to jail hasn't accomplished anything." To me, that was a pretty stunning claim. The Whampoa Military Academy had been China's version of West Point, a hallowed institution where China's first generation of modern officers received training in the 1920s and 1930s. Equating a prison term served by a businessman with a military education completed by a patriotic Chinese cadet was blasphemous. You'd think that in these circles doing time was a black mark and that Whampoa would be revered. But here was the son-in-law of the fourth most powerful politician in China venerating penal incarceration. Everybody else nodded in solemn agreement, clinked glasses, and downed a flute of Krug Champagne. While I was pretty amazed at David's chutzpah, I wasn't particularly worried. Whitney and I had always been careful in our dealings to stay within the boundaries of the law.

Whitney had directed me to put on a show for the group and once we landed at our first stop, France, it began. On the evening of June 10, 2011, I organized a dinner at Pavillon Ledoyen, one of the oldest restaurants in Paris, situated in gardens east of the Champs-Élysées. Here, in the city's tony 8th arrondissement, was where Napoleon first met Josephine, I told my guests, and where duelists came to bury the hatchet with a feast after shooting at each other in the nearby Bois de Boulogne.

On three sides, the dining room looked out on well-manicured grounds through generous windows festooned with white curtains. The tables shimmered with white tablecloths and silver cutlery. The clientele that night included a smattering of French couples, Saudi princes, German industrialists, a table of Japanese businessmen, and some underdressed Americans. We were ushered into a private room. Chef Christian Le Squer was renowned in culinary circles as having worked his way up from serving fast food to deckhands on a trawler to being a Michelin-starred chef.

I'd invited a French friend, François, who has one of the biggest private collections of pre-1960 wine in France, no mean feat in a nation of oenophiles. I'd asked François to curate the meal in tandem with Chef Le Squer because I wanted to show my friends how delicately the French treat their wines and the care they put into the gastronomic experience. China's Communist revolution had shattered our ties to the famed craftsmanship and connoisseurship of Imperial China. This was my way of exposing my traveling companions to the beauty of tradition and to some really fine wine.

In addition to three champagnes and a bottle from the private collection of the Rothschild family, François engineered a vertical tasting of six vintages of Château Lafite, all magnums, starting with a 1900, then a '22, a '48, a '61, a '71, and a 1990. Chef Le Squer paired these with grilled mullet, braised turbot, spring lamb, and smoked eel toast, finishing with a citrus sorbet. The wines alone ran more than $100,000 and we ate and drank for hours. Yes, this was conspicuous consumption, but for Whitney and me it was conspicuous with a purpose.

In China, politics is the key to riches, not the other way around, and David Li was wired into the system politically. Whitney and I were there to make a connection. Whitney could always use another piece on her chessboard. Both Whitney and I were pleasantly surprised by David's wife, Jia Qiang. Despite her Party pedigree, she was easygoing and approachable.

Whitney was singularly focused on burnishing our personal brand and in perfecting how we as a couple could distinguish ourselves from the crowd. She played the role of a woman with access to the East, epitomizing Chinese learning. I played the role of a man with an entrée to the West and its way of life. In Europe, I opened doors for our group that normally would have been locked. To highlight my knowledge of the world outside China, I curated every step of the trip. Why stay here versus there? Why eat here and shop there? Why drink this but not that? I had the answers. From that perspective, the price of the evening was part of the show.

After Paris, we traveled to Bordeaux to visit an estate that belonged to the Rothschild family. I'd gotten to know this branch of the Rothschilds during earlier travels to Europe while engaged in my family legacy project. At the property, seventy-year-old Eric de Rothschild, the New York–born scion of the clan, and his wife,

Maria-Béatrice, hosted us for a meal. Banker, vintner, philanthropist, Eric was a man of many talents. That day, Eric wore a well-tailored and clearly well-loved suit that was dotted with patches, not just at the elbows. My companions were astonished. Another teaching moment. This, I observed to my fellow travelers, is old-money style. Back in the day, it'd been a bespoke tailored suit. It was getting on in years, but Eric, reluctant to part with it, had treated it with care. To a group of slightly vulgar nouveau riche Chinese, the story of that suit was an opportunity to learn how to cherish the things we owned.

After Bordeaux, we flew to the Côte d'Azur along the Mediterranean Sea. Property developer Xu Jiayin wanted to look at a boat. Xu was a self-made man, born in a village in rural Henan Province in 1958. Xu's father had been a warehouse worker, like my dad. His peasant mother died when he was eight months old and he was raised by his grandparents. By the time he was twenty, Xu was working in a steel mill in southern China.

Xu rose to become the plant's general manager. In the late 1980s, when the factory was privatized, Xu quit. Work at a foundry is dangerous and Xu had put together a strong team. He convinced the team to leave with him and go into property development.

That was in 1992, the year that Deng Xiaoping, China's paramount leader, went to the southern Chinese city of Shenzhen to revive economic reforms and ease out hard-liners who'd led the crackdown on pro-democracy protests around Tiananmen Square in June 1989. Xu and his team caught the real estate development wave just as it was cresting. By the time we were in Europe, he'd made billions, selling apartments to China's burgeoning middle class.

Xu's technique for winning over connections was, I thought, more bald-faced than ours. One day after Whitney had gone out with Xu and Auntie Zhang for a meal in Beijing, he'd invited Whitney to a jewelry store and offered to buy her a ring for more than $1 million. Whitney declined, knowing that she'd have to pay for it somehow in the future. Xu then bought two of the exact same rings. Obviously, they weren't both for his wife. In China, there are several ways to get the attention of those in power. Xu's preferred method was through giving outrageously expensive gifts.

Xu wanted to go to check out a $100 million pleasure ship docked off France's southern coast. The ship belonged to a Hong Kong business mogul (also worth billions). Like David Li, Xu was interested in opening his own private club, but Xu figured that a waterborne establishment would be more secluded than one like David's on a Beijing side street. Xu envisioned a floating palace to wine and dine officials off China's coast, away from the prying eyes of China's anti-corruption cops and its nascent paparazzi.

It tells you something about that special time that none of us were floored by the $100 million price tag. Dropping this type of money among these jet-setters had become, if not routine, at least not totally out of the ordinary. But when we arrived dockside and saw the vessel, what struck me was the modesty of the decor. For sure, it was a huge boat. To man it, you'd need a dozen cooks, maids, and waiters. But for $100 million you'd expect more elegance, dangling chandeliers, and the type of inlaid wood that had mesmerized me on my first ride in a Rolls-Royce with my dad and his boss years ago in Hong Kong. "Is this all you get for one hundred million dollars?" I asked. Needless to say, Xu didn't buy the boat.

During the trip, our gang expressed little curiosity about Europe's history or culture. My companions were part of the first generation of China's wealthy: up-from-the-bootstraps entrepreneurs, like Xu; hard-nosed developers, like Little Ningbo; and members of the Communist aristocracy, like David Li. Daring was rewarded. Jail time was an occupational hazard. Education wasn't a requirement. People like them weren't interested in famous paintings in museums. They were all about putting their mark on the world. Anyway, it was time to shop.

Following the French Riviera, we set our sights on Milan. We men holed up in the Bulgari hotel while our wives hit the Quadrilatero della Moda, Milan's fashion district, in a frenzy of consumption. They were like gladiators at the Coliseum, vying over who could afford what. I'd never thought of shopping as a blood sport, but what did I know? At the airport in Milan readying for our return to China, it took three hours to process their value-added tax refunds because they'd spent so much. In the meantime, I was called back to the card table in the VIP lounge. This time I dropped $200,000. Luckily, no one ever called in those debts.

On the way home, reclining in a leather bucket seat, thirty thousand feet above Eurasia, I reflected on the amazing course our lives had taken. "Just a few years ago," I mused out loud, "we'd be lucky to be pedaling around on Flying Pigeon bikes. Now we're in private jets. From there to here in less than a lifetime, it's enough to make your head spin." The others nodded. Arriving back in China, Whitney and I decided that the time wasn't ripe for a wine club.

Auntie Zhang also loved to travel and Whitney and I arranged trips for her while her husband was in office. "Once the old man retires, they won't allow me to leave China," Auntie Zhang observed at one point, "so I'd better travel overseas while I have the chance." It's a peculiarity of China's system that the Party bans most retired senior leaders from leaving the country. For example, former premier Zhu Rongji was stopped from taking up a position as a visiting scholar at Harvard. In other countries, former senior officials often play a useful, behind-the-scenes role in hashing out compromises, floating proposals, and channeling criticism that current officials cannot. But the Party, ever obsessed with total control, has closed off that avenue to itself.

On the road Auntie Zhang was a whirlwind of energy. We took her to the pampas of Argentina, the fjords of New Zealand, Australia's outback, the castles of France's Loire Valley, and on jaunts to Switzerland, where she disappeared inside exclusive spas for longevity treatments.

On one adventure we flew into Zurich in 2007 and I drove Auntie Zhang halfway across the country to the Clinique La Prairie spa between Montreux and Vevey on the shores of Lake Geneva. She had an appointment for a facelift and injections of sheep's placenta to ward off the vicissitudes of old age. I checked her in and took a seat in the spa's waiting room. A procession of women in bathrobes, their faces swathed in gauze, paraded by. Hours later, Auntie Zhang emerged similarly bandaged and we returned to the hotel.

After a few days, the bandages came off and Auntie Zhang, paying no heed to the prominent incision marks around her ears, was primed to hit the road. She was far hungrier for life than my entrepreneur friends. And she set a grueling pace.

Rising at 5:00 in her suite at a five-star hotel, she hailed the new day by trundling into the dining room with the rice cooker she'd brought from Beijing. Under the bewildered gaze of European waiters, she prepared rice porridge, seasoning it with pickled Chinese vegetables she'd brought in her carry-on. By 6-ish, breakfast was ready and Auntie Zhang dispatched one of her underlings to wake us up. Sleeping in or ordering a Western breakfast was taboo. For me, this was particularly painful. I like my croissants.

A curious band of hangers-on attached themselves to Auntie Zhang. Ex–factory manager Huang tagged along everywhere; we never caught him sneaking into Auntie Zhang's room, but everyone assumed hanky-panky was ongoing. Another fellow, who called himself Sunshine and was a pal of Auntie's son, Winston, accompanied us, too.

Breakfast over, by 7:30 we were on the road, in a big van with a Chinese driver, gallivanting across Europe's countryside. Auntie Zhang was also not a museum person, but she fancied the great outdoors. From early morning until 9:00 at night, she went non-stop. For lunch or dinner, I had to find a Chinese restaurant, which was often a challenge in the boondocks of Switzerland or the ranch country of Argentina.

To me, this was a frenetic way to travel. I put Auntie Zhang up in the best hotels in Europe and found her some of the best restaurants to boot. I routinely paid more than one thousand Euros a night for a bed, but we never spent any time in the rooms, rarely ate in the best restaurants, and we'd be out the door almost at the crack of dawn.

Auntie Zhang never traveled with a Chinese security detail.

And it didn't seem to us that the security services of the nations we visited had any idea who she was. On a trip to New Zealand's fjords we tittered as Auntie Zhang downed a cup of instant noodles while we and a gaggle of Western tourists took in the scenery. Those people had no idea that the elderly lady slurping next to them was the wife of China's premier.

CHAPTER FIFTEEN

I'VE WRITTEN BEFORE THAT LUCK LIES AT THE HEART of most fortunes. Whitney and I had a lucky strike with the Ping An IPO. Then we had another.

Early into his tenure as the airport chief, Li Peiying had signed a memorandum of understanding with a big state-owned enterprise, the Beijing Tourism Group, to buy a hotel that BTG held in central Beijing. Li wanted to redevelop the site and locate the headquarters of the Beijing Capital International Airport Group downtown. It would've been a massive vanity project, but it never went anywhere. About a year into our joint venture at the airport, Li Peiying told me about the deal.

Li said he was no longer interested in building on the site. I didn't know it, but Li had been under almost constant investigation by the Party's Central Commission for Discipline Inspection for corruption. So, naturally, his dream of a second HQ for the airport conglomerate—just around the corner from his favorite sushi bar—had fallen by the wayside.

I asked Li whether our joint venture could buy the project

from the airport. He thought that was a good idea. We proposed the deal to the Beijing Tourism Group.

The site in the Chaoyang District of Beijing ran five hundred yards along the Liangma—or Bright Horse—River, which at the time was a foul-smelling waterway that iced over in the winter and was the scene of noxious algae blooms in spring. The Huadu Hotel, a somewhat shabby three-star four-story facility with a surprisingly good canteen, anchored the site.

We got the land appraised by an independent auditor and ran the numbers through the Party committees at both the airport and the Beijing Tourism Group. Whitney and I didn't know where real estate prices were heading, but we were optimistic that things were pointing up and we were intent on controlling as much land as we could. Once the two sides agreed on the value of the land and the hotel, about $100 million, our joint venture bought it with loans from a state-owned bank.

We, too, let the project sit for years. All my energy and all of our capital were being consumed by the airport. Then Whitney left for New York to have Ariston. Finally, by 2010, I was ready to build. But politics got in the way again.

Following Li Peiying's arrest, new regulations came down banning the airport from involving itself in anything outside of its core business, especially real estate because land deals had become such a font of corruption. So just as I was turning my attention to developing that site, the Beijing Capital International Airport Group, our biggest joint-venture shareholder, got cold feet.

The airport approached us and practically ordered Great Ocean to buy the land from the joint venture. The airport said it first wanted the land to be reappraised and would then sell it to us at its new value. Of course, the airport was looking to make a killing. In the interim, the value of land in Beijing had skyrocketed, particularly in prime locations such as a big plot along the banks of the Liangma River.

We counteroffered to buy the land at the original price the joint venture had paid plus interest. We observed that the airport was essentially forcing us to take the land off the joint venture's hands. We'd wanted the joint venture to develop it. Why should we have to buy the land from the joint venture at an inflated price?

Under the rules, the land could only be sold after public bids had been solicited. But the process could be managed to scare competitors off. First, the item for sale wasn't actually land; it was a holding company that owned the Huadu Hotel, which itself owned the land. None of the potential buyers, except us, knew the liabilities of this holding company. To them, it was a black box. In the end, our bid of $130 million was the only bid. Whitney and I pulled together the funds. This time, Auntie Zhang actually put up some money, about $45 million.

In the end, the redevelopment project—which included a hotel, residences, office space, and a museum—would amount to an enormous windfall. The Huadu Hotel had taken up about 450,000 square feet. When we built it out, the new site contained four buildings and almost 1.5 million square feet above ground and 800,000 square feet below. I can only guess at the total value today. But it's got to be somewhere between $2.5 and $3 billion. No one knew that real estate prices in Beijing would appreciate like they have. A lot of it was luck.

For me, the project was a joy. Overseeing the airport buildout had been my boot camp. Now that I'd made it through, the redevelopment project was where I could put my training to use, avoid rookie mistakes, and exercise my creativity.

Our first impulse was to build the tallest building in Beijing. Whitney and I held a competition involving some of the world's most famous architects. We received a proposal from the architect Norman Foster for a 1,250-foot-tall tower. But regulations demanded that the residential apartment blocks across the street from the project receive two hours of sunlight during the shortest day of the year. So we were forced to cut the height in half and utilize every square inch of land we controlled. Whitney offered the painter Zeng Fanzhi the opportunity to locate his studio on the top floor of a museum we were planning and to add a space for entertainment next door. On the floors below, the museum would showcase Zeng's works, many of which were selling for millions of dollars around the world. Most of the museums in China were run by the state. To have a privately owned one would change the way you curated a show.

In the end, we secured permits to build four buildings. A hotel and condo apartments would share one twenty-story structure. Then there'd be two office towers and the museum. Office space would take up almost three-quarters of the project, with another quarter devoted to the hotel and the remaining quarter to the condos. We only had limited storefronts; China is overbuilt with malls. We planned the museum on a lot just a few feet from the banks of the Liangma River.

In my view, the site was one of the best in Beijing. The whole southern side of the project ran along the riverbank. One of Beijing's oldest embassy districts was located on the other side of the river, a tree-lined neighborhood of two-story houses and chanceries surrounded by ample grounds. On good days without smog you could gaze out from the site onto a sea of green, like you can from 59th Street in Manhattan looking north into Central Park. In addition, the Beijing city government was cleaning up the river. Gone was the putrid smell.

Whitney and I had stayed in the world's most exclusive hotels all of our professional lives. We knew how they operated and understood what made a great room. Unlike with the airport project, we didn't need to travel the world to research hotels because our lives had been unconsciously devoted to that work. Whitney and I hired an all-star collection of interior designers, lighting designers, architects, and engineers. For the job of designing the project's surrounding landscape we interviewed a Japanese monk who'd inherited his Zen monastery from his father. We ultimately went with a team from Australia. To design the museum, we signed up Pritzker prize winner and autodidact Tadao Ando. For the office complex, hotel, and residences, I used the New York architectural firm of Kohn Pedersen Fox, which has built skyscrapers around the world.

We were on a mission to make this the best real estate project China had ever seen. We spared no expense to make it happen. We consciously set ourselves apart from other rich developers who hired designers and then let them make the decisions. The problem with that model was that designers and development company executives had never lived a life of luxury. Whitney and I had—for a decade. We knew that if we could mix our aesthetic with the professionalism of our team, the results would be hugely impressive. I named the project Genesis because I believed we could write a new chapter in global real estate development.

In January 2011, we held a kickoff meeting with our design team in Beijing. Some seventy people from all over the world packed into a conference hall. I began the meeting with a speech. I was wearing a dark blue suit. I was also wearing a pair of bespoke crimson shoes called Sergios fashioned by the French cobbler Atelier du Tranchet. "Have you ever seen an owner dressing the way I am dressing coming to a meeting like this?" I asked. "Look at these shoes! This is the style I want to bring to the entire project." The whole hall had a good laugh. But they knew I was serious. For them, it was inspiring to work on a project they could put on their resumés. They'd never seen an owner ready to spend so much to do the best, to never cut corners, to pursue perfection, with bright red shoes.

China is awash in hotels partly because Chinese businessmen like them almost as much as they like private clubs. Executives at state-owned enterprises love to build hotels because they can use them like clubhouses to entertain contacts or woo mistresses, all at state expense. Even after retiring, former executives from a state-owned firm swim in the pool, dine at the restaurant, or book rooms free of charge. Beijing has more five-star hotels than any other city in the world. I knew if I was going to include a hotel in the project, I wanted one of limited size—to give it at least a fighting chance of turning a profit. I settled on a partnership with Bulgari, a crown jewel of world hotels and a brand that would enhance the value of the entire development. Initially, I argued for a sixty-room hotel; Bulgari wanted more. We settled on one hundred and twenty rooms.

I delved into every aspect of the room design. I wanted my hotel to give guests things they couldn't get anywhere else, little touches that would improve the often-enervating experience of traveling. For example, most five-star hotels barely provide enough space for one open suitcase. But travelers often come in pairs. I directed my construction team to make sure that all of my rooms would come with enough space for two suitcases. This extra five square feet proved a big expense, but it was worth it.

We argued with Bulgari over who'd get the top floors, the hotel or the condos. We wanted the top floors for residences because with such a prime location they'd fetch the highest prices in Beijing. Bulgari eventually bent to our wishes. Whitney and I took the penthouse, a sprawling ten-thousand-square-foot pad equipped with an indoor swimming pool for me and Ariston. It was going to be our home.

Whitney returned to work in 2010 as we launched the project. We began to bicker openly over project details in front of our staff. She seemed to relish contradicting me. We'd talk about it at night and she'd agree that it didn't look good, but the next day she'd do it again. Finally, we decided to split responsibilities to limit our interactions inside the office.

I took charge of marketing, planning, strategy, and sales and she took on construction, cost, and quality control. Still, there was lots of crossover. And in joint meetings, she'd still openly shut me down. One meeting concerned the size of the residences, which involved detailed financial and political calculations. What type of clientele did we seek? People who'd buy smallish units of fourteen hundred square feet for $3 million or people who'd buy a whole damn floor for twenty times more? Don't forget, these were China's go-go years. Maybe somebody wanted a center city mansion in the air. We certainly did.

In terms of social status, those would be completely different clients. The simply rich versus the megarich. Should they even mix in a common elevator and a common lobby or should there be separate entrances? And when it came to politics, would it be wise in an allegedly Communist country for people to shell out tens of millions of dollars on an apartment? Would people be scared to spend money like that in China? How should we bet on the social and political trends?

My team spent months on this topic and we shared our findings with Whitney and her group. They were, after all, the builders. Whitney wasn't impressed. She didn't like the mix we suggested. But I sensed underneath that she was uncomfortable with me calling the shots. She went around the room asking her team what they thought of our plan. They hemmed and hawed. I felt like I was back in the airport with the GM who'd replaced Li Peiying. Everybody had a different opinion, and the lack of consensus meant we wouldn't get anything done.

Whitney then announced that she wanted to shelve the decision for the time being. I was livid. "You think you're so damn smart, you do it," I yelled, adding, "I'm done with this." I walked out. This was about more than just a difference of opinion. Whitney was openly disrespecting me in public, and given my lifelong concerns about face, this was particularly painful.

My relationship with Whitney had always contained echoes of my relationship with my parents. When Whitney and I first met, she criticized me non-stop, much like my parents had. I took that censure to heart and changed the way I lived, dressed, talked, and moved in an attempt to follow her recipe for success. But once I succeeded, I confronted, as I had with my parents, this gap between my private world, which was colored by Whitney's disapproval, and my public world, which was filled with accolades and accomplishments. Something had to give.

In hindsight, I believe that Whitney felt the need to assert her authority. She'd been away from China to have Ariston, and as my position in our company had grown she felt that her position had weakened. I'd built the management team myself. I'd made all the hires, except the CFO. Starting with the airport, I'd put together the group from scratch. And when I sold our stake in the airport, part of the deal with Prologis was that the entire management group would leave with me. Building that team was one of the greatest things I've accomplished. Whitney focused on relationship building with Party bigwigs. But my team and I actually carried out the work. Whitney was not involved in much of that labor and that magnified her insecurity.

My team and I worked to create a hybrid culture of East meets West. Unlike most Chinese bosses, I believed in weekends off. At the same time, I wasn't a multinational corporation imposing values from three thousand miles away. I designed everything from the ground up. I believed in personal growth. It would have been hypocritical of me not to. After all, I'd spent a lot of time in Shanghai after the collapse of PalmInfo and later at the Aspen Institute trying to better myself. I matched the benefits package of international firms. I paid for some of my senior staff to earn MBAs. I also didn't hire relatives. Whitney had helped her half brother's real estate business in Tianjin, but he never was on my payroll. As a result, we avoided the factional strife that bedeviled so many other Chinese firms.

Despite being married, and business partners, Whitney and I

competed intensely. She'd shaped me and facilitated my success, but now she felt that I was challenging her authority and she worried that I no longer needed her. She had a point. I believed that time was on my side and that, with my expertise as the driving factor, our firm would soon be vying with Chinese or international firms on a level playing field for development projects in China and abroad. I also looked forward to the day when Whitney and I would share our wealth in a more balanced manner. But Whitney was apparently unwilling to change. She viewed playing the *guanxi* game as her only skill and she feared the day when it and, by extension, she were no longer needed.

Once we obtained approvals to construct the Bulgari in 2012, the project wasn't as reliant on connections as the airport had been, so Whitney had a smaller role. Foreigners dominated the work. All my contractors were international. We didn't muck about with wining and dining. I'd left Moutai in my rearview mirror—though the team welcomed it when, on occasion, I'd crack open a vintage red.

Despite the joy I felt at work, my relationship with Whitney began to deteriorate. It was ironic, even tragic, that a project that could have brought us closer together seemed to be pulling us apart. With perspective, I can now see that we were never emotionally close enough and were too pragmatically analytical about our ties. Whitney had always argued that passion should take the backseat in our relationship and that as long as the underlying logic was strong we, as a couple, would endure.

But my view is that logic wasn't enough. In life, we approach key relationships by mixing a jump off a cliff with calculated self-interest. There's no perfect formula. But Whitney and I clearly didn't have the right one. There was too little emotion invested in our union. In retrospect, that was the glue that would have kept us together. Emotion could have functioned as the soft tissue so that, when the skeleton was weakened, there was still a vital layer to cushion our fall.

CHAPTER SIXTEEN

ON OCTOBER 26, 2012, THE *NEW YORK TIMES* PUBlished a front-page article detailing the immense wealth belonging to the family of Wen Jiabao. Based on corporate records, the exposé estimated that the Wen family was worth close to $3 billion. At the beginning of the twentieth paragraph was Whitney's name. Talk about a blow to the skeleton of our relationship.

Three days before the story ran, the *Times* reporter, David Barboza, reached out to Whitney, informing her that she was going to be a focus of the piece and requesting comment. Whitney huddled with Auntie Zhang to come up with a response. Barboza told Whitney that he'd be reporting that Great Ocean had been the vehicle used to purchase Ping An stock and that, later, more than 100 million dollars' worth of shares in Ping An had been transferred to an account belonging to Wen Jiabao's mother, who was a retired schoolteacher with no source of income other than a government pension.

Whitney and Auntie Zhang initially decided not to comment on the story. Then Whitney contacted Barboza's Taiwanese wife through her connections in the art world. For several hours,

Whitney pleaded with her to convince Barboza to shelve the story. "We're all Chinese," I overheard Whitney say to her. "We should be able to settle this amicably. I have children; you have children; you know how much this is going to hurt my family. You wouldn't wish this on any family." This was another example of the breach between Whitney's culture and that of the Western world. But she was desperate. It was a shot in the dark. Needless to say, the Barbozas weren't interested

Auntie Zhang changed her mind and ordered Whitney to take responsibility for the Ping An deal. She instructed Whitney to talk to Barboza and to tell him that all of the stock held in the names of the premier's mother and other relatives actually belonged to Whitney and that she'd placed the stock in their names to conceal the size of Whitney's fortune. "When I invested in Ping An I didn't want to be written about," Whitney told the *Times*, "so I had my relatives find some other people to hold these shares for me." Whitney's statement was far-fetched, to say the least. Obviously, it beggared belief. But Whitney's loyalty to Auntie Zhang compelled her to follow orders. Of course, originally, the stock had all been in Great Ocean's name to protect *the Wens*, not Whitney. Only after Whitney and I sold our shares in 2007 did Auntie Zhang make the wrongheaded decision to transfer ownership of the shares to her mother-in-law and others in the clan. That move created a paper trail. If the shares had stayed in Great Ocean's name, Barboza wouldn't have had much to hang his story on.

In the back of my mind, I always knew that at a certain point Auntie Zhang would sacrifice Whitney. I'd imagined, however, that by the time that pivot occurred, Whitney would have better protected herself. But I was wrong. Whitney had invested too much of herself in her relationship with Auntie Zhang. She'd also embraced what we Chinese called *yiqi*, the code of brotherhood, the same code I adhered to with my buddies in Shanghai. She willingly became the fall girl to prove that Auntie Zhang had been right to trust her for all these years.

Most people would have run for the hills, figuring now was not the time to be a hero. But Whitney didn't. I saw her action as a deeply personal choice, equal parts desperation and courage. Whitney's Christianity might have played a role. But more than that was her commitment to the relationships that she'd built. I urged her not to talk to Barboza. But she made the decision to do it because her relationships were all she had. In the end, it boiled down to how she saw herself as a person.

For the Wen family and, more broadly, the upper ranks of the Chinese Communist Party, the story struck like an earthquake. The piece marked the second time that year that a Western news agency had detailed the wealth of a leading Communist family. Several months earlier, in June 2012, the Bloomberg news agency had run a similar story about the fortune held by relatives of Vice-President—and soon to be Party chief—Xi Jinping. Interestingly, no one fell on his or her sword for that piece, like Whitney would for Auntie Zhang.

The Party reacted to the Wen story by blocking the *New York Times*'s website. A Foreign Ministry spokesman accused the *Times* of intentionally smearing China and harboring "ulterior motives." Internally, the Party circled the wagons. True to its paranoid roots, the Party's leadership viewed the two stories as part of a concerted attack on China's political leadership by the US government. If the story on Xi's family hadn't run, the Party might have reacted differently and Wen could have been targeted. But the Xi story convinced everyone that the United States was somehow to blame for the pieces and that the best response was the animal one: to close ranks.

In private, Wen Jiabao was livid at the revelations about the business activities of his family members, especially Auntie Zhang and his son, Winston. (Wen's daughter, Lily, was not named in the original story, but would be in later pieces in the *Times*.) Whitney and I believed that Auntie Zhang and her children had kept Wen in the dark about many things. We also understood that Wen earlier had discovered some of his family's business activities and had voiced his disapproval.

This time, we were told, Wen demanded a divorce. In a rage, he declared to his relatives that he was preparing to shave his head and enter a Buddhist monastery after retirement. At that point, Party authorities stepped in—to stop both the divorce and Wen's impulse to, as Buddhists say, "see through the red dust" of human desire and become a monk. That last move would have looked especially bad for a Party that was officially, at least, atheist.

The fallout from the story built like a tsunami, which starts with a low tide. Our relationship with the Wen family changed. Auntie Zhang informed us that the family was no longer interested in taking 30 percent of our projects. We'd only recently broken ground on the Bulgari hotel and suddenly Auntie Zhang told us she was pulling out. We didn't know how to take it; we thought she'd change her mind. We'd never signed any contracts with Auntie Zhang. Like so much in China, everything was implicit.

Following the *Times* exposé, Whitney shut down her networking activity. She didn't reach out to anyone and no one reached out to her. She didn't want to put people in a difficult spot. Meanwhile, I tried to assess how much risk we faced. I had a sense that there'd be ramifications, but I didn't know what they'd be or when they'd hit. We waited for a month and continued to work on the hotel. No one from the security services or the Party's feared Central Commission for Discipline Inspection darkened our door.

Auntie Zhang told us that she had directed her son and daughter to get out of the spotlight. Winston Wen went to work for a state-owned enterprise. Lily Chang shuttered her consulting business and joined the State Administration of Foreign Exchange. Auntie Zhang also dropped a plan to use a big swath of land in northern Beijing to build a jewelry vocational training center. She turned it over to her son, Winston, who set to work building the Keystone Academy, a school with pretensions of becoming Communist China's finest boarding school.

Auntie Zhang told Whitney she was convinced someone was trying to destroy her family. She searched for a source of the story. Citing contacts inside China's government, Auntie Zhang said that she believed her husband's reputation had become collateral damage in a life-and-death power struggle inside the Party.

The struggle pitted Xi Jinping against an official named Bo Xilai. Both were sons of Communist "immortals," veterans of Mao's revolution. And both owed their careers to a Party decision made in 1981 and pushed by a high-ranking Communist named Chen Yun to establish a special office in the Party's personnel department called the Young Cadres Section. That section's purpose was to ensure that the sons and daughters of senior Party members were given good positions in the government and the Party. "If our sons and daughters succeed us," Chen Yun declared, "they won't dig up our graves." The Tiananmen Square crackdown of 1989 gave this work added urgency. A key lesson that the red aristocracy drew from that turmoil was that, as the saying went, "you can best depend on your own kids." Each leading family chose an heir to be groomed for future political leadership. Nominated by their fathers, Xi and Bo rose through the Party ranks.

Xi's father, Xi Zhongxun, was a hero of the Party's civil war against Chiang Kai-shek's Nationalist forces in the 1930s and 1940s. In the late 1970s and early 1980s, he played a key role in establishing economic policies that transformed China into the factory of the world.

Bo Xilai was the son of Bo Yibo, another of Chairman Mao's lieutenants. Bo Yibo also battled Nationalist forces. Bo Yibo was more conservative than Xi Zhongxun when it came to economic reforms, but in the 1980s he oversaw the creation of China's two stock markets, in Shanghai and Shenzhen.

By the early 1990s, Bo Xilai had risen to prominence as the dashing mayor of the seaside city of Dalian. He subsequently served as governor of Liaoning Province, minister of commerce, and then in 2007 he was appointed Party secretary in Chongqing, a massive city in China's southwest once known to Westerners as Chunking. With a mane of slicked-back black hair and a radiant, million-dollar smile, Bo was a media darling, always ready with a pithy quote. If Bo had been an American, he'd have been the guy who parlayed a successful string of used-car lots into a seat in Congress.

Xi Jinping was less flamboyant and far more careful. When he was an official in Fujian Province in the 1990s, his coworkers had no idea he was wooing and would ultimately marry the Chinese army singer-celebrity Peng Liyuan. Xi had split with his first wife, the daughter of a Chinese diplomat, over her desire to stay in Britain, where she'd gone to study.

Xi's resumé, which included top government and Party posts in Shanghai and Zhejiang provinces, was no less impressive than Bo's. Still, to the media, Xi was a relative unknown when he burst on the scene in November 2002 as a member of the Party's Central Committee. Bo also won a coveted spot on the Central Committee that year following intense lobbying by his father. Five years later, however, Xi pulled ahead in the race to be China's next ruler. Although Bo Xilai won a seat on the Politburo in 2007, only Xi was elevated to the Politburo's Standing Committee, China's top political body.

Whitney and I heard a lot of stories about Bo's desperation to get back in the race and the attention-getting activities he organized to do so. As Party chief in Chongqing, Bo raised his profile by launching political campaigns redolent of the mass mobilizations that occurred under Chairman Mao during the Cultural Revolution. Playing on the nostalgia for China's early revolutionary days, he'd organize huge rallies where thousands of city residents would gather to participate in sing-alongs belting out old Communist tunes.

But Bo's ambition brought him down. His fall began on November 15, 2011, when the body of British businessman Neil Heywood was found in room 1605 of the Lucky Holiday Hotel, a threadbare guesthouse in Chongqing. The initial report on Heywood blamed "sudden death after drinking alcohol" and his body was cremated without an autopsy.

Heywood had been a longtime business partner of Bo's glamorous second wife, Gu Kailai. When Chongqing's police chief,

Wang Lijun looked into the case, he discovered that Bo's wife had poisoned Heywood over a business dispute.

Wang went to Bo Xilai's office and told him. Bo took that as an implicit threat. In his mind, as a loyal police chief, Wang should've just quashed the case and made it go away. Bo jumped up from behind his desk and slapped Wang with a force hard enough to puncture Wang's eardrum. Bo then fired Wang and had him placed under investigation for corruption.

Fearing that he'd be the next murder victim, Wang fled Chongqing and on February 6, 2012, knocked on the door of the US Consulate in nearby Chengdu, where he told his story to American diplomats and requested political asylum. As Wang made his case inside the US mission, police officers representing various competing political factions ringed the consulate in a tense standoff. A day later, US officials handed Wang over to a vice-minister from the Ministry of State Security, who took Chongqing's top cop to Beijing. All of this unfolded at an inauspicious time—as the Party readied for the annual meeting of the National People's Congress the following month.

Auntie Zhang revealed to us that following Wang Lijun's arrival in Beijing, the nine-member Standing Committee of the Politburo met to discuss the scandal. Zhou Yongkang, the Standing Committee member in charge of China's security services and an ally of Bo Xilai, spoke first, arguing that the investigation should stop at police chief Wang. Silence descended on the meeting, Auntie Zhang said. Zhou's declaration meant that there would be no investigation of Bo Xilai. Members of the Standing Committee pondered Zhou's view. When no one spoke up, Xi Jinping, who was relatively low in seniority, broke with protocol to speak. He asserted instead that the Party investigate not only Wang but also anyone else who might've been involved. He didn't need to mention Bo Xilai or Bo's wife, because the implication was obvious to everyone at the meeting. Xi knew if he didn't speak up then, he'd lose a golden opportunity to rid himself of his archrival.

As number two on the Standing Committee, Wen Jiabao had a key say. He concurred with Xi Jinping. Next, Party chief Hu Jintao, ever cautious, also backed a complete investigation. And that's how the tide shifted. When the Standing Committee of the Politburo finally voted on how to handle the situation during a subsequent meeting on March 7, only Zhou opposed a plan to expel Bo Xilai from the Party, hand his case to China's prosecutors, and investigate Bo's wife for killing Neil Heywood.

The decision to purge Bo set the stage for a dramatic press conference at the close of the National People's Congress on March 14. This was Wen Jiabao's final news conference after a decade as premier. Responding to a question from the *New York Times*, Wen rebuked Bo Xilai and called on the Chongqing municipal Party committee to "reflect seriously and learn from the Wang Lijun incident." That was a bombshell. Not only had Wen backed Xi in his battle with Bo behind closed doors, but now he was publicly shaming Bo. A day later, Bo was dismissed from his post as Chongqing Party boss. On April 10, he was kicked off the Party's Central Committee and out of the Politburo. In September, a Chinese court sentenced him to life in prison. And on November 15 of that year, Xi Jinping became general secretary of the Chinese Communist Party.

Auntie Zhang believed that her husband's support for the investigation and his participation in the public shaming of Bo Xilai put him on a collision course with Bo's allies, some of whom were in China's security services. Other information that came to our attention supports Auntie Zhang's view. In February 2012, Whitney and I heard chatter that Bo had hired Chinese journalists and academics to dig up dirt on Auntie Zhang and her children. Barboza, when asked how he came to write his story, has always denied obtaining information from Party insiders looking to help Bo get even with Wen Jiabao. But Auntie Zhang said she'd learned that security officers loyal to Bo Xilai handed over boxes of documents to Barboza in Hong Kong.

In 2013, about a year after Xi Jinping had launched his anti-corruption campaign and a year after the *Times* story on the Wen family wealth, Auntie Zhang told us that she and her kids had "donated" all of their assets to the state in exchange for a guarantee that they wouldn't be prosecuted. She said other red families had done the same. There was another reason behind this action. The Party wanted to rewrite history. In the future, if the Party faced allegations of tolerating systemic corruption, it could claim that these red families, in "donating" their wealth to China, had only been serving the state. All this seemed pretty surreal to Whitney and me. But then again, China's Communists had a long record of stealing private property and distorting the truth.

The *Times* story strengthened my case that Whitney and I should put a substantial portion of our investments overseas and stop relying on our ties to the Party to do business in China. We were skilled enough, I argued, to compete in the open market. We'd had great success playing the *guanxi* game, but, I thought, it was time to transition to a new model. My position was bolstered by some of our Western partners who'd become close friends.

International players like Paul Katz, CEO of the Kohn Pedersen Fox architectural firm, were impressed with our work and encouraged us to vie for projects overseas.

Whitney didn't agree. She was afraid of going international. And she argued that, because Wen had played such a crucial role in Xi's rise, Xi would protect Wen and his family—and, by extension, us. She thought our future remained bright in China, using the old methods to make our way.

Other issues arose between us. One evening as we lay in bed, she showed me the divination of a fortune teller. Getting one's fortune told was all the rage among China's elite. People at the top of China's pyramid hired soothsayers, qigong masters, and purveyors of all sorts of hocus-pocus. In its seventy years in power, the Party had destroyed traditional Chinese values and had essentially outlawed religion. In the vacuum, superstition took hold. In an unpredictable system, where a person can go from top to bottom in a flash, totems promising to make sense of life become very appealing.

Whitney brought out a small red booklet in which the soothsayer had written her fortune with a calligraphy brush. What caught my eye wasn't the prognostication; it was her year of birth. The fortune teller had written "1966." All along Whitney had told me she was born in 1968, the same year as me.

My birthday was in November 1968 and I'd been led to believe that Whitney was born in December of that same year, making me about a month older. Suddenly I discovered that she was actually two years my senior. She'd concealed her real age from me, but not from the fortune teller. Without her true date of birth, he wouldn't have been able to give her an accurate reading.

"What the heck is this?" I asked, pointing to her date of birth. Whitney blanched slightly. "I've been married to you for ten years and I never knew your real age," I said.

She paused. "I'm still me," she said sheepishly.

"Yeah, but not exactly," I said. "The most basic information a person can give is their name, birthday, and gender. If you fill out any form, those are the first three questions asked. If you change any one of those, and say you're the same person, well, that's not actually true."

"I'm still me," she repeated.

Whitney explained that she'd discussed the issue with her mother when we first started going out. Her mother had observed that we seemed to be a perfect match. "Don't tempt fate by telling him your real age," her mother advised. Both women worried that if I knew Whitney was older than me, given China's patriarchal society in which wives are invariably younger than their husbands, I might walk away.

Learning about the deception so late into our relationship was another blow. We were at loggerheads over the future of our work together and were constantly bickering in front of our staff. And now this.

We also clashed over another project that Whitney was eager to do. We were considering bidding on a deal to redevelop a huge site next to the China World Hotel that anchored Beijing's Central Business District. It promised to be a massive enterprise of almost 5 million square feet, with skyscrapers and malls. No other chunk of property was worth more in China.

As we carried on negotiations to redevelop the land, I got a sense of the heat we'd be under. I found myself getting wined and dined by businessmen and their Party contacts for a piece of the project. A representative from the Hong Kong developer Sun Hung Kai Properties, one of the world's leaders in the field, came to Beijing and lunched with us and Auntie Zhang. As soon as the meal ended, Whitney's cell phone rang and it was Chen Zuo'er, who was then serving as deputy director of the State Council's Hong Kong and Macao Affairs Office. Whitney put Chen on speaker, and I sat there listening to him urging us to sell a controlling stake in the project to Sun Hung Kai. That was pretty shocking. Chen was a minister-level official in China's government. And here he was brazenly lobbying on behalf of a Hong Kong business for a real estate deal in Beijing. It showed how cozy the ties were between Communist Party officials involved in Hong Kong's affairs and the Hong Kong business elite. We said we'd consider the request.

I evaluated the situation and got a sense of how complicated the project would be. The approval process would make the airport look like a cakewalk. We'd probably need not just one but at least two allies on the Standing Committee of the Politburo to have any chance of garnering all the permissions to make it work. And even then, there'd be political pressure. I told my staff to pull back from the deal. Whitney wasn't happy.

Then another deal pushed us further apart.

In early 2013, I lent a friend $30 million to buy a Hong Kong–listed company, with a commitment for a second tranche to help him finish the transaction. I'd known the friend, Ding Yi, for years. Like me, he was born in China but grew up overseas, in his case Australia. We'd met in the 1990s, after I first returned to Hong Kong. We spent a lot of late nights together in Hong Kong's Lan

Kwai Fong entertainment district and on Beijing's Bar Street. I considered him one of my best pals.

Ding Yi had worked for a Swiss bank and a Chinese investment firm, made a fortune, and then lost it during the Asian Financial Crisis in 2007. His wife represented an international metals-trading company that did business in China.

At one point, his wife's firm got tangled up in a business dispute. Then a Chinese bank paid the police to arrest his wife and hold her hostage, a common occurrence on the mainland. After the police tossed her in a village lockup in faraway Xinjiang in the northwest corner of China, Ding Yi spent years trying to free her. He ultimately succeeded, something I found particularly impressive, considering that in the meantime he'd divorced his wife and married her receptionist, a former bar girl from Shanghai who'd taken the English name Yvonne. But this was China and people led contradictory lives. Anyway, I figured that someone who'd go to bat for his ex-wife would be trustworthy.

In October 2013, the second tranche of my loan was due. I went to Whitney for the money, but she refused. "We had a deal," I told her during a heated meeting. "I don't want to do it anymore," she responded. I went back to Ding Yi with the bad news. He wasn't happy. Incapable of raising money to complete the transaction, I asked him to sell his stake in the company and return the $30 million. He balked. Ding Yi's second wife, Yvonne, apparently played a role here. During a party at a Hong Kong nightclub that her husband had thrown in my honor, she'd propositioned me and I'd turned her down. Again, this was China, where no one missed an opportunity to try for a bigger fish, and, if snubbed, no one forgot a slight. I figured that she'd urged Ding Yi not to pay me back.

I felt Ding Yi was trying to play me. I went to Hong Kong a lot. Each time, we'd go out, have a meal, and hit the bars. Ding Yi was unfailingly buddy-buddy. Finally, I confronted him about the money and he just up and disappeared. I had no recourse but to get a lawyer and take him to court. He denied that the money he'd invested in the listed company was mine.

At home, things weren't any better with Whitney; our interactions grew more forced. By this time Whitney and I were living in the residences attached to the Four Seasons Hotel to be nearer to the Bulgari site. In late October 2013, I moved out.

CHAPTER SEVENTEEN

ON JULY 31, 2013, A FEW MONTHS BEFORE WHITNEY and I separated, I addressed the Aspen Institute at a Leadership in Action program in Aspen, Colorado. I noted that in China there was "a rising tide" of people interested in their rights, but I also observed that the Chinese Communist Party was opening up and trying to adapt. Each Communist ruler, I said, had shared more power with his comrades than the last.

I argued that although China was nominally a Communist state, "how it's being run is completely different." Each successive administration, I observed, had to be more responsive to public opinion. "Mao was one man. When Deng Xiaoping came in, he had to consult with two or three elders. Jiang Zemin had to listen to even more. Power is more dispersed—just looking at China as a single state never changing is not correct." Dressed in my casually hip style—a sunset-colored T, dark jacket, and designer sneakers with no-show socks—I embodied the idea that China would dovetail with the West. But privately, the concerns I harbored about China's system were growing with the rise of the Party's new leader, Xi Jinping.

I had initially been optimistic about Xi's rule, in part because I knew he was close to Chen Xi, who'd been the Party boss of Tsinghua University when we made our donations there. Soon after Xi became vice-president, he asked Chen, his college-days bunkmate, to serve in his kitchen cabinet. Chen had refused Xi Jinping before. In 1999, Xi had offered him a post in Fujian Province when Xi was governor there. But this time the prospect of working for the paramount leader of China at the center of power was enough to convince Chen Xi to leave Tsinghua behind.

Xi had Chen appointed vice-minister of education and then engineered a quick elevation to deputy Party boss of Liaoning Province for a mere seven months to pad his resumé with a compulsory tour in the hinterlands. In April 2011, Chen was brought back to Beijing. Two years later, Xi placed him in the Party's Organization Department, a key post that handles the promotions of all senior Party members. In 2017, Chen became chief of the Organization Department. With an ally in that slot, Xi was able to insert his followers into Party posts all over China.

Another reason why I was initially comfortable with Xi was that Whitney's tea partner, Wang Qishan, also appeared to be close to the new Party chief and had praised him in conversations with Whitney. We were thinking that if both Chen and Wang liked Xi, his term could even be an improvement on the cautious rule of Hu Jintao.

Soon after Xi became Party boss in November 2012, though, he launched a massive anti-corruption campaign. We felt that he was being far too aggressive. He wouldn't be appointed to his government post as president until March 2013, but he was already instigating criminal investigations of thousands of officials. This type of grandstanding wasn't usual in China and it marked a break with Party tradition. We supported the fight against corruption. China could use a thorough housecleaning. But after Xi's campaign had lasted for a year, we broached the subject with Chen and others. Their conclusion was that Xi Jinping would extend the battle into the middle of his first term and then wind it down. He'd *have* to, they said, because the current campaign was affecting the economy and damaging morale inside the bureaucracy. People were so scared of being investigated that they didn't want to make decisions. It couldn't last forever. Also, Xi's arresting a few hundred officials was one thing. But once he'd incarcerated tens of thousands, people would conclude that it wasn't just a few bad apples; the whole system was rotten to the core. By 2020, China's authorities had investigated more than 2.7 million officials for corruption and punished more than 1.5 million, including seven national-level leaders and two dozen generals.

Other developments began to concern us. In July 2012, as Xi prepared to take power, a document circulated from the Party's General Office titled "Briefing on the Current Situation in the Ideological Realm." The report, known as Document Number 9, warned that dangerous Western values, such as freedom of speech and judicial independence, were infecting China and needed to be rooted out. These ideas, the document said, were "extremely malicious" and would, henceforth, be banned from being taught at China's schools and universities. The document also blasted the move to a more independent media, ordering Party organizations to redouble their efforts to rein in muckraking periodicals.

The security services followed this with a withering crackdown on lawyers and other proponents of a civil society. The last vestiges of a somewhat independent media were either shuttered or turned over to Party hacks. And at the Chinese People's Consultative Conference, I witnessed other disquieting changes as well.

In early 2013, delegates to the Beijing municipal CPPCC were summoned to a meeting. I could tell things were different. For one, the chairman of the Beijing conference was in attendance. We were treated to a speech by a senior Party official who took the opportunity to dispel any fantasies about political loosening in China. He directly criticized Yu Keping—whom we'd hired to run our think tank, the Kaifeng Foundation—for suggesting that democratic reforms would make China stronger. He blasted the idea that the CPPCC would ever function as a second house of parliament. The speech knocked everyone back. It was another example of the nasty hard-line turn that we'd see more of under Xi Jinping.

China's foreign policy became far more aggressive. I saw those changes personally on trips back to Hong Kong. Under the terms of the "one country, two systems" arrangement that China had agreed to with Britain to honor as part of the deal that returned Hong Kong to Chinese rule in 1997, the Chinese government had promised to let Hong Kong manage its own affairs for fifty years. China had also agreed that it would grant Hong Kong a significant measure of democracy and continued freedoms of religion, speech, and assembly—rights that were denied inside China. But under Xi Jinping, China began to break these promises.

Xi's government curtailed Hong Kong's democratization. It dispatched security officers to Hong Kong to kidnap publishers and booksellers who'd printed and sold material about China's rulers that the Party didn't like. And it began to actively undermine

Hong Kong's political system. The Party enlisted me and other Hong Kong members of the CPPCC to serve as foot soldiers in that campaign.

In meetings at the conference, officials ordered us to involve ourselves directly in Hong Kong's political life. These demands intensified in 2014 when the Umbrella Movement erupted in Hong Kong. These protests were sparked by a Communist Party ruling mandating that any candidate for chief executive of Hong Kong, the top post in the territory, be first vetted by a committee composed of people loyal to Beijing. The irony was clear: What good was one man, one vote, when the only candidates you could vote for had first been vetted by Beijing?

No sooner had the Umbrella Movement started with demonstrations in September than we were directed by CPPCC officials to go to Hong Kong and organize and fund counterdemonstrations. Those who had businesses in Hong Kong were told to pay employees to march in support of China's position. On a hot day in October 2014, I participated in one of these counterprotests.

We gathered at Victoria Park in Causeway Bay, which, ironically, was the starting point for every pro-democracy rally before or since. Representatives from scores of Communist-front organizations, village associations, CPPCCs from other parts of China, and other pro-PRC groups patrolled the crowd.

I made sure that I was seen by representatives from the Hong Kong Liaison Office, the PRC's main government body in the city. I didn't want my efforts to go unrecognized. Those officials gathered us into a group photo. They wanted Beijing to recognize their efforts, too. Liaison Office apparatchiks handed out Chinese flags and the march began.

We walked down Hennessy Road, a main thoroughfare on Hong Kong Island. We ran into the pro-democracy march and exchanged good-natured wisecracks. Relations between pro-Beijing and pro-democracy groups in Hong Kong hadn't yet become so antagonistic. By the time we got to the neighboring Wan Chai District, some of our group started to slip away.

While most members of the Beijing chapter of the CPPCC lived in Hong Kong, I'd flown down from Beijing to join the group. I'd skipped so many organized activities that I thought I'd better show up for this one and stick it out to the end. I walked a little over a mile from Victoria Park to Admiralty, named for an old British naval dock. I made sure that the officials from the Liaison Office were aware I'd completed the march.

I found the whole exercise laughable. Everyone, from the Liaison Office officials to all of us marchers, was acting. Few, if any, believed in the main idea underlying the action—that Hong Kong needed less democracy or less freedom. Everyone was there because of self-interest and to gain brownie points in Beijing. In my heart, I never believed that China should interfere in Hong Kong's affairs. I never thought that Hong Kong needed China's guidance. We'd been doing fine without China's interference.

For the Legislative Council elections in Hong Kong in November of 2013 and 2015, Party officials gave us lists of preferred candidates and directed us to return to Hong Kong to organize people to vote for them. At one point, a copy of the Party's instructions appeared on someone's WeChat social media account. That was embarrassing, so the Party stopped distributing those. Instead, to give themselves plausible deniability, Party officials handed us lists of candidates from a newspaper with the Party's choices underlined in red. They demanded that we report back on our work. "How many people did you organize to vote for our candidate?" we were asked.

One of the peculiarities of Hong Kong's system was that certain professions had their own legislative representative who could only be elected by members of that field. Doctors made up one of these so-called "functional constituencies." Because many graduates of Queen's College had become doctors, I was instructed to use my alumni network to convince my former classmates to vote for candidates in the medical profession who'd been approved by Beijing.

Although I had my doubts about Xi Jinping and the direction he was taking China, at the time I wasn't very sympathetic to the Umbrella and the Occupy Central movements. They seemed too radical and divorced from reality, a copycat version of the quixotic Occupy Wall Street movement in the USA. I didn't feel that the bulk of the population in Hong Kong supported them, either.

I also believed that China's central government was being manipulated when it came to handling Hong Kong. I decided to do what I could to assist the Party to better rule Hong Kong. Following my participation in the counterdemonstrations, I returned to Beijing and wrote a report, which a friend handed to the office of Xi Jinping. In the document, I took aim at what I called Hong Kong's "plutocrats," the rich families that had used their connections to leading Communist officials to turn Hong Kong into their personal piggy banks to the detriment of the territory's people. Hong Kong was, I wrote, controlled by "crony capitalists." The rich were getting richer while the wages of normal college graduates hadn't risen in a generation. What needed to happen, I suggested, was some democratic loosening, particularly in the organization that nominated Hong Kong's chief executive. Allow representatives of democratic groups and the youth to sit on the committee, I advocated, not simply members of the pro-Beijing business elite. I also attacked the notion, popular on the mainland, that the unrest in Hong Kong had been influenced by the Color Revolutions sweeping the Middle East and had been stirred up by "hostile Western forces." That misinterpretation of the nature of the problem, I predicted, would lead to unworkable solutions. China's government needed to reach out to all parts of Hong Kong's society and not simply allow Hong Kong's moneyed class to monopolize political power. It was ironic, to say the least, that the Chinese Communist Party, which had come to power on the backs of the masses in China, had so neglected the masses in Hong Kong.

My friend told me that my report had been read at the highest level of China's government. In the end, the Party ignored my advice. Instead, it tightened control, sparking massive protests that began in 2019 and stretched into 2020. Ultimately, the Party imposed a national security law on Hong Kong that has basically nullified the right of free speech. Like all laws born in mainland China, it was purposely vague, full of gray areas, that gave the Party wide latitude to prosecute anyone it disliked.

Thousands of people from Hong Kong were members of CPPCCs on the national, provincial, city, and county levels. And all of us were being directed to facilitate China's direct meddling in Hong Kong's elections. What amazes me is that none of us ever came out publicly and said, "This is what I did and it was wrong." If you think about it, that is deeply troubling—that so many of

Hong Kong's people were selling out the territory's future and no one felt enough remorse to say, "It's time to stop." We were doing China's bidding purely out of self-interest. But it also tells you how much we feared the Chinese Communist Party and the possible repercussions of saying no and speaking out. Maybe it was the same conundrum that faced officials like Chen Xi, Xi Jinping's former roommate at Tsinghua University. We all went along with a system that we knew was wrong because to do otherwise would have cost us—and everyone around us, including loved ones—their livelihood, freedom, and, who knows, even their lives. The price just seemed too high.

As Xi's corruption campaign played out, I finally concluded that it was more about burying potential rivals than about stamping out malfeasance. Xi had already played a role in locking up his fellow princeling, Bo Xilai. He followed that by jailing Bo's ally on the Standing Committee of the Politburo, Zhou Yongkang. He then turned his attention to destroying another faction within the Communist system, something called the Youth League.

The Youth League had been led by Xi's predecessor as Party boss, Hu Jintao. Hu's right-hand man, Ling Jihua, the father of Ling Gu, the young man who'd once borrowed my racing cars, was set to replace Hu as the public face of the Youth League when Hu retired in late 2012.

Ling Jihua had served Hu Jintao as the director of the General Office of the Party's Central Committee, the same "chief eunuch" position that Wen Jiabao had held in the early 1990s. He was expected to ascend to the Politburo, and maybe even to its Standing Committee, in November 2012 when Hu stepped down.

Always planning for the day when Wen Jiabao retired,

Whitney had been very interested in cultivating Ling Jihua, so she got to know the family. She had me mentor Ling Gu. And Whitney befriended Ling Jihua's wife, Gu Liping, who at the time was the founder and chief secretary-general of Youth Business China, a Youth League charity that bankrolled budding entrepreneurs. Whitney donated several million dollars to the charity with the idea that Gu Liping and husband Ling Jihua could one day serve as pieces on her chessboard.

Then disaster struck. Before dawn on March 18, 2012, Gu Liping and Ling Jihua's son, Ling Gu, was at the wheel of a Ferrari 458 Spider (it wasn't mine) about a mile from his apartment when the car spun out of control and crashed, killing Ling and two female passengers who were found in various stages of undress. The car crash became juicy fodder for Chinese-language tabloids in Hong Kong, which crowed about the debauchery of the sons and daughters of the red aristocracy. But I'd known Ling Gu and felt something was amiss. Although Ling Gu definitely liked fast cars, he was also interested in ideas and he didn't have the nihilistic wild streak that I'd seen in other Chinese redbloods.

The episode unfolded days before the Standing Committee of the Politburo was set to decide whether to promote Ling Jihua to one of its seats later that year. Thus, Ling Jihua always believed that his son hadn't actually died in an accident and that the whole crash had been orchestrated to destroy him and the rest of the Youth League faction. When I raised this theory with Western friends, they discounted the possibility that the Party would engage in such chicanery. But many people have trouble fathoming the depths that the Party plumbs when power is on the line.

Following the accident, Ling Jihua made a fateful error. According to Auntie Zhang, he convinced Zhou Yongkang, the top Party security official, to block information about the crash. Somehow, Party boss Hu Jintao got wind of the accident. When he asked Ling Jihua what had transpired, Ling denied that his son was involved.

Hu Jintao ultimately learned the truth when his predecessor Jiang Zemin confronted him with the facts. With Ling's falsehood exposed, Hu Jintao could no longer protect him. With that, Hu lost the chance to leave behind an ally at the height of power in China.

Ling Jihua's kneecapping began in earnest six months later in September 2012 when he was removed from his post as "chief eunuch." Then on November 15, 2012, at the 18th Central Committee meeting of the Chinese Communist Party, Ling Jihua failed to win a seat on the Politburo as well.

After keeping Ling in political limbo for two years, the Party announced in December 2014 that he'd been placed under investigation by the Party's Central Commission for Discipline Inspection. He was kicked out of the Party and charged with corruption. In July 2016, he was sentenced to life in prison.

The charges included allegations against Ling's wife, Gu Liping. The prosecutors claimed that Gu had received bribes from a company seeking political favors from her husband. But Whitney and I had known Gu Liping for years and found those charges to be far-fetched. For one, she barely ever saw her husband. As the "chief eunuch," he spent most of his nights sleeping inside Party headquarters at Zhongnanhai. He had no time to create a corrupt business empire with his wife.

Second, in addition to meeting Gu often in Beijing, Whitney had accompanied her on shopping trips to Hong Kong and noted how uncomfortable she was parting with large sums of money for watches and clothes. That bolstered Whitney's belief that neither Gu nor her husband was particularly rich or particularly corrupt. One day, Whitney took Gu to the Carlson Watch Shop in Hong Kong's Central shopping district. Carlson sells watches that can cost half a million dollars. But Gu blanched at one with a $20,000 price tag. Whitney brought Gu to the Chanel shop nearby and they checked out a suit. Gu peeked at the price and announced that it also was too expensive. Afterward, Whitney told me that it seemed like Gu had never been in a Chanel shop. Back in Beijing, Whitney and Gu would meet for tea at the Grand Hyatt. Whitney would sometimes bring along people with business proposals. Gu Liping was an eager listener but never pulled the trigger. Whitney actually stopped going out with her because she thought Gu lacked the political backing, the vision, and the will to get anything done. "She's all talk and no action," Whitney complained.

Other allegations against their deceased son, Ling Gu, seemed dubious as well. The state-run press accused Ling Gu of establishing a secret political society. What a joke. He ran a book group. I personally observed the whole process. I even suggested a few titles.

In China, the Communist Party can fabricate evidence, force confessions, and level whatever charges it chooses, untethered to the facts. And, of course, many people gullibly believe the Party's charges because the system is so opaque. It's like China's economic growth rate. The Party sets a target and every year China miraculously hits the bull's-eye, down to the decimal point. Everybody mouths the same lie, including foreigners, because the Party is so adept at concealing the truth and silencing dissenting voices. It's almost impossible to separate fact from fiction.

But our personal familiarity with the Ling family made us conclude that the allegations against them were ludicrous and the estimates of their wealth, reported in the state-run press, were fake. The popular consensus was that Ling was purged not because he was any more corrupt than the average official but because he represented a competing political force.

Then there was the case against Sun Zhengcai. Sun had been in the running to succeed Xi Jinping after Xi's second term as China's president and Party boss ended in 2022–2023. After the fall of Bo Xilai in 2012, Sun had taken over the leadership of Chongqing and had been praised by the state-run media for his work.

But starting in February 2017, Sun's career took a turn for the worse. The Central Commission for Discipline Inspection criticized him for not sufficiently purging Bo's influence in Chongqing. In early July 2017, he lost his job in Chongqing to a man who'd been Xi Jinping's propaganda chief when Xi ran Zhejiang Province. In typical Communist fashion, censors began to airbrush Sun's presence from photographs and video clips. At the end of July, the Party announced that Sun was under investigation for violating Party discipline, making him the first sitting member of the Politburo to be hit by corruption allegations since Xi took power in 2012. (Zhou Yongkang was prosecuted after he stepped down.) By September 2017, Sun had been expelled from the Communist Party, and on May 8, 2018, he was sentenced to life in prison for allegedly receiving bribes worth $24 million.

Sun's main competitor, Hu Chunhua, fared only a little better. He was never thrown in jail, but Xi stymied his rise, too. In 2017, Hu should have gotten a seat on the Standing Committee of the Politburo, but he was kept one level below.

We believed the allegations against Sun and Ling were manufactured by the Party security services to do the bidding of Xi Jinping to ensure that neither Hu Jintao nor Wen Jiabao would succeed in placing allies on the Politburo's Standing Committee. We thought that the charges of how much they embezzled or whether they'd even embezzled had been pulled out of a hat. Xi gave the order to purge them and the Party's Discipline Inspection Commission followed his commands. State prosecutors then made use of the infinite fungibility of Chinese laws to bundle them off to prison. This was how Xi Jinping consolidated power.

Taking out Ling and Sun in succession made it clear to anyone who had the slightest understanding of China that this wasn't about corruption. In my opinion, these were political hit jobs. The campaign spared people Xi preferred not to take on, for example red aristocrats, particularly those associated with the head of the Shanghai Gang, Jiang Zemin. In January 2014, the Party ordered high-end nightclubs to shut down in Beijing. But David Li's Moutai Club didn't close its doors. David's father-in-law, Old Man Jia, was Jiang's iron ally. And Jiang's support had been critical to Xi Jinping's rise.

In Sun's case, from the day he made minister of agriculture in 2006 he'd focused like a laser on moving up the chain. He'd told Whitney that as long as he didn't slip up, he was going to end up on the Politburo's Standing Committee and if he wasn't going to be president he'd be the premier. He made every move with his eyes on the prize.

The Party alleged that Sun paid for prostitutes and took bribes. But we knew him well. He didn't lust for money or sex. He lusted after power. Why would he run after women or a few million dollars when he had a nation of 1.4 billion people potentially in his grasp?

From what Whitney and I had observed, the guys who succumbed to the temptations of corruption were usually about to retire and seeking to feather their nests, not the ones vying to rule the country. We'd watched Sun spend his career carefully insulating himself against allegations of malfeasance. While he was in Shunyi, he *had* done influential people favors by doling out land parcels, but in a strictly legal sense that wasn't corruption. But Xi Jinping and his minions had apparently decided to concoct a case against him, so there was nothing he could do. Throughout China's history, so many emperors have killed off princes. This was just more of the same.

If Ling Jihua and Sun Zhengcai hadn't been purged, they'd both be on the Standing Committee of the Politburo today. The Chinese Communist Party would have maintained the idea of a collective leadership that was instituted by Deng Xiaoping in the 1980s. It wasn't a perfect system, but it had avoided returning China to the time when one man, in this case Chairman Mao, called all the shots. Now, with competitors and potential successors sidelined or in jail, Xi Jinping moved to amass even more power. In March 2018, he rammed through an amendment to China's constitution that ended term limits on the presidency, thereby opening the way for him to be emperor for life. His acolytes at the Ministry of Propaganda labeled Xi "the people's leader," a throwback to the cult of personality that had surrounded Mao. Xi's face began appearing on posters, teacups, and plates. Xi's name became a daily fixture on the front page of the *People's Daily*, the Party's mouthpiece. He grabbed so much power that Chinese began calling him "the chairman of everything."

CHAPTER EIGHTEEN

THERE'S A CONFERENCE ROOM IN THE FOUR SEASONS residences in Beijing that for Whitney and me was neutral ground. We used to meet there from time to time to discuss Ariston's upbringing and other issues. One afternoon in August 2014, Whitney summoned me. Whitney was always direct and this time was no different. "I want a divorce," she said.

I wasn't surprised. Little things had signaled that she'd been moving in that direction. She'd changed the code on the Austrian safe we'd installed in our apartment. Her message was clear: "I don't want to give those things to you." I hadn't been thinking that we were going to get back together, so I didn't have a strong emotional reaction to her declaration. Still, I was sorry it had come to this.

Later on, I interpreted her moves as a way to force me to come back to her on her terms. While we'd been separated, Whitney had sent her mother to prod me to move back in. She'd enlisted my mother to help us patch things up. I made it clear that I wasn't going back to her unless she offered to make real changes in our relationship. I wanted our playing field to be level, not tilted in her favor. She'd grown accustomed to making the decisions in our professional and personal lives. That had to change. Granted, Whitney had been a key guide and teacher to me during some very dark hours. But as I evolved, I needed her to grow with me, to make space for me, and to see me as an equal.

My sense that she was intent on forcing me back into the marriage on her terms was reinforced by her proposed divorce settlement. All she was offering was the $30 million I'd lent my old friend Ding Yi in Hong Kong. But that money was locked up in a court dispute.

During one particularly acrimonious meeting at the Oriental Plaza, she told me that, if we were divorcing, she wasn't going to give me a dime. "Get money from your friend," she told me. "You did the deal. He's your pal."

"But," I countered, "if you hadn't pulled out suddenly, there wouldn't be a problem like this."

"Tough luck," she replied.

Basically, Whitney wanted me to be so lacking in funds that I'd be forced to return to her on my hands and knees. We'd always kept our money in accounts held by Great Ocean. I possessed very little of my own. My name wasn't on any documents. I was in a real fix.

Battling a two-front war with my erstwhile wife and erstwhile best friend, I faced the most difficult period of my life. This was far worse than the failure of PalmInfo, or the firestorm sparked by the disappearance of airport boss Li Peiying, or even the *New York Times* story. To help me cope, I recalled the lessons I'd learned during those crises. I resumed meditation. I returned to the philosophical texts I'd studied before. I began to detach myself from the daily goings-on of life, insulate my emotions, and, like my parents had when they first immigrated to Hong Kong, do what needed to be done to make it through.

There's a hill on the outskirts of Beijing called Xiang, or Fragrant, Mountain that's dotted with pavilions first built in the twelfth century. Thousands of stone stairs lead to the top and I took a lesson from the mountain into my daily life. Instead of focusing on the peak, I fixed on the step in front of me, knowing that if I did that, I'd get where I needed to go. This lesson remains relevant to me today. *Control what you can control. Don't bother with the rest. You will always,* I tell myself, *get out of the pool.* Still, it was a hard time. A friend of more than two decades was intent on screwing me. And the mother of my son was trying to turn me into a pauper.

Ding Yi, the old friend from whom I was trying to recover $30 million, didn't help things by highlighting, in documents he filed with the court in Hong Kong, the *New York Times* story on the Wen family wealth. He apparently wanted to scare the judge into dropping the case. Luckily, it didn't work. But Ding Yi still had a card to play. With my suit still unadjudicated, he declared bankruptcy, and I suspect that he may have put the money in his second wife's name. Years later, we're still in court.

Whitney also vowed to fight me tooth and nail. Although we'd been married in Hong Kong, she succeeded in getting a Beijing court to take our divorce case because inside China it would be easier to lean on the judge. In China, there's no such thing as joint property. She counted on total victory and wanted to cut me off from any form of financial security.

My only option was to play hardball. I debated whether to take this step. In the end, I threatened to release damaging information about her. I leveraged the *New York Times* story, too. Our businesses were on the radar of the Chinese authorities and, given the purposely pliable nature of Communist law, there were always things that could be interpreted in a negative light. Despite the reality that Whitney strived to keep her nose clean, my threats compelled her to accept a settlement that provided me with enough to live comfortably. On December 15, 2015, we finalized our divorce.

Those two ordeals taught me a lot about the vagaries of life, especially in China. I learned that friendships aren't reliable. Nor are marriages. What kind of relationship is left?

Obviously, these issues arise *outside* China, too. But a few things set these stories apart. One is the hard-hearted, zero-sum, winner-take-all approach pursued by Whitney, Ding Yi, and even Ding Yi's second wife, Yvonne, the former bar girl who, after her husband declared bankruptcy, succeeded him to become the chairwoman of the company listed on the Hong Kong Stock Exchange. Yvonne's bizarre story was yet another example of the type of "great leap forward" not unusual in China of the day.

That give-no-quarter feature is a function of the Communist system. From an early age, we Chinese are pitted against one another in a rat race and told that only the strong survive. We're not taught to cooperate, or to be team players. Rather, we learn how to divide the world into enemies and allies—and that alliances are temporary and allies expendable. We're prepared to inform on our parents, teachers, and friends if the Party tells us to. And we're instructed that the only thing that matters is winning and that only suckers suffer moral qualms. This is the guiding philosophy that has kept the Party in power since 1949. Machiavelli would have been at home in China because from birth we learn that the end justifies the means. China under the Party is a coldhearted place.

The second is how much politics played a role in these events. Whitney got the divorce case moved to Beijing because she thought she could play her *guanxi* game and determine the settlement. Right in the middle of one hearing, the judge excused himself to take a call. *Here it comes*, I said to myself. *She's making a move behind the scenes to get the judge to rule in her favor.* I never learned the content of that call, but it helped convince me that threatening her was the only way out. Ding Yi, too, sought to capitalize on my notoriety, courtesy of the *New York Times*, to gain leverage in the case I'd brought against him. One confrontation was a divorce proceeding and the other a financial dispute, but politics infected both. And so, as the divorce and court case unfolded, I began to wonder whether it was time for me to leave China again.

My alienation from China's system intensified in other ways, too. Encouraged by Whitney, I'd gotten to know members of the red aristocracy. When I first met the well connected, like David Li, I was mesmerized. But over time, I became increasingly dismayed by the members of this class.

The sons and daughters of China's leaders were a species unto themselves. They lived by different rules and inhabited what seemed at times like a different dimension, cut off from the rest of China. Their homes were behind high walls. They didn't shop with the masses. Their food came from a different supply chain. They traveled in chauffeured limousines, attended schools that were closed to normal Chinese, were cared for at special hospitals, and made money through political access, which they sold or rented out.

Thanks to Whitney, I came across these people with great regularity and got to know them. There was Liu Shilai. He was the grandson of Gu Mu, a veteran of China's revolution and an ally of Deng Xiaoping. Gu Mu served as a vice-premier in the 1970s and 1980s and was a key figure in jump-starting China's economic reforms. Liu had been a neighbor of ours.

Liu apparently made his money in a fashion typical of many Chinese redbloods: he seemingly sold his political connections. He obtained fire department permits for discos and medical licenses for plastic surgery clinics. In exchange, he got a cut of the profits.

Liu wanted redbloods like himself to be seen as genuine nobility. He played polo around the world, winning cups in Thailand and hosting tournaments in Beijing. There the crème de la crème of Communist Chinese royalty rubbed elbows and the Chinese ladies—channeling their upper-crust role models in England—donned enormous hats.

I remember a conversation Liu and I had about the June 4 crackdown on pro-democracy protests in 1989. Liu was just a teenager then, but he remembered how scared his relatives had been that the demonstrators would actually succeed in overthrowing the Chinese Communist Party. Liu was living in a courtyard house in central Beijing with his grandfather, Gu Mu. He spent the evening of June 3 on guard at the house with an AK-47 in his lap. Outside, the People's Liberation Army attacked the protesters and cleared Tiananmen Square.

Another redblood was a friend I'll call Wolfgang. His grandfather was one of the top leaders of the Chinese Communist Party in the 1930s and 1940s. After the revolution, the grandfather served in key posts but fell afoul of Mao in the late 1950s when he criticized the ruinous Great Leap Forward that cost the lives of millions to starvation. The grandfather spent decades in the political doghouse until he was rehabilitated by Deng Xiaoping in the 1980s.

Given his experience, the grandfather insisted that his son—Wolfgang's father—avoid politics, so he studied science and took a job at a research institute. When Deng launched market-oriented economic reforms, Wolfgang's father started a small manufacturing company that made a product that was widely used and highly regulated in China. Given his lineage, Wolfgang's father won government contracts.

Wolfgang grew up in Beijing as a member of the red aristocracy. He attended the elite Jinshan Elementary School with the rest of the children of high-ranking Party members. When he was a teenager his family left China. Wolfgang was educated in the United States. When he graduated, his father brought Wolfgang, his only son, back to China and into the firm.

The firm continued to make solid profits. In fact, Wolfgang's business benefited from almost every single transaction made in China, from buying a coffee in Starbucks to purchasing a multimillion-dollar mansion in Shanghai. By this time, another company, run by the People's Liberation Army, had moved into the same space, but there was room enough for two firms to prosper. This type of duopoly was common in China, with a state-run player sharing the market with a company controlled by a descendant of the red elite.

Wolfgang expanded his company's production line and got involved in services that gave it access to reams of data. The data was of particular interest to China's police. Wolfgang shared the data with the police, who trusted him implicitly because of his pedigree. In exchange, the security services brought Wolfgang's company more business.

Wolfgang and I used to talk about the Chinese system and he regaled me with stories of plying Party bigwigs with prostitutes. He noted that a particularly effective way to bond with a Party official was to share a room with him and several girls at once. He saw the shortcomings of the system, its corruption, and how it twisted people's souls. He wouldn't defend China in terms of ideology or values, but he was happy to be mining his bloodline to make a mint. I imagined him as being a bit like Michael Corleone in *The Godfather*. In my view, Wolfgang was a reluctant mobster.

On the surface, he was thoroughly Westernized. He spoke perfect English and his wife was from Taiwan, but he didn't question the system. In fact, he helped to sustain it, sharing his data with the cops and chasing contracts with state security.

At the same time, however, Wolfgang had an overseas passport and had invested a good chunk of his wealth abroad. I debated politics with him. "Where does your capital sit?" I asked once, knowing that the bulk of it was outside China. "What kind of passport do you have?" I asked, aware that it wasn't Chinese.

For years, Western commentators insisted that people like Wolfgang who'd been educated overseas were agents of change in China—that they'd import universal values from the West and push China in a better direction. But people like Wolfgang never saw themselves in that role. His interest was in China's remaining the way it was. That's what made him a very rich man and allowed him to reap the benefits of two systems at once, the freedoms of the West and the managed duopolies of authoritarian China.

The more I saw of Wolfgang and others like him, the more I viewed them as highly competent enablers of an increasingly toxic affliction, Chinese Communism. In exchange for a pot of gold, they'd sold their souls. Whitney and I had played by the rules they and their parents had set, and we'd prospered. But we knew the rules were skewed. Whitney was comfortable staying inside this skewed system; I wanted out.

Despite my battling with Whitney in court, she and I maintained a semblance of unity over Ariston's upbringing. Soon after he was born, Whitney had mapped out his education. She started him in kindergarten at a small international school in Beijing called 3e. She signed him up for horseback riding lessons at Liu Shilai's equestrian club, an avocation fitting his status as a member of China's elite. After kindergarten, she'd planned to send him to a top-notch school attached to People's University in Beijing. For college, he'd be heading overseas to either the United States or England.

But Beijing's noxious air pollution—coupled with my desire to leave China—prompted Whitney to change her mind. In 2015, Ariston and I moved to England. Whitney and I found a school for him and by April he was settled in.

Later that year, Whitney came over to England for a few months and rented a town house near us to get Ariston further accustomed to such a dramatic change. I'd already begun devoting myself to being Ariston's primary caregiver. If I'd learned one thing from my research into family legacies, it was this: no parent ever regretted that they'd spent too much time with their kids.

I also worked to improve my relationship with my parents. I took them on vacations around the world. I planned every step of the itinerary and made sure they were comfortable, well fed, and looked after. Over lunch in Florence during a vacation to Italy, my mother, staring off in the distance as if she were speaking to no one in particular, said, "You know, I'm surprised. You've turned out to be a good son."

Whitney still dropped hints to my mother that she was interested in patching things up. After such an acrimonious divorce, it was ironic that she still wanted me back. It showed that on some level, she really valued what we'd built together and what I'd brought to her life. Underneath it all, I suspected, was a loneliness and a fear of having to fight the business battles and the Chinese system on her own. Whitney was nothing if not complicated. When she was looking to purchase a car during her trip to England, she asked me to come to the showroom and help pick one out.

"This is your car," I said.

"But you choose," she countered. "You know what's best."

At another point she turned to me and said, "I'm not good at relationships, I'm very insecure." I was unmoved. What I wanted was a sincere apology, but she was too proud.

Despite everything, she still believed she was superior to me in judging China and that I still needed to be schooled in China's ways. One day in 2016, we met for coffee. We were both in Hong Kong. I suggested again that she should diversify her risk and move some of Great Ocean's assets out of China. I was just trying to offer some friendly advice. I noted that everyone was doing it. In fact, so many people wanted to take money out of China that the government had slapped controls on the movement of capital. Whitney smirked. China, she said, "is going to continue to go great guns." Then after a somewhat pregnant pause, she added, "People need to have foresight"—as if she had it and I didn't. In 2017, during a trip I'd made to Beijing, she let it slip that Party authorities had banned her from leaving China. She didn't seem concerned and again dismissed my pleas for her to get out of China. "This," she said, "will soon pass."

AFTERWORD

IN AUGUST 2017, A FRIEND CAME TO THE APARTMENT I used to share with Whitney to pick up Ariston and take him home to England after a summer with his mom. Whitney came downstairs to say goodbye. As a car waited outside to whisk them to the airport, Whitney offered a wan smile. "I am the body that delivered him into the world," she said. "Now he's going to go on without me."

It's hard to say whether Whitney had any premonition that she'd soon disappear. If she had, she probably would've better arranged her affairs or tried to protect herself. Still, that lonely image of a woman handing over her son stuck with me. Did Whitney sense that they were coming for her? So many thousands of people had been caught up in Xi Jinping's anti-corruption drive. Whitney faced a travel ban. She didn't seem to take it seriously. But by the time she'd told me about the ban several months earlier, we'd long since stopped talking as honestly as we once had.

Might things have been different if I'd tried harder to remain in her life as a sympathetic ear and trusted counselor, if not a husband? I can't help wondering. After I'd moved out and we'd divorced in 2015, Whitney lost the one person in the world with whom she'd shared everything. Yes, she had other close relationships. But no one read her like I once could. She rode a wild ambition. She dreamed big and went for it all. I often stopped her from doing things that seemed too dangerous or risky. But once we split up, she lost her sounding board, her guardrail, and perhaps her caution, too. When she was grabbed from her new office in the Bulgari hotel complex that we'd built, I tried all my contacts in China, but nobody had any answers.

I've heard rumors. A leading Chinese economist told me he believes that Whitney was drugged, probably beaten, and, if she ever emerges alive, the Communist secret police will inject something into her spine that will turn her into a walking zombie. If she comes out, he said, she'll never be the same. The Chinese businessman turned dissident Guo Wengui announced that Party authorities had killed her, but he's a gossip and his allegations rarely hold. Even the *New York Times* reporter David Barboza, in an attempt to get me to talk, passed along rumors that Whitney was dead. Part of me thinks that one reason she hasn't appeared is that she's refused to admit guilt. She always used to say, "If you pulled my corpse out of my coffin and whipped it, you'd still find no dirt." Whitney is (or was) as strongheaded as they come.

Whitney's disappearance cemented my evolving view of Communist China. I was raised to love China and the Party. Patriotism came naturally to me, as it did to many of my generation. From the days when I hoarded comic books detailing the exploits of Communist revolutionaries, I'd unconsciously committed to the cause of making China great again. Studying in the United States in the late 1980s, I waived the right to get an American green card so that I could hew my path in Greater China. In Beijing in the 2000s, I devoted myself literally to building the capital—vastly improving the airport and constructing what is arguably the nation's finest hotel and office complex.

But what type of system allows for extralegal kidnappings of the type that befell Whitney Duan? What type of system gives investigators the right to disappear people and not even inform their parents or their son? Obviously, Ariston misses his mother, but what is torturing him and all of us is not knowing what has happened to her. Where is Whitney Duan? Is she even alive?

China has rules for how suspects should be treated. Its 1997 Criminal Procedure Law allows the police to hold a suspect for up to thirty-seven days before either releasing or formally arresting him or her. But that's a cruel joke. Whitney has been gone for *years* and still not a peep.

Also calling into question the system's essential morality is the Party's opaque mechanism for investigating its members. The process is run by the Central Discipline Inspection Commission. In 1994, the Party instituted an investigative system called *shuanggui* that allows investigators to hold people suspected of violating Party regulations. But *shuanggui* is not limited by any law. Technically, detentions can last forever. I believe Whitney is being held under that structure. Again, what type of system allows a political party to operate above the law and keep its suspects incommunicado for years? Whitney isn't the only one suffering this fate, but she's the longest-held captive without a sound.

My views on China began to sour in 2008 during the second term of Party boss Hu Jintao and Premier Wen Jiabao. The logic of China's Leninist system, essentially unchanged since the days of Chairman Mao Zedong, demands that the Party seek total control. Only in times of crisis does the Party loosen its grip, allowing more free enterprise and more freedom. It always does so reluctantly and then reverts to form. From 2008 on, the Party began reexerting its control—over the economy, the media, the Internet, and the educational system. Editors were sacked, publishers were arrested, professors were fired, the Internet was censored, and Party committees were forced on all private businesses. China's growing economy presented the Party with an opportunity to reassert its dominance.

I concluded that the Party's honeymoon with entrepreneurs like Whitney and me was little more than a Leninist tactic, born in the Bolshevik Revolution, to divide the enemy in order to annihilate it. Alliances with businessmen were temporary as part of the Party's goal of total societal control. Once we were no longer needed—to build the economy, invest overseas, or help restrict freedoms in Hong Kong—we, too, would become the enemy.

China was moving in this illiberal direction long before Xi Jinping took power in 2012. Xi has simply accelerated the process. Not only has he maneuvered the Party to maximize its control inside China, he also has pushed the Party to export China's repressive system overseas. This, too, conforms to the logic of China's system. As its capability increases, the Chinese Communist Party will seek to defend itself in an ever-expanding sphere. We see this in Hong Kong with the passage in 2020 of the national security law, which, although purposely vague, effectively outlaws comments criticizing the Hong Kong government by anyone anywhere. Talk about imperial overreach.

There's a lie perpetrated by the Chinese Communist Party

that it prioritizes the collective over the selfish interests of the individual. Many in the West, unhappy with the West's obsession with individual rights, buy into this fantasy that the Chinese Communist Party focuses on the common good. The reality is that the Party's main purpose is to serve the interests of the sons and daughters of its revolutionaries. They are the primary beneficiaries; they are the ones sitting at the nexus of economic and political power.

Thirty years ago, my parents brought me out of a communist state to Hong Kong. I grew up and studied in a liberal, capitalist, Western-oriented culture, learning the possibility and the value of human potential. Starting in the late 1970s, when the Chinese Communist Party gave everyone a breather so it could recover from its own disastrous mistakes, it opened the window a crack and allowed the world to imagine what a freer, more open China could be. Whitney and I squeezed ourselves through this crack and seized a unique opportunity—one that gave us the chance to extend ourselves, realize our dreams, and build China, too.

Now that the Chinese Communist Party has the resources, it's back to showing its true colors. At the same time, I've come to realize that, more than wealth or professional success, basic dignity and human rights are life's most precious gifts. I want to live in a society that shares that ideal. So I've chosen the Western world over China—not only for me, but also for my son.

ACKNOWLEDGMENTS

This is a book project that was started by courage and love. Love, loving, and being loved.

I wrote it because of my love for my son, Ariston. He has given me the chance to be the father that I've aspired to be. I want him to know who his father and mother truly are, what we've achieved, and what we've been through.

Being loved. Without the support of my loved ones, I never would have had the guts to see this through. Ci Sun, my better half, has truly been a blessing in my life. Without her, it would have been so much harder to get my footing after turning the page on China. She has been forgiving and encouraging in every step I've taken.

She is also sacrificing part of her life to face with me whatever storms may hit us after this book comes out. She has prepared herself not to return to China. This is a very heavy decision she's made.

I also want to thank my ex-wife, Whitney Duan. I wouldn't be what I am today without her. She is my silent partner in this book. Then there are my parents. They love me in their own way. They also have been supportive of this project by readying themselves for possible persecution from the Chinese Communist Party.

Courage. It takes all the courage I can muster to stand up and speak truth to this unscrupulous power, the CCP. Many have helped me prepare for this undertaking. Keith Berwick was my mentor at the Crown Fellowship Program at the Aspen Institute. He inspired me when I was looking for a higher calling in life. He showed me the path of courage, righteousness, and love. He continues to motivate and encourage me. My fellows at 9th Symphony class inspired me with their dedication to help others and their desire to live a life for someone other than themselves. I still remember Jordan Kassalow's story about facing a storm from an open window. Another Aspen Crown fellow, Bill Browder, has been an inspiration with the courageous publishing of his book, *Red Notice*. That memoir and Browder's subsequent actions blazed a path for all those who confront unscrupulous authoritarian regimes. Then there is Matthew Pottinger, who served for four years on the US National Security Council. The image of him reciting in flawless Mandarin a line from an ancient poem by Fan Zhongyan—"Better to speak out and die than keep silent and live"—has stayed with me until today. Fan's poem has been the motto of this book-writing journey, and that line serves as the book's epigraph.

Of course, I can't leave out the undaunted Hong Kongers who have sacrificed themselves in pursuit of human dignity. I have been in awe of their bravery, and I want to do my part for the city that I used to call home.

This book wouldn't have been possible without my writing partner, John Pomfret. His knowledge of and experience in China made our exchanges smooth and fruitful. His thoughtfulness and diligence made working with him a delight. I look forward to continuing our friendship.

I also want to thank my friends who have exchanged ideas with me throughout the project. Andrew Small has been a friend since he graduated from Oxford. As he rises to be a leading researcher in geopolitics, I look forward to more conversations; I know I'll always find novelty in our exchanges. Ken Zhou is a leading thinker and writer on Taiwan politics and cross-strait dynamics. His out-of-the-box thinking has been an inspiration for me over the past decade. Thomas Eymond-Laritaz has always been a supportive and thoughtful friend. His knowledge of global politics and business is truly exceptional. There are others as well, but I'll keep their names to myself given the CCP's lamentable tendency to punish dissenters' friends and family.

Fashion and style are things that I've enjoyed since early adulthood. They have emboldened me to shoot for the stars, to reimagine what's possible. My lifelong friend Stephen Luk is the person who brought me into that world. After forty years, we still swap fashion ideas and exchange information about the best craftsmen to make our beloved items.

I am forever thankful to ChinaVest, the leading private equity firm in the greater China region in the early 1990s. Jenny Hui hired me. Dennis Smith and Alex Ngan helped polish my business plans and investment acumen.

I want to thank my Great Ocean colleagues; together we created leading real estate projects in China. But, out of fear of retribution from the CCP, I can't name them. You know who you are. I'm grateful for all your support.

I also want to thank my agents, Amy and Peter Bernstein. They saw the potential of my story and brought it to the attention of major publishing houses. They guided me through the process. Scribner has been an ideal partner. My editor, Rick Horgan, has been extraordinarily tolerant of this novice writer. His wisdom and patience have been exemplary. I also want to thank the whole team at Scribner who just seemed to get the urgency of our story. That includes publisher Nan Graham, director of publicity and marketing Brian Belfiglio, rights director Paul O'Halloran, senior marketing director Brianna Yamashita, senior production editor Mark LaFlaur, art director Jaya Miceli, and editorial assistant Beckett Rueda. Meg Handler did a great job on the photos.

NOTES

Chapter Three

50 *"enlightenment can flow through the taps like water":* David Sheff, "Betting on Bandwidth," *Wired*, February 1, 2001, https://www.wired.com/2001/02/tian/.

53 *Robertson reportedly boasted about Feng Bo's family ties:* Charles R. Smith, *Deception: How Clinton Sold America Out to the Chinese Military* (La Porte, Ind.: Pine Lake Media Group, 2004), 166.

Chapter Six

85 *Party elders had already decided to purge him:* Philip P. Pan, *Out of Mao's Shadow: The Struggle for the Soul of a New China* (New York: Simon & Schuster, 2008), 4.

Chapter Seven

91 *J.P. Morgan paid Fullmark $1.8 million:* David Barboza, Jessica Silver-Greenberg, and Ben Protess, "JPMorgan's Fruitful Ties

to a Member of China's Elite," *New York Times*, November 13, 2013, https://dealbook.nytimes.com/2013/11/13/a-banks-fruitful-ties-to-a-member-of-chinas-elite/.

93 *"disgusted with his family's activities":* Consulate Shanghai, "Carlyle Group Representative on Leadership Issues." Wikileaks Cable: 07SHANGHAI622_a. Dated September 20, 2007. https://wikileaks.org/plusd/cables/07SHANGHAI622_a.html.

94 *"constrained by the prominence of his position":* Consulate Shanghai, "Carlyle Group Representative on Leadership Issues." Wikileaks Cable: 07SHANGHAI622_a. Dated September 20, 2007.

97 *Rumors swirled that much of Xu's wealth was ill-gotten:* Michael Forsythe, "Chinese Businessman Linked to Corruption Scandals Dies in Prison, Reports Say," *New York Times*, December 6, 2015, https://www.nytimes.com/2015/12/07/world/asia/china-xu-ming-dies-prison.html.

101 *Huang landed another $3 million from Deutsche Bank:* Michael Forsythe, David Enrich, and Alexandra Stevenson, "Inside a Brazen Scheme to Woo China: Gifts, Golf and a $4,254 Wine," *New York Times*, October 14, 2019, https://www.nytimes.com/2019/10/14/business/deutsche-bank-china.html.

Chapter Eight

108 *contract to provide a kind of mineral water, called Tibet 5100:* Cao Guoxing, "Everest 5100: The Political and Business Alliance Behind a Bottle of Mineral Water." Radio France Internationale, July 7, 2011.

Chapter Ten

141 *Li Peiying was all in. He used his muscle and charisma:* "Beijing Capital International Airport Air Cargo Clearance Base Lays Foundation," PRC Central Government Official Website, June 29, 2006, http://www.gov.cn/jrzg/2006-06/29/content_323047.htm.

Chapter Twelve

170 *A painter, Deng Lin had made a small fortune:* Patrick E. Tyler, "China's First Family Comes Under Growing Scrutiny," *New York Times*, June 2, 1995, https://www.nytimes.com/1995/06/02/world/china-s-first-family-comes-under-growing-scrutiny.html.

Chapter Fourteen

205 *His purported corruption was also the stuff of legend:* Bill Savadove, "Jia Qinglin: Tainted survivor with a powerful patron," *South China Morning Post*, October 23, 2007, https://www.scmp.com/article/612592/jia-qinglin-tainted-survivor-powerful-patron.

211 *That was a license to print money:* Sean O'Kane, "EV startup Canoo's mysterious backers named in new harassment lawsuit," *The Verge*, October 8, 2019, https://www.theverge.com/2019/10/8/20899436/discrimination-lawsuit-canoo-foreign-backers-ev-startup-british-chinese-government.

212 *identified in the Panama Papers as the sole shareholder:* Juliette Garside and David Pegg, "Panama Papers reveal offshore secrets of China's red nobility," *Guardian*, April 6, 2016, https://

www.theguardian.com/news/2016/apr/06/panama-papers-reveal-offshore-secrets-china-red-nobility-big-business.

213 *cables also linked Yu to a questionable loan:* Consulate Shanghai "Pension Scandal Claims More, Politics as Usual." Wikileaks Cable 06SHANGHAI16957_a. Dated Oct. 27, 2006, https://wikileaks.org/plusd/cables/06SHANGHAI6957_a.html.

Chapter Sixteen

235 *the Wen family was worth close to $3 billion:* David Barboza, "Billions in Hidden Riches for Family of Chinese Leader," *New York Times,* October 25, 2012, https://www.nytimes.com/2012/10/26/business/global/family-of-wen-jiabao-holds-a-hidden-fortune-in-china.html.

237 *the fortune held by relatives of . . . Xi Jinping:* "Xi Jinping Millionaire Relations Reveal Fortunes of Elite," Bloomberg News, June 29, 2012, https://www.bloomberg.com/news/articles/2012-06-29/xi-jinping-millionaire-relations-reveal-fortunes-of-elite.

239 *sons and daughters of senior Party members were given good positions:* Yuan Huai, "Chen Yun Appointed Me to Work under Li Rui of the Central Organization Department," Mirror History Channel, November 10, 2020 https://www.mingjingnews.com/article/48411-20.

Chapter Seventeen

251 *I addressed the Aspen Institute:* "Leadership in Action Series: David Rubenstein; The China Model; Madeleine Albright,"

The Aspen Institute, July 31, 2013, https://archive.org/details/Leadership_in_Action_Series_-_David_Rubenstein_The_China_Model_Madeleine_Albright.

Chapter Eighteen

272 *He was the grandson of Gu Mu:* Wu Ying, "A man, his horse, His mallet, his life," *China Daily*, October 26, 2011, http://www.chinadaily.com.cn/cndy/2011-10/26/content_13976808.htm.

272 *the crème de la crème of Communist Chinese royalty:* John O'Sullivan, "China: Wealthy elite revives the spirit of the emperors," *Financial Times*, May 26, 2012, https://www.ft.com/content/f6ace4c8-9da1-11e1-9a9e-00144feabdc0.

INDEX